CLEARED FOR TAKE-OFF

Stephen Barlay escaped from Budapest after the Hungarian revolution in 1956. He made his name as an author of documentary books, including *Double Cross* and *Fire*, and as a novelist with bestsellers including *Blockbuster, Cuban Confetti, Tsunami* and the highly acclaimed *The Ruling Passion*.

He is the author of two internationally successful books on air safety, *The Final Call* (now also a university text book in America) and *Aircrash Detective*. While writing *Cleared For Take-Off* he travelled widely and conducted hundreds of extensive interviews with various specialists.

He is married with two grown-up sons and lives in England.

CLEARED FOR TAKE-OFF

Behind the Scenes of Air Travel

STEPHEN BARLAY

KYLE CATHIE LIMITED

For Gloria Ferris
and Rivers Scott

First published in Great Britain in 1994 by
Kyle Cathie Limited
20 Vauxhall Bridge Road, London SW1V 2SA

This edition published 1996

ISBN 1 85626 173 5

Stephen Barlay is hereby identified as the author of this
work in accordance with Section 77 of the Copyright,
Designs and Patents Act 1988.

A Cataloguing in Publication record for this title is
available from the British Library.

Typeset by York House Typographic Ltd, London
Printed and bound in Great Britain by Cox & Wyman Ltd,
Reading, Berkshire

Contents

CONTENTS

Acknowledgements

I am indebted to more than 200 individuals, including aviation, medical and travel specialists, lawyers, pilots, cabin crews, security and customs officers, airline, airport and government employees in eleven countries, many of whom have permitted me to quote them in this book, while others wished to remain anonymous for a variety of reasons – above all because their employers deem it best to offer 'no comment' on their trade practices.

For granting me access to their records and facilitating lengthy interviews, I am most grateful to numerous organizations, particularly the Air Accident Investigation Branch, Air Safety Group, Air Transport Users' Committee, Airport Operators' Association, All Nippon Airways, American Airline Pilots' Association, Association of British Travel Agents, Aviation Consumers Action Project, Boeing, Britannia Airways, British Airline Pilots' Association, British Airports Authority, British Airways, *Business Traveller*, Cabin Crew 89, Campaign for Freedom of Information, Civil Aviation Authority, Cranfield Institute of Technology, Dulles International Airport, Emirates Airways, Fairchild Aviation Recorders, Federal Aviation Agency, Flight Data Co., Flight Safety Committee, Flight Safety Foundation, Frere Cholmeley, HM Customs and Excise, Institute of Aviation Medicine, International Air Transport Association, International Airline Passengers' Association, International Civil Aviation Organization, International Federation of Airline Pilots' Association, International Society of Air Safety Investigators, Kuoni Travel, Lufthansa, Malév, National Transportation Safety Board, Pannone and Partners, Royal Aeronautical Society Library, SCI-SAFE, Singapore Airlines, Speiser-Krause-Madole, Swissair, US Air Transport Association, US Association of

Flight Attendants, US Department of Transportation, and Willis-Corroon Aerospace Division.

For guidance and advice my special thanks are due to Jerome Lederer, President Emeritus of the Flight Safety Foundation, Tony LeVier, President of SAFE, Ira Rimson of ISASI, and Dr James Vant – as well as Chris Mason, Alan Pollock and Dick Stafford who patiently answered my endless questions and organized interviews with executives of the CAA, NTSB and FAA respectively.

I am also indebted to Beverley Cousins, editor of this book, and Janos Reeves, who helped me with the preparation of the index.

Picture Acknowledgements

Associated Press for Hawaii 29.4.88 (page vi); Boeing Defense and Space Group for super-jumbo and hypersonic (page i) and *Air Force One* (page iii); CAA for Air Traffic Control Operations Room (page ii); Canadian ASB for computer screen reconstruction (page v); Loral Data Systems for black box and air-gun (page v); Quadrant Picture Library for front cover, Wright brothers first flight (page i) and planes in the Arizona Desert (page viii); Press Association for Hong Kong 18.11.93; SWISSAIR for glass cockpit of an Airbus (page ii) and catering (page viii). Pictures of wreckage in hangar, upholstery in wreckage and scratches on two pieces of wreckage (page iv) courtesy of Eric Newton.

1

The Joy of Flying

You chose your destination. You bought your ticket. The long queue at the check-in desk made you fume. Like taking the number 49 bus, you hopped on a plane. To most people, a mere routine. Yet even the mundane contemplation of such practical necessities fails to destroy the fairy-tale quality of air travel. If you watch passengers during take-off, if you note the facial signatures of anticipation, fascination, incredulity and the increased flow of adrenalin, you will recognize that deep down in the human psyche vibrant and exciting airports still represent the gateways to the wide world, and that a seat on a jet makes us bit-players in, rather than witnesses of, the performance of something supernatural. Perhaps it is because we associate the freedom from gravity with the idea of going to Heaven, with the mythical images of Daedalus and Icarus, with the effortless soaring of Michelangelo's winged angels and wingless saints, the freely floating, puckish cupids of Raphael. After all, we have not had enough time to grow jaded and blasé about it all.

Mankind's presence on the planet has been short: not a million days have passed since AD 1. Ninety years are but a blink in history. Yet it was just nine decades ago that at 10.35 in the morning of 17 December 1903, the Wright brothers' *Flyer No. 1* achieved the first man-carrying, powered, sustained flight – it took about twelve seconds to cover a distance of 120 feet. The same day, three more flights broke the record repeatedly, and increased it to 852 feet in fifty-nine seconds.

It seems equally incredible that it was only eighty-five years ago that a Madame Peltier, having been flown in an aeroplane near Turin, Italy, over the staggering distance of 500 feet, entered the record books as the world's first woman passenger. Barely a year later, in 1909, American-born British air pioneer Samuel Cody took the first British woman passenger, his wife, for a joy-ride in Army Aeroplane Number 1. The press reported the event with envy and yearning, speculating on the exhilaration of leaving the ground, of touching the clouds and reaching for the sky. That joy of miraculous ascent has never left mankind, even

1

though flying has become air transport, a mere convenience, the quickest means of being conveyed from A to B.

The acceleration of developments in man-made speed through the air is breathtaking. From throwing a stone or a spear it took thousands of years to create the lightning strike of a catapult and an arrow. It took another 3000 years to achieve, in the 1940s, the unimaginable 500 m.p.h. flight, but not quite a decade to break the 1000 m.p.h. dream, and the sound barrier.* By 1969, 600 million people could watch the televised launch of a missile leading to Neil Armstrong's first steps on the moon, and today the technology is available to fly us twenty-five times faster than the speed of sound. (The only comparable acceleration of human achievement was brought about by computers. While it took almost four millennia to enable us to do arithmetic 300 times faster in 1940 than we did in 2000 BC, in just another fifty years that speed was multiplied by several million.)

The brevity of commercial air transport history becomes obvious when you realize that there are still many people alive who knew the young Lindbergh prior to his first non-stop solo flight across the Atlantic in 1927, and when you think of it how very recently some randomly chosen firsts have occurred.

DID YOU KNOW

That in 1911 a box of Osram lamps was the first recorded carriage of freight by air?†

That the Mediterranean was first crossed by air in 1911?

That the first all-metal aircraft, a German Junker, known as the 'tin donkey', took off in 1915?

That international air mail service began between Vienna and Kiev in 1918 – but only a year later in the United States?

That the first American international scheduled passenger air service was inaugurated in 1920 (from Florida to Cuba), when Britain's Biggles-lookalikes had already been offering international transport for almost a year? (In their converted bombers 'they charged £42, then 20% of a teacher's annual salary, for a one-way trip . . . between London and Paris. A lunch basket cost extra' (*The Economist* 12.6.1993). French fliers then undercut them with the help of government finance – state subsidies for aviation are as old as air transport

---

*See Glossary at the end of the book for an explanation of aeronautical terms and abbreviations.
†An excellent source for more 'firsts' is *Air Facts and Feats: A Record of Aerospace Achievement* by F.K. Mason and M.C. Windrow (Doubleday, 1970).

itself – and Britain countered by setting up Imperial Airways, the subsidized forerunner of the first British flag-carriers.)

That in 1933, after Imperial Airways had completed the first 10 million miles of flying, passenger accident insurance was reduced from twelve to one shilling per £1000, a rate comparable to that applied to ground transport?

That the first round-the-world flights were made by Douglas World Cruisers in 1924? (Four aircraft set off from Seattle, Washington; two completed the course – in 175 days.)

That even after World War II, it took seven days – albeit in great comfort – to reach Singapore from London by BOAC flying boats?

That regular passenger transport by Comets, the first pure-jets in airline service, began in 1952?

That *Sputnik*, the first man-made satellite, orbited the Earth in ninety-six minutes in 1957, whereas in 1993 it is being contemplated how to send cargo, and later passengers, by a hypersonic aircraft from London to Sydney in just one hour – including launch and re-entry into the atmosphere?

And that the first pilot to smoke while flying was Hubert Latham? (Creating something for true connoisseurs of trivia, in 1909 he rolled his cigarette and puffed away merrily in the slipstream of his open cockpit!)

Another aspect of the air transport miracle is safety almost beyond belief. Any mode of transport, indeed any human activity, is a considered compromise to varying degrees. Otherwise a truly safe car would be a tank, a truly safe tank would be a fortress. An absolutely safe aircraft would never get off the ground. So you need a certain amount of faith in the thousands of decisions taken by armies of faceless strangers – just as you trust the 'other driver' not to swerve into your path on the road, your mechanic not to have forgotten to check your brakes, or for that matter your surgeon to be a master of his trade and sober on the day. And yet you need *some* knowledge beyond idle curiosity to choose your car, pick your surgeon, and decide which airline and what aircraft will fly you. Regarding the latter, the choice ought to depend on four criteria: safety, reliability, price and convenience. Most people's initial compromise is to take safety and reliability for granted, and promote the price as the number one decisive factor. Disregarding the bad apples of aviation, to be discussed later, that promotion is justifiable only because flying is generally so safe that – as Carl Vogt, Chairman of the US National Transportation Safety Board, put it, 'If you took a scheduled flight every day, it would take 4000 years before you were likely to be in some, probably minor, accident – and still have a fifty-fifty chance of survival.'

Consider just one more thought: an aircraft can be described as 'a million spare parts flying in close formation'; if only 99.9 per cent perfection was achieved, 1000 components would fail after each flight. The fact is only two- or three-millionths of all the parts need frequent, quick-fix repairs – and more often than not they are the soap dispenser nozzles in the toilets.

Technology in passenger aircraft has improved at break-neck speed from 1920, the year of the installation of the first automatic pilot (nicknamed *George* ever since) to the invention of the unimaginable, such as instruments for 'blind' landing, weather radars, ground proximity warning and fly-by-wire systems. No wonder that ever more affordable air transport has grown so astoundingly fast, particularly in the United States, despite the much-publicised and hard-to-forget occasional mishaps caused by ignorance, mistakes or negligence. In the mid-1930s there were a thousand flights a day in America. Today, there are twenty times more, and it is projected that by the turn of the century US airlines will carry 800 million passengers a year (as many as those transported by the whole of the world's aviation industry in 1984). On average, every US citizen over eighteen now takes two trips by air annually. (That disregards, of course, the dwindling part of the population that has never flown – about one in every five souls in the industrially advanced countries.)

If you took just one flight in 1993 you could be proud of having contributed to the statistics by being one of the 1.1 billion people who travelled safely by air in that single year. It would also give you a share in the miracle of flying – but the individual experience, however joyous, will not earn you a mention in the record books next to Madame Peltier or Mrs Cody. Which is just as well. There is much to be said for flights that are a mere routine of breaking through clouds into the sunshine of a 200-mile horizon at 25,000 feet, watching glorious formations of cotton wool and floating icebergs, skating on what looks like the vast expanse of the Antarctic, coming upon green lagoons to catch a glimpse of fields, villages, people, and a snaking procession of cars in miniature, feasting on a bird's-eye view of Mount Fuji, the shore-line of Rio or the gold-plated ant-hills of Hongkong.

Joy of flying? You mean the pleasure of being conveyed to that faraway beach really fast? Passengers have more tales to tell about the hassle of getting to an airport, and petty disappointments with that 'plastic lunch' in the air, than about just another routine flight. Air travel can be soured, indeed, by the niggly package it comes with. Choosing your destination, finding the best deal, packing, selecting your attire for the trip, losing your way in the maze of the airport, delays, doubts, feeling like a ninny when everybody else seems to be a seasoned globe-trotter or flash-Harry jet-setter, not quite knowing or understanding what goes on around you on the ground and in the air, can cause persistent irritation and uncertainty. Words such as 'routine flight' and 'being conveyed' reinforce most people's impression that once they have decided to fly somewhere, their lives, and the outcome of innumerable potential inconveniences, are entirely in the hands of strangers. Not so.

We passengers can, in fact, do a great deal for ourselves, for the smoothness of a holiday or a business flight, for the choice of the cheapest, most advantageous arrangements, and even for our safety, by 'knowing the ropes', learning what questions to ask, discovering what goes on behind the scenes and who is supposed to do what for us – by graduating from *tourists* to *travellers*.

2

The Fear of Flying

Let's face it: the air is not the natural habitat of our species. There is something blatantly unnatural in humans travelling where angels may fear to tread. But then what is natural in zapping along motorways at 70 m.p.h., flicking a switch to let there be light or dwelling in skyscrapers where we may bump into clouds? Modern ways of living have brought about a new set of hazards, but while we have been desensitized to most of those by habit, to the extent that we may forget the risks, we are not yet quite used to the idea of leaving the ground. (Incidentally, while it is true that travelling by car *is* infinitely more dangerous than by aeroplane, the concept is false because it compares private means of transport with public ones, and flying takes us into a different world where miracles and trepidation come hand in hand.)

The unknown and the invisible, the darkness of the night, the deep sea and underground caves have always given birth to great myths and mysteries. The skies have been full of good and bad omens for us, gifts such as babies borne by storks, and the menace of thunder, lightning and monsters.

Pterodactyls, the massive pre-historic reptiles, were born to fly like birds. Mankind was not. The lure of the sky, and a varying degree of pterophobia,* the fear of flying, are parts of our heritage.

At the Royal Aeronautical Society, an aviation insurance specialist once began his lecture saying, 'I'm always asked when will aircraft insurance come down?' He flashed three colour transparencies on to the screen: an eagle was diving, catching its prey an inch from the ground and flying off in one clean swoop. 'My answer is that when you fly like this, the rates will come down.' We may be a long way from the accomplishment of this task, but the specialist had to admit that whereas

---

*pter(-o)-: in composition feather, wing.

6

THE FEAR OF FLYING

some three decades ago a pilot's life insurance cost ten times more than that for ordinary mortals, the rates for his life now more or less match everyone else's – and he may even get a special reduction in view of his frequently monitored good health.

The worst pterophobia sufferers confess their debilitating fear, but only with unnecessary embarrassment. Most people deny it, but aviation physician Dr Alan Roscoe is convinced that four out of every five *regular fliers* have some apprehension when stepping on to an aircraft. Questioned by Swedish researchers, only a quarter of 2000 people admitted such apprehension, but when they were asked if any of their friends or relatives either refused to fly or would do it with trepidation, the figure almost doubled – it was probably easier to be truthful about 'somebody else'. (This author has flown in all sorts of contraptions all over the world, but still experiences a certain tightness of the stomach when taking off for the first time after a few months' gap in flying.)

Relatively few people are hit by outright panic at the thought of taking to the air or when actually boarding an aircraft, but even a mild form of pterophobia can put them at a serious disadvantage. They bear the 'guilt' of ruining family holidays, and the 'shame' of being unable to see the world and visit loved ones.

Many well-known factors may trigger their fear. On a ship, they think they can swim or take to the lifeboats. In a car, they feel they are in control. On a bus, they see where they are going, pass recognizable landmarks, know they can get off at any time, even jump out if necessary. In the air we have no control over our fate, we are in the hands of pilots and thousands of others who make that flight possible; we experience unusual movements only acrobats are used to – pitching, rolling without the reassurance of ground contact. To children, it is natural to entrust their lives to others; to adults, it is not. Yet from the moment we step into an airport, we seem to lose control. In the bewildering ant-hill of a terminal building, we are channelled, tunnelled, guided, directed, processed, checked, examined, herded, even searched and seemingly suspected – all in the good cause of getting us safely and speedily from one place to another.

'Yet you do have control,' says Anthony Broderick, Associate Administrator of the US Federal Aviation Agency (FAA). 'First of all you can *choose* who should take you on your journey. It's a matter of trust in their safety record, care and punctuality. My advice to apprehensive first-time fliers is that they should at least once visit the airport at their leisure, sample the relaxed mood of most travellers and those who work in the industry – they don't want to die either, do they? – understand what's going on, find out what seat to ask for, what the boarding routine is, and read something basic that lifts the shroud off the mystery of flying.'

Fear of the unknown is hereditary.* Many of our worries are an infection by others who have lived to tell tales of truly rough rides (a rare experience these days), and of air-sickness (airlines do need to replace those bags in the seatbacks but mostly because people use them for rubbish). Claustrophobia in the cabin may, indeed, affect some passengers who would also be prone to suffer from it in enclosed spaces on the ground. Some spectacular events, such as the Lockerbie sabotage disaster, would overwhelm many people with fear. The industry counters it with impressive and true statistics of safety, but figures on a slip of paper can never eliminate subjective concern.

Jerome Lederer, one of the great gurus of air safety, once quoted airline pioneer Harold Harris, Vice President of the then thriving PanAm, to describe the task of air transport: 'Anxiety never disappears in a human being in an airplane; it merely remains dormant when there is no cause to arouse it. Our challenge is to keep it forever dormant.' Three million people who fly safely to their destination every day are a testimony to that remarkable achievement.

Those who are worst afflicted by the pains of the irrational may suffer alarming symptoms such as vomiting, sweating, diarrhoea, serious palpitations or fainting. They can turn to pyschologists, relaxation exercises (like those at ante-natal clinics), Yoga, supportive group therapy, and other treatment, even hypnosis, but most of these cures are time-consuming, require regular practice (learning to reduce blood pressure, transfer thoughts from threats to pleasures), and tend to be expensive. That is why many victims of pterophobia seek help from anti-fear courses that claim an encouraging success rate.

For example, Britannia, a charter company, Britain's second biggest airline, runs a Flying With Confidence course at East Midlands Airport. The cost is reasonable, considering what is on offer: £95 for lectures, discussion over a buffet lunch, a special ninety-minute flight, followed by more food, tea and sympathy with an opportunity to put individual questions to the pilots, experts and cabin crew.

It was a moving experience to watch the arrival of those about to enter the lions' den. One who came by car forgot to switch off her engine, and left her door wide open until reminded by a fellow sufferer. They shared a nervous laugh. Others were dropped off by husbands, wives or friends. A reassuring touch, a kiss, the sweetness of sorrow. Some of the drivers would rejoin their passengers after the lectures – they could accompany them on the flight only, and hold their hands, for £45. There was no discernible pattern of age, class or intelligence. A beefy six-footer

---

*A New Guinea tribe, witnessing the arrival of the first aircraft, felt utterly convinced that the pilot was God himself. They begged him to take them to the other world where they would meet their dead relatives. Those early magnificent men and their flying machines were idolized and treated as brave demi-gods.

walked through the throng to reception with oozing macho self-confidence. He mumbled some all-too-transparent excuses (he had driven the eighty miles there instead of telephoning), and opted out. He was offered his money back, but he declined it. It would be held with a place for him on the long waiting list for the next course. Perhaps the second time round he could make it beyond reception. There was a priest on the course. He was greeted with gasps and clearly secular *oh-my-gods*. He smiled bravely, and comforted everybody with the little joke that he was not present in a professional capacity. Small groups huddled together, as if to share shelter in a storm – making friends was as easy as in a hospital ward.

When their papers and documents were distributed, the receipt of their boarding cards was a shock. It transpired that many of them had already flown several times – but each occasion had been torture, and sometimes their anxiety grew with each flight. Others were victims of a variety of phobias. (Nureyev started out as 'fearless flier', and could not have danced many times around the globe without air travel, but gradually he was overcome by panicky pterophobia. He would shrink into a corner of his seat and bury his face in his hands, praying silently, whenever the aircraft began to move.)

Captain John Galyer's light-hearted talk on the technical aspects, safety procedures, maintenance and engineering back-up, and the secret of flying, offered plenty of reassurance, but was not without pitfalls: it was the first time that some of his listeners had heard of or thought about certain conceivable risks. Dr Alan Roscoe then spoke. He revealed that their fears were far from unique, suggested techniques to fight them, explained how inaccurate exaggeration by others (and the press) could feed the irrational, and praised his audience for having taken the first, most important steps towards cure: 'You have not only recognized and freely admitted your anxieties – you're here, that's the proof – and have already begun to discuss them without embarrassment.' Finally Debbie Clifford, who is in charge of Britannia's cabin staff training, talked about care in the air, and invited everybody to visit a cabin mock-up so that boarding the aircraft should hold no surprises.

The atmosphere was relaxed now, the laughs sounded more genuine, but sweaty hands and brows were still in evidence. A young woman ('Flew three times, and was uncontrollably hysterical on each occasion') had to be supported by a stewardess and others to stay upright and walk to lunch. She was incredibly determined to go through with it, come what may: her fiancé had booked their honeymoon in Hongkong, but would cancel the trip if she failed to improve. An attractive woman of apparent composure could hardly open her mouth to speak, let alone eat. (Her husband, a high-powered executive flies regularly to exotic destinations, and she could have a free ticket to accompany him every time.) Some people were shaking so badly they could just about hold their plates. A couple, trembling in unison but longing to see faraway places, virtually had to feed each other – they would not stop holding hands. There could be no doubt about it, their fear of flying was an illness, far beyond 'normal' anxieties. But amazingly, food and frank answers brought relief to many people, and there were shared expectations and excitement in the rising crescendo of their chatter. Whatever happened, nobody would laugh or point a finger at them.

When it came to boarding the coach to the aircraft, three people went missing. It happens every time. On the steps to the *Sir Sidney Camm*, a freshly washed B737, some passengers hesitated, sighed, then almost dived in through the door. A man and a woman manoeuvred to be last. They reached the top of the stairs, but could go no further. A stewardess embraced them: 'Well done. Next time round you'll fly, I'm sure.' While they were escorted back to the terminal, she explained, 'On a previous course, the same two could not even board the bus. Now they've almost made it. We had others on the course who went through the same trauma until a new world of freedom opened up for them . . . the third time round.'

The take-off brought a hush. The woman who could get free trips seemed amazingly at ease – until we felt a bump. 'Turbulence,' she whispered, hanging on to the arm-rests for dear life. That was the one word that held terror for her. Numerous Britannia staff were available to reassure her that the bump had been caused not by the air but the retraction of the undercarriage. (On the way down she was told that the undercarriage would soon be lowered: when it happened, she noted it with immense relief. If only she had been forewarned about those frightening non-events in the air (see Chapter 10), she might never have developed her phobia.)

By now, we were high up, and passengers were encouraged to walk about. Reluctantly, they began to leave their seats. And then they were invited to visit the cockpit. Some refused. Those who did not returned from their journey with the beaming broad smiles of salvation. They were full of stories. 'Would you believe it? It's like a caff up there,' exclaimed the girl who would honeymoon in Hongkong. She had expected to see white-knuckled pilots peering intensely through their windscreen. 'They were sipping tea, turned to chat to me, and the plane was flying itself!' The hand-holding couple would not move an inch. Halfway through the flight, the husband tore himself away and staggered to the flight deck. A few minutes later he returned and took his wife by the hand all the way down the aisle. Colour began to return to the cheeks of a boy in his late teens. When we landed, he burst out laughing: 'I can't believe it! This was fun!'

I wish I could convince myself that they all found it fun. Or that all would fly without fear from then on. They were clutching their personal

THE FEAR OF FLYING

initiation 'certificates' that had been issued to prove that they had, indeed, owned up to and faced their fears, completed the course, and got over the first, probably their greatest, obstacle to flying.

In 1991, at an international seminar in Lisbon, Jerome Lederer defined air safety as a 'systematic process for identifying hazards and risks in order to eliminate, control or reduce them to acceptable limits'. The same could be said about people's struggle against pterophobia. Instead of sneering remarks on 'cowardice', and a light wave of dismissal at their predicament, they deserve nothing but the encouragement and compassion any other patient receives in the fight against illness.

3

Travellers and Tourists

This is how many travel agents classify us – the travellers and the tourists. The dividing line? A traveller asks questions to obtain information far beyond the sun-and-sand-seeker's preoccupation with the fares, price and package, resorts, the hotel's star-rating and the weather, i.e. nothing that cannot be found in the brochures. Most people pay less discriminating attention to the purchase of their annual holidays and occasional flights than they do to shopping in a supermarket where they have learned to enquire about the additives and calories in their food, and to check the 'sell by/use by' dates on the wrapping. Perhaps that is why they get only what they demand from those who, in turn, could be classified as . . .

. . . TRAVEL AGENTS AND PACKAGE-PEDLARS

Most of these may well be trustworthy, but the quality of their service varies enormously.

In economically advanced countries, the trade is regulated to a great extent. In Britain, for instance, no scheduled, charter or freighter airline may be set up without an Air Operator's Certificate issued by the CAA (Civil Aviation Authority), for which the airlines have had to prove their expertise and sound finances. The CAA also monitors their safe performance, and will intervene if their freely set fares appear to be too high or too low. To protect passengers, charter tour operators (some 700 of them) are also controlled by the CAA's Air Travel Organisers' Licence (ATOL). This cannot be obtained without depositing a hefty bond: if the company collapses, leaving its clients stranded abroad, that money (more than £25 million in the Air Travel Trust) is used to bring them home, and compensate them for their losses, including a paid-in-advance holiday that never happened. When booking a trip, it is well worth looking for the logo of ATOL and ABTA, the Association representing nine-tenths of all British Travel Agents. (ABTA members must conform to strict regulations such as the minimum standards laid down in their Code of Conduct, the propriety of their relationship with tour operators, and financial requirements.) AITO (Association of Independent Tour Operators) and IATA (International Air Transport Association) offer similar protection.

If travel agents go out of business, a client's money is protected as long as the agents were ABTA or IATA members. If an airline goes bankrupt, only credit card payers are safe. When Air Europe went bust recently, only those who had chosen that method of payment were safeguarded by general credit regulations. (The same happened in America with Braniff: the airline was declared bankrupt on 2 July 1992, and only those who had paid by 'plastic' prior to that date were entitled to a refund.) When the non-bonded tour operator Land Travel packed up, several thousand people lost their holidays without any reimbursement – or found themselves stranded abroad without cover.

The recession certainly took its toll among independent travel companies. The CAA had to call in the bond to rescue and refund thousands of customers when the Airbreak Leisure Group was placed in administration and lost its licence. And while most DHG (UK) clients were safe when the company ceased trading under its various operations, such as Flights Delight and Turkish Delight Holidays, those who had booked with the Florida Shop in Reading or Flightsavers in Devon were not so lucky: the latter two were not members of ABTA, and Flightsavers closed with an 'out to lunch' sign on the door (*The Times*, 30.9.1992). It would be possible to insure individually against loss due to bankruptcies, but the premium could be substantial. (Some US travel agents offer such protection – Travel Guard charges $5.50 for every hundred dollars' cover.)

Germany and Britain have more stringent regulations than the rest of Europe. A new EC Package Directive aims to give greater security for all (including the clients of the thousands of 'cheapies' that do not belong to a professional body) but fails even to mention agents' duty to warn people about health hazards, and does not go as far as ABTA's rules. Leaving the implementation to governments is peppered with loopholes, and may result in the lowering of some standards. A leading independent travel agent complains: 'It could render us *criminally* responsible for giving misleading or ambiguous information. So what do we do? Minute each conversation and make the passenger sign it?' A good question, for the right to display a professional logo is no guarantee against an agent's ignorance.

Almost anyone can become a *tour operator*, but those who want to set up as *travel agents* must prove their competence and pass exams. However, as profit margins are low, the agents will often employ poorly paid, inexperienced school leavers as counter clerks who are attracted by the perks of a fun industry – people who may not know their 'products' because they have not even read their own brochures properly. ABTA claims that 90 per cent of their members' customers are satisfied with the services, but the Consumers' Association discovered fundamental flaws in agents' 'knowledge, competence and willingness to help' (*Holiday Which?* magazine, April 1992). Of those tested, 79 per cent could not find a readily available cheap BA fare to Nice, 38 per cent could not give useful advice about a holiday in Mallorca. Big chains and upmarket firms invest heavily in training (basic geography, familiarization with resorts and health regulations) but local conditions at their clients' destinations can remain a mystery to their staff.

The agents may not actually recommend holidays in war-torn Sarajevo, but political turmoil in Egypt, Cambodia or Myanmar (Burma), and fighting in some of the former Soviet republics may be news to them. Few British agents can warn about terrorism in Peru, kidnappings in Colombia, ivory poachers preying on tourists in Kenya, uprisings in Sri Lanka, the frequency of mugging in Spain, Italy and Jamaica, or even the much publicized murders in Miami. They often fail to pass on Foreign Office advice about 'potential difficulties' in seventy countries, and warnings 'not to visit' (at the time of writing) Afghanistan, Bosnia, Iraq, Libya and Zaire. In America, the State Department issues travel advisories about social and political unrest in various countries, and publishes a telephone number (202–647–5225) to find out if a relevant notice is in print.

INSURANCE AND MEDICAL REQUIREMENTS

may be revealed only to inquisitive passengers. A third of holiday-makers fail to take out insurance, which is sold mostly by travel agents. Policy premiums and contents vary a great deal. Tourists are usually advised, sometimes compelled, to buy the one that pays agents the best commission – up to 40 per cent! (Annual company policies for business travellers can save money but only if a firm's employees make about six dozen trips a year.) The small print on a policy is essential reading: for what and to what extent are you covered? *Holiday Which?* found that only four policies were adequate out of thirty-two on offer as many omitted the kind of small print that could, the magazine reported, 'sink a claim if disaster strikes on your holiday'. (ABTA countered that the magazine was alarmist, and set standards that were too high and unnecessary for the average traveller.) Those who want peace of mind can, however, obtain a 'top up' – at a price.*

UK agents' knowledge about medical emergency treatment (what is and what is not free in EC and other countries) can be rather hazy. It is best to contact the consulate of the country to be visited, but *Health Advice For Travellers* (prepared by the UK Department of Health and the COI,

---

*The Consumers' Association recommends the following minimum cover for holidays: medical expenses of £250,000 in Europe, £1 million worldwide; personal liability: £1 million Europe, £2 million worldwide; full cancellation cost; luggage and possessions £1,000; £250 cash.

updated daily on Prestel, and available free of charge, by calling 0800-555-777) is a comprehensive guide with a country-to-country checklist. It also gives sensible, general health principles, warnings about various diseases, and necessary or mandatory immunization. Airlines and clinics, such as the one run by Thomas Cook, can also advise. MASTA, the Medical Advisory Services for Travellers Abroad, charges for up-to-date information.

Vaccination requirements have been relaxed due to the success of the smallpox and leprosy eradication (and because not all vaccines are foolproof!), but it is vital to safeguard against hepatitis A and B, tetanus, polio, typhoid and rabies. Special care is needed in the Third World: a drug-resistant strain of malaria is now rampant in 100 countries, including normally low-risk areas of Africa. (Some new types of vaccines are free of adverse side-effects, though not yet available worldwide.)

The risk of excessive reliance on vaccines can be reduced by the adoption of the early Victorian adventurers' commonsense attitudes to local food and water. Ethnic minorities in the West need extra reminders of protection, because many of them are under the illusion that they are immune from diseases such as cholera that are prevalent in their native lands. Muslim pilgrims on the *hadj*, for instance, ought now to be vaccinated against meningitis because of a recent outbreak in Saudi Arabia.*

WHAT SORT OF AIRCRAFT?

Those who want to know what sort of machine will fly them, may face a brick wall. Operators do not guarantee that the type you booked on will actually be the one used. That may give rise to concern among those who dislike the idea of crossing oceans in modern, long-range aircraft with two engines, favoured increasingly by the carriers because of economic considerations and their good safety record to date (see Chapter 4). Once again, those who ask questions may influence the thinking of the airlines. When Air Seychelles started up, it used refurbished B707s ('hush-kitted' to comply with noise regulations) but had to revise its policy because most people preferred the B747s of British Airways. Travel agents' brochures are printed at least a year in advance and changes may occur in the published details (less likely in the case of charters). However at the time of booking, if the client is inquisitive, the agent *should* be able to find the type that is at that moment scheduled on the computer.

---

*The Traveller's Health, edited by Dr R. Darwood (OUP, 1991) is a most helpful book, *Travelling Healthy*, the US bi-monthly, brings the latest news on worldwide health risks such as a yellow fever epidemic in Kenya in 1993. The World Health Organization advises diphtheria immunization for visits to Russia, particularly Moscow, St Petersburg and Kaliningrad. (Those who had their last jab more than ten years ago need a booster dose.)

The cabin layout of the aircraft should also be available on request. The International Airline Passengers' Association discovered, for instance, that certain airlines were 'using short-range cabin configuration in Boeing 767, 757 and Airbus 310 aircraft for long-range flights of up to eight hours. Doing this – in order to gain a few extra seats – leaves passengers with insufficient toilet facilities and other unhealthy conditions' (*IAPA World*, Winter 1991).

AIRCRAFT	ENGINES	PASSENGERS	SEATS ABREAST
Airbus A300	2	201–375	9
A320	2	150	6
A330	2	440	9
BAC 1-11	2	119	5
BAe 146	4	70–82	5–6
B 727	3	189	6
B 737	2	115–149	6
B 747	4	550–660	11
B 757	2	178–239	6
B 767	2	290	7–8
B 777*	2	440	9–10
Concorde	4	128–144	4
L 1011	3	330	9–10
DC 8	4	269	6
DC 9	2	115–139	5
DC 10	3	380	10
Fokker 100	2	107	5
MD 80	2	172	5
MD 90*	2	172	5
MD 11	3	405	10
TU 134	2	84	4
TU 154	3	154–180	6

The table above gives a basic idea of the most widely used types of aircraft. Seating capacity varies not only with the range of operation (maximum fuel instead of maximum load) and the different versions of a type (e.g. a B747-400 may carry 110 more people than a B747-200), but also from airline to airline, depending on their keenness to economize with legroom by the reduction of pitch to cram in more seats. (An extra inch or two can make a great difference in comfort on a long flight.) The number of seats abreast may vary with the layout chosen by the carriers, and indicates whether the aircraft is wide- or narrow-bodied.

A knowledge of cabin layout is also an advantage if one seeks a smoking or non-smoking seat. On many short-haul flights (all domestic

*To enter service in 1995.

ones in the US) smoking is banned. No pipes or cigars are allowed on any flight. On long-haul, the number of seats for smokers is shrinking. In America, a non-smoking seat *must* be given on request, so smokers are advised to make seat reservations in good time. Satisfying local demands, certain Far Eastern carriers allocate less than half their seats to non-smokers, and so do some European carriers serving Far East destinations. On a B747 of All Nippon Airways, however, flying between Tokyo and Sydney or Honolulu, two-thirds of the passengers may smoke. And while the World Health Organization and ICAO wish to outlaw all smoking in the air by 1996, Lufthansa and KLM have relaxed their restrictive rules because of public dissent in 1993.*

INTO THE JUNGLE OF FARES

It has long been a maxim of the industry that 'fares, not fears, prevent people from flying'. Because of the surfeit of seats and half-empty aircraft on popular routes, competition among the proliferating airlines is fierce, and fares have tumbled to the extent that only those with the greatest reserves can endure the crippling losses. In 1992, United Airlines, the largest US carrier, and American Airlines, its nearest competitor, each suffered a billion-dollar deficit; Delta, the third leading US line, lost half as much. In 1993, Delta chairman Ronald Allen said, 'We're talking about survival now.' Stephen Wolf, chief executive of UAL, admitted that the industry was in a state of chaos: 'rational pricing' would have to return, and barriers to international competition needed to be removed. The latter demand could, however, aggravate the former one. It is tempting to see throatcutting competition as a pure benefit to the passenger, but inevitable economizing could undermine the high safety standards maintained by the best carriers (see Chapter 4).

Be that as it may, the punters *are* laughing. Allegedly, hardly anybody pays the full fare on popular routes, such as between India and the West or Europe and the North American continent. (The transatlantic flights alone may be responsible for the bulk of the massive financial losses of the airlines.) Special offers are in abundance. They may come as straight reductions, free flights for frequent fliers, or two seats for the price of one, particularly on first and business class, the vanishing mainstay of airline profits. At the same time, depending on market conditions, there are many anomalies. One may pay a great deal more in Europe than America for flying the same distance. On business class, at the official rates, a flight from London to Mexico would cost 14.7 pence per mile, but twice as much to Cairo. Within the former Communist bloc, air fares were kept artificially low. From Budapest, the distance is the same to Moscow as it is to London, but the latter used to cost ten times more.

Travel In Tolerance – A Guide to Smoker-friendly Aircraft was published in London by FOREST, the Freedom Organization for the Right to Enjoy Smoking Tobacco,

So it pays to shop around. Discounted APEX (Advance Purchase Excursion) tickets must be bought seven to thirty days in advance. The money is non-refundable. Unlike those who pay the full fare, APEX users are offered no flexibility, although lately it has become possible to circumvent even those restrictions by paying a small penalty for a last-minute change of departure or return date – and even the penalty variations are subject to competition. Charter flights are often obtainable at the last minute at vastly reduced rates – but, of course, those who wait the longest take the greatest chance. Scheduled flight tickets are not reduced so suddenly, but the differences can be considerable: special offers are likely to be more attractive early in the day as opposed to later, when a flight is already filling up. In America, published fares are frequently referred to as prices because they may fluctuate weekly like those of groceries.

'Crafty business travellers, flying frequently to East Europe, can take advantage of differences in exchange rates,' says Péter Kárász, Communications and Publicity Manager of MALÉV. 'Though fares are set by bilateral agreements, a return ticket between Budapest and Paris costs more in Paris, a more expensive city, measured in dollars. So a frequent French flier may buy a single ticket to Budapest – or a special return that may be cheaper, and throw away the return half – then start buying returns Budapest–Paris–Budapest . . . and save some 15 per cent on each trip from then on.'

Passengers are always shocked when they discover they are surrounded by people who have paid much less for the same trip. What they often overlook is that the lucky ones had gambled on whether they would get away on the intended day, that the special offers may hide a trap (such as an almost free flight but compulsory use of an expensive hotel), and that some people might have accepted a longer flight with a stop-over, a lengthy detour and the inconvenience of transfers. A first- or business-class passenger, who goes to Chicago or some other American destination via Frankfurt instead of direct from London may save up to £800 on a round trip. Germans and Swedes may save by flying economy via London across the Atlantic or to Australia. It is also possible to save time: London to Beijing may take seventeen hours with BA via Hongkong, five hours less with SAS via Copenhagen.

Airlines may be so keen to fill seats that they slightly undercut their own cut-price agents. But when shopping around, it is essential, once again, to ask questions and read the small print: there may be special restrictions, weekend exclusions, minimum stay, for example. In November 1992 in London one could find economy tickets for a particular UAL flight to Washington ranging from £224 to £266, well below the official APEX fare. But when one looked closer, differences in the profit margin became visible: one included airport tax, the other did not; the tax was sometimes £11, sometimes £17. BA tickets, for a flight departing half an hour earlier, ranged from £249 to £301. NorthWest Airlines offered a £30 saving – via Boston, taking a few extra hours. If the price difference is startling, as can be the case for long-haul and round-the-world travel, *beware* – the greatest saving may be offered by the airline with the poorest reputation for punctuality, service, legroom and safety.

In order to protect the smaller airlines that could be forced out of business by deliberate undercutting, the international law states that only the bilaterally agreed fares can be advertised openly. However the sale of discounted air tickets has long been an ongoing, well-planned, yet not easily admitted strategy. Airlines can estimate many months in advance the number of seats they are likely to fill at full fare on any particular flight. It may depend on the competition for the route, the season, even the day of the week or the time of departure. So apart from their own 'special offers', they use discount outlets. Some of these advertise cut-price tickets, and sell directly to the public, adjusting their profit according to demand: the outlets may make no more than £10 on a £300 ticket, but rely on the *volume* of sales – some airlines market up to a third of their discounted seats through them.

What airlines are most coyish about (to say the least) is the use of consolidators, wholesalers who sell discounted tickets through their agents, also at very tight profit margins. The list of consolidators is regarded as a closely guarded trade secret. Many carriers deny outright their existence, yet the practice is extremely widespread, and hardly any airline fails to take advantage of it. On some of the most competitive routes, tickets might be released to consolidators several months in advance. On other routes, where the airline hopes to sell more seats at the full, published price, the consolidator may get only last-minute left-overs. Most airlines use an average of five consolidators per destination or just one for a particular flight exclusively. Some airlines work with up to forty consolidators for much contested routes, such as between Europe and the USA. (Allegedly, AA, UAL and Virgin use numerous, and BA has a dozen such outlets.)

'I find it irritating that airlines insist on secrecy, when virtually everybody knows that there's no need to pay the full fare to certain destinations,' a consolidator told me, insisting on anonymity to protect his business that may be worth around £3 million a year. 'After all, we're the ones who take the risk, relying on a network of bucket shops that are unbonded, unlicensed, often ethnic agents who have minuscule over-heads – newsagents, grocers selling tickets only as a sideline, with the whole family serving customers and living above or in one room behind the shop. While a big, licensed travel agent works with a minimum of 9 per cent profit, bucket shops start with discounted tickets, and may be satisfied with 3 or 4 per cent on top: £10 on a flight to Bangladesh. They often sell only within their own ethnic groups, but may produce a turnover of £30,000 to £40,000 in five days.'

Overall, it is the passenger who benefits – in Britain saving 30 per cent or more – but there are certain risks involved. American consolidators have often sold 'dodgy' tickets that were for 'stand-by' but appeared to be confirmed seats. They advertised low fares that were unavailable or were then 'supplemented' by trebling the airport taxes or they raised excessive cancellation charges that amounted to as much as 75 per cent of the fare.

Because of their tight profit margins, discount sources try to save on everything, even on the postage stamp to issue confirmation of the booking in advance. If it is a last-minute booking, it is best to visit the bucket shop and pick up the ticket there and then against payment. They may charge up to 2 per cent for accepting credit cards because it costs them money. But if they refuse to accept cards, *beware* – it may imply an urgent need for cash, and therefore instability. And, once again, if a bucket shop goes out of business, only those who are already in possession of a ticket or have paid by plastic are safe.

In 1992, British Airways decided unilaterally to come out into the open and make discounted tickets available to licensed travel agents. The CAA, also opposed to clandestine trading, turned a blind eye to this break of the bilateral agreements, and said it would interfere only if the airline was seen dumping tickets to blatantly undercut and force a competitor out of business. It was a move in the right direction, but did not eradicate the use of consolidators and bucket shops.

OVERBOOKING – BUMPING

The multiplicity of outlets contributes to the passenger's nightmare of getting bumped off a flight. An airline may give the same seats to different consolidators who, in turn, may sell, illegally, more tickets than they are allocated. But overbooking scheduled services by anything up to 30 per cent is a standard, premeditated, but legitimate airline stratagem.

When I asked a major international airline press office, 'What is the position with overbooking?' they replied 'Sorry, the question is too general to be answered.'

'OK, so how many consolidators do you use on a New York flight, and how many seats do you overbook?'

'Sorry, it's company policy not to discuss specifics and individual cases.' (Japanese airlines claim they do not need overbooking, because Japanese passengers are disciplined and will turn up at the appointed time.)

The airlines' excuse for overbooking is the need to fill their aircraft. They know from bitter experience that according to the season, the day of the week and the hour of the day, a varying percentage of passengers will not show up. Those who paid the full fare could simply take another flight – or a refund!* Others on, say, an APEX ticket, might produce a doctor's certificate, and reclaim their loss from the insurers. Overbooking will often equal the no-shows. When it does not, bumping begins.

The British Air Transport Users' Committee deems this 'no-show' philosophy a myth: cases reported to the AUC were statistically incompatible with the airlines' explanation. The French Chamber of Commerce found that 80 per cent of denied boardings had other causes (if a late block booking came in, individuals might be left behind). 'The uncritical acceptance of the airline story has been a major obstacle to improving the situation' (*AUC Annual Report*, 1989/90).

'The practice of overbooking is, supposedly, to the passenger's benefit,' said Hoyte Decker, Assistant Director for Consumer Affairs of the US Department of Transportation, 'because if the airline achieves a higher yield factor, it will, hopefully, lower the fares. In the United States, 1.03 persons per 10,000 get bumped, based on 1992 data. The figure is low, but when it happens to you, you'd better be sure of your rights. Our *Fly-Right* leaflet costs a dollar, but at least one airline distributes it free on request. The regulations are clearly defined. No compensation is due if they can get you to your destination by an alternative flight within an hour of your planned arrival time. Then there are different provisions for compensation. To minimize the trauma, airlines usually ask for volunteers who can take another flight. They may get cash or a free additional ticket. Some people actually look for compensation – a business traveller, using the same route frequently, may accept a brief delay if he gets his next flight free. But before you volunteer, find out whether they will pay for meals, telegrams or accommodation if necessary. In 1992, we had 718,346 volunteers, and only 45,732 people suffered involuntary denial of boarding. It's well worth making a complaint to us if, for instance, they fail to offer you the obligatory minimum compensation, because we can bring action against airlines that seem to do it regularly.'

At American airports, airline officials walking round with a fistful of dollars are not an unusual sight. They tempt passengers, upping the offers, to make them volunteer, and those who hold out longest seem to get the most. Except for flights originating in the United States, airlines used to be free of obligatory compensation for denied boarding. In Britain, many carriers followed the advice of the AUC on how compensation should be calculated. Since 1991, the Association of European Airlines has standardized the victims' entitlement: they could choose a full refund of the cost of the unused portion of the ticket or, alternatively, accept rerouteing at their convenience, plus cash compensation

---

*On Swissair's Zurich to Washington inaugural flight eighteen first-class seats were booked – twelve showed up. 'On Fridays, businessmen want to get home early,' said Peter Gysel, Deputy Chief of the airline's Corporate Planning. 'They book an afternoon departure – hoping to make it, but safe in the knowledge that they could always switch to an evening flight.'

(proportionate to the delay on a set scale), meals, hotel accommodation if necessary, and a free phone call/fax/Telex message to their destination. So finding volunteers is now easier because a family of four could collect up to £1000, maybe half the cost of their entire holiday, for the loss of a day.

Although in other parts of the world the bumped passenger's rights are ill defined (if defined at all), the American Aviation Consumer Action Project's advice may come in handy anywhere: *be assertive*! If an airline tries to pay you off or arrange a seat with another carrier to take you to your destination, clarify what is on offer. Airline personnel often have the discretion to pacify insistent passengers one way or another, but an alternative flight may cost extra, and the offer must cover the difference. Seasoned travellers have a trick up their sleeve: smartly dressed women, men who wear a tie, couples with no children, have the best chance of being bumped up to first class, free of charge, instead of getting left behind.

DEFENSIVE FLYING

is an excellent concept advocated by the American Consumer Affairs Office. It recommends that defence should start at the booking:

- try to check out the agent from whom you buy the ticket
- pay by credit card whenever possible
- when selecting a flight, remember that departures early in the day are less likely to be delayed than a later flight because of the 'ripple' effect
- if punctual arrival is essential, try not to book the last possible flight or you may miss that wedding or important business meeting
- if you book the last flight of the day, and there is overbooking, you may be stranded overnight
- try to pick up your ticket instead of having it mailed to you because your 'lost in the post' claim may cause much inconvenience
- if there is a choice between two connections (and the fares are equal), select the less congested connecting airport where the risk of delayed landing and misconnection would be reduced
- reconfirm your reservation with the airline itself, whenever possible, a day or two before departure.

(Contact with the airline is also useful because it is probably connected either to an American computerized booking network or the international British Airways Business System that can handle 20 million instructions a second, holds details of more than a quarter of a million flights, hotels, visa and health requirements, airport information and other key facts.)

THE TICKET

Above all, it is essential to read and scrutinize all the details. Check your name and initials, flight numbers, departure dates and times, class (F for first, Y for economy/coach or some other euphemism, such as

World Traveller, favoured by the airline), and the airports to be used. (The name of Dulles Airport was changed by President Reagan to Washington Dulles International Airport because previously, many passengers found themselves at Dulles when they had intended to fly to Dallas, Texas. Airports are denoted only by a code such as LHR for London Heathrow, CIA for Rome's Ciampino and the misreadable CTA for Sicily/Catania.)

Query immediately if the ticket is not marked 'OK' (i.e. seat confirmed) in the 'status' box because you may only be on the waiting list (if there is a dispute with the agent, ask for your 'locator number', the reference number of reservation that should be, in any case, at the top of the ticket). Also check that there are separate flight coupons for each sector of the journey. (When changing aircraft en route, it is useful to count your remaining coupons because check-in clerks may accidentally remove two instead of one.) See if the endorsements are correct: for example, APEX, non-transferable, travel restrictions. Keep a note of the ticket number because that makes it easier to get a replacement if lost. Check in early (certainly by the time specified) for if anybody is to be bumped it is most likely to be the last one to show up.

Unfortunately, certain important pieces of information are never given on the ticket, and hardly anybody reads the small print.*

What information is missing from the ticket? First of all, everything that may be relevant to the safety of the carrier or its aircraft (see 'Bill of Rights' in the next chapter). It omits any reference to the taxes included in the fare. Apart from the fiddle some agents use to profit by overcharging airport tax, governments use taxes on air transport in curious ways. Dr Hans Krakauer revealed in *IAPA World* (Winter 1991) that in some cases taxes constitute a third of the fare. 'IATA knows of over 600 different types of ticket and airport taxes, charges and fees. They range from fees to fund animal and plant health inspection services, to a fee to rebuild a bridge damaged in a hurricane – there even exists a fee to celebrate the martyrs of a national revolution . . . Unless consumers become more vocal in expressing their concern at rising ticket taxes and charges, governments will take little notice of airline industry protests.'

Tickets (and agents/airlines) say nothing about the tax that may be payable at the last minute before the return flight at a foreign airport. This often comes as a surprise demand to the traveller who has already used up his foreign currency, and must now change more money. (It is

---

*The size of the print is regulated because of the Lisi case. Some thirty years ago, a blade of a turbofan engine came off, and Mr Lisi suffered minor injuries aboard a New York-bound Alitalia DC8. He argued that the print on his ticket was illegibly small, and so he was deprived of vital information. Although it was arguable that he would have rejected flying because of any of the details, the American court ruled in his favour, and from then on 10-point print has become the minimum acceptable size.

particularly irritating when one has only large denomination traveller's cheques, and the exportation of left-over local currency is banned!)

The check-in time may or may not be on the ticket, but there is certainly no outright warning that what is considered a 'late' check-in may lead to the loss of the ticket without compensation. Airlines do not guarantee their schedules: if a flight is delayed because of weather, heavy air traffic or anything beyond their control, there is nothing to be done. Airlines retain the right to substitute alternative carriers or aircraft, and alter or omit stopping places without notice. If there is an unscheduled stop-over to pick up extra passengers (because the airline has suddenly combined two half-empty flights), only full-fare passengers can change their reservations to avoid the annoyance of the delay, and carriers accept no responsibility for missed connections. (Because of an unscheduled stop-over in Rome, an American passenger witnessed a fatal shoot-out with terrorists and suffered a heart attack while he was kept locked in an aircraft without air conditioning. Most unfortunate? Yes. But the airlines disclaim responsibility even for scheduled stop-overs, though arguably every additional landing and take-off, the phases of flight during which most accidents occur, may constitute an added hazard.) So if you really want a *direct flight*, for which there is no official, legally binding definition, examine the indicated flying time: a stop-over may be revealed by the extra sixty or ninety minutes.

The ticket shows the codename of the airline with which you booked, but may say nothing about the company that will actually fly you, particularly in Europe. 'Wet leasing' (subcontracting the aircraft and its crew) is practised by many major airlines that lend only their much publicized good name to the flight. In that sense, the passenger may be misled by the ticket, and even more by the subcontractor's aircraft being painted in the major carrier's corporate colours, with only the crew's uniform or foreign tongue revealing the truth. Passenger organizations have long campaigned for the right to refuse flying if such undisclosed arrangements are made. In France it has been every passenger's legal right since 1990 to receive all the facts about subcontracted aircraft, whether it is a scheduled long-term deal or a charter at short notice to cope with strikes and heavy high-season traffic.

The small print on the ticket – concerning mostly baggage and injury liabilities, hand-luggage allowance and dangerous articles – is an extract from your unseen contract with the airline. It is based on the standard IATA Conditions of Carriage that ought to be freely available to any passenger on request, but copies are often hard to obtain. (Out of eighteen booking agents of sixteen major airlines, only one knew what I was talking about when I asked to see that document. Just two others volunteered to make some enquiries, and eventually sent me the full text. The rest either treated the request as another nutty phone call or, under pressure, representatives of household names such as Aeroflot and Qantas simply forwarded photocopies of the standard ticket.

The Conditions do contain, however, some interesting facts. The airlines may refuse carriage if in their opinion the passenger misbehaves or represents a health hazard to himself or others. But probably the most startling sentence (included in the standard IATA ticket) reveals that the airline is not obliged to *fly* you to your destination: 'Carrier undertakes to use its best efforts to carry the passenger and baggage with reasonable dispatch.' *But not that it will transport you by air.* It is unlikely that in the case of a strike, for instance, any airline would resort to chartering a raft for an Atlantic crossing, or an elephant to carry you over the Alps, but if there is a diversion to a distant airport for any operational reason, a long coach ride to the original destination would still be 'reasonable dispatch'.

Contracts set out the obligations and rights of both parties – valid even if unseen. (British Rail tickets are 'issued subject to conditions' though inquisitive passengers might by lynched if they hold up a long queue, demanding to see the document.) An Indian domestic airline took a huge risk when it flew the participants of an international convention to the Taj Mahal with cardboard numbers issued in lieu of tickets. It could have been sued out of existence for the slightest mishap or inconvenience – no ticket, no contract – particularly because all the passengers were lawyers!

THE LAST RESORT

Whenever you encounter problems with air travel, it is essential to resort to making a formal complaint instead of just brooding and spreading the word about the airline or agency that did something wrong – though the latter also helps in the long run.

The British AUC receives about 1300 complaints a year – a surprisingly low figure in proportion to the 100 million journeys undertaken. Almost a fifth of those concern flight cancellations and delays. The second largest group complains about tickets and reservations (including false 'OK' status), but very often the resentment is due to the agent's neglect to explain, and the passenger's failure to query, the restrictions on the ticket: they entered a contract without revealing and, on the other hand, asking to see the booking conditions. Other common reasons for complaint are in-flight service, overbooking, schedule changes, and, above all, insufficient compensation offered for lost luggage. The AUC investigates all complaints against airlines, but can act only as an intermediary even if the passenger has a good case. Professional bodies of travel agents, such as ABTA, can handle complaints but only against their members.

In America, the periodic Air Travel Consumer Report is known as the 'hit parade'. It identifies airlines by name if there are more than ten complaints against them. Though 31,000 agents sell three-quarters of all tickets, worth some $40 billion, they are regarded as middlemen – except when they make unauthorized, indirect sales – and it is the airline that is held responsible for generating the problems.

'We regard all complaints as justified,' says Hoyte Decker, 'but in 40 per cent of the cases, an explanation to the passenger clears the air. He might have asked for a ticket to Chicago but failed to check that the agent wrote one for Minnesota. Another 40 per cent warrant calls to the airlines, and that usually speeds up a response or outright settlement. As a matter of fact, airlines visit our office, and utilize our reports, particularly when they're named, to stem a trend, such as frequent bumping or the rudeness of staff, that dents their reputation.'

The reasons for American passengers' complaints are similar to those in other parts of the world, with delays high on the list, even though all American agents have on their computers – and must reveal – the current punctuality ranking of each domestic carrier. (A '6', for instance, shows that in the previous month only 60 per cent of its flights departed on time, i.e. not more than fifteen minutes behind schedule. If someone wants to fly at nine a.m., there may be four departures for the same destination within a few minutes of each other, and the airline with an '8' will enjoy preference.)

THE WARSAW CONVENTION AND THE HAGUE PROTOCOL

A crucial part of the ticket and the Conditions deals with the airline's liability in case of a passenger's injury or death. It is not a subject most people are keen to contemplate, but it is worth a brief review, because the antiquated laws and anomalies will never be changed without a public outcry. For currently, it can make a vast difference who kills or maims you and where – rather odd subjects for consideration when booking a ticket.

Airline liability used to be limited to $10,000 per passenger by the Warsaw Convention 1929, later doubled by the Hague Protocol. The Montreal Additional Protocol which aimed to raise it again was not ratified by enough governments because the poorer airlines could not or would not afford the ensuing higher insurance rates, and chose to live in the hope that they would not have an accident. It was an obvious anachronism, and America threatened to leave the Convention unless a compromise was reached: all airlines carrying passengers to or from the USA, and all with a planned stop-over in the USA, would have to raise the limit to $75,000. Even that isn't much, but most airlines stick to it, and their tickets barely refer to 'liability according to the Warsaw Convention'. *Some* carriers have, however, quietly adopted a new limit of 100,000 Special Drawing Rights* (now about US $130,000) by special

*The value of SDR varies, but it is often close to the sterling/dollar exchange rate of the day.

contract, and hardly anybody notices, for instance, that in BA's Conditions of Carriage the limit is now raised to 130,000 SDRs.

With these *limits*, the airlines waive their defence, and declare the maximum they will pay in compensation for personal injury or death without any need for litigation or admission of liability. In this way, they hope to avoid costly, humiliating court procedures that draw protracted, potentially adverse publicity. But, difficult as it may be, the limits can be broken whenever a victim can prove an airline's aggravated negligence – wilful misconduct or, occasionally, intentional or reckless misconduct – or simple negligence by the aircraft, engine or components manufacturer, or some other third party. Even then, serious anomalies could arise. In the 1960s, a young person's life was valued at three or four thousand dollars. In America and Japan, it is now up to half a million. The loss of a child is horrible, but the compensation is next to nothing. A non-working mother's death pays far less than a breadwinner's that depends on age, earning power, commitments, loss of pension rights, children's educational needs, et cetera. After the Lockerbie bombing disaster, PanAm offered $75,000 for each victim. The relatives sued in America, and PanAm was convicted of failure to comply with FAA security measures. So the liability became unlimited, and up to $7 million damages were awarded per passenger. It's high time to bring such anachronisms to an end. In November 1992, all Japanese airlines offered compensation on an *unlimited* liability basis in their Conditions of Carriage. That might break the ice; others would have to follow suit and bear increased costs of insurance. If not, it will tell passengers a great deal about the operator they are flying with.

'It may sound ridiculous, but it is a fact that even though air transport is a vast, international industry, the difference from country to country can be even greater than in a car accident,' explained Malcolm Keogh, a legal specialist in air safety. 'If you're knocked down by a car driven by a rich plastic surgeon in Los Angeles, the compensation would be many times more than if the culprit was a taxi driver in Karachi. That is why in certain circumstances lawyers are forced to go forum-shopping in the country or state of the airline, aircraft or engine manufacturer – or, for instance, the defendant's place of business. Take a crash in Germany by an African airline, with a French aircraft, flown by a British pilot. If we can prove that a *faute grave*, some gross negligence, arose in America – say, out of commercial considerations, the US engine manufacturer failed to warn users or put sufficient emphasis on a *known* potential hazard – those liability limits could be greatly exceeded.'

In December 1991, an MD-81 of SAS crash-landed and broke into three near Stockholm. Fortunately nobody was killed – yet another testament to the strength of aircraft and the survivability of accidents – but it could have led to a major legal spectacle. The investigation revealed that ice had accumulated on the wings, and remained undetected before take-off. It broke away in flight, damaging the engines which then surged. The pilots saved their passengers (see page 199) though without noticing that the throttles had advanced, i.e. increased power, of their own free will, destroying the engines. The reason was simple: the MD-81 was equipped with an automatic thrust-restoration system, but its existence was unknown to the pilots for it was hidden in the computer program. (Had it not been there, the pilots could have returned to the airport.) SAS claimed it had not ordered the aircraft with that system, and knew nothing about that computer program. The manufacturers countered: it was there for all to see in their flight procedure manual. The investigators did find it mentioned – tucked away under 'noise abatement'. Had there been any fatalities, the ensuing legal wrangle would have earned a fortune to the lawyers – and huge embarrassment to all other parties. (Belatedly, pilots were then duly alerted.)

Airlines never mention safety, beyond claims such as 'We take good care of you', but Don Madole, the well-known American aviation lawyer, believes that 'Airline advertising ought to be the first step towards breaking and eliminating that unrealistic $75,000 limit. If at least they were more open about their favourable and special Conditions of Carriage, their advertising would imply: *We fly you safely, but if anything goes wrong, we pay you more, and more readily, no questions asked.*'

The fine print on an airline ticket, just as with the law in general, is a quagmire on which the legal profession thrives. In 1992, a relatively minor injury case in Britain went all the way up to the High Court. An airline employee was pushing the wheelchair of a passenger who had just landed at Heathrow; at the end of the trevelator the wheels got stuck, and the plaintiff was trapped and injured. According to the Warsaw Convention, the carrier was responsible for the passenger 'in the course of embarking and disembarking', so was the passenger still in the care of the airline? Though the passenger had not yet gone through immigration or customs, the court held that within the meaning of Article 17 of the Convention, she was not in the course of disembarkation when the accident occurred.

The cost of litigation and necessary investigation in a major accident case is enormous. It is, therefore, often tempting to accept the quick settlement of a claim, and let the wrongdoers hide behind the 'liability according to Warsaw Convention' clause. That is why the once pooh-poohed American-style 'no-win-no-fees' legal deals look more and more attractive to victims and surviving relatives who can get nowhere without a shrewd, experienced and preferably rich lawyer who might take the risk, and invest a great deal of time as well as cash 'on spec'.

4

A Matter of Trust and Choice

Despite the occasional, disastrous hiccups, the overall safety record of aviation is excellent. So does it make any difference which airline you entrust with your life?

Consider three crashes, and the questions arising from them. (The cases have been picked at random, to illustrate potential problems rather than point a finger.)

- In 1983 a B727 of the Colombian Avianca was flying over Mount Otiz when the voice recorder in the cockpit taped a curious exchange: the GPWS (Ground Proximity Warning System) began shrieking, *Whoop . . . Whoop . . . Whoop*, and then, in a metallic voice, *Pull up . . . Pull up . . .* The captain, preoccupied with landing checks, answered the busybody American contraption with obvious irritation: 'Shut up, gringo!' A few seconds after this laughable dialogue, the aircraft crashed, killing 148 people. Basic and refresher training of pilots was always expensive – had it been drilled into that captain to respect and take advantage of that revolutionary safety device?

- In 1992 an Air Inter A320 crashed into Mount Saint Oddily near Strasbourg; eighty-seven people on board were killed. The French magistrate in charge of the investigation (which is still in progress) charged the airline's operations manager with criminal negligence because the Airbus was not equipped with GPWS even though other operators of the type were using that device. The carrier's defence was that at the time the GPWS was not mandatory in France, that the system was prone to give false warnings, and that the manager followed the company policy which, based on 'long and extremely careful analysis', had gone against fitting the device. In 1992, there were twenty-six CFIT (Controlled Flight Into *high* Terrain) catastrophes – more than four times as many as in 1982; and a Civil Aviation Directorate letter had expressed concern about Air Inter flying without a GPWS a month before Strasbourg. Question: is it possible that the evaluation of that analysis and the resultant policy were tinted by cost considerations?

- In 1989 175 people were killed (eleven survived) when a Surinam Airways DC8 crashed on approach to Paramaribo. The US NTSB specialists, who helped the Indonesian investigation, discovered that the captain of the all-American crew was sixty-six years old, unqualified on the grounds of age, and his last proficiency check had been on a twin-piston Grunman aircraft. It then came to light that in the previous six months, two other contract pilots over the age limit of sixty had been flying for Surinam Airways, that the Miami agency, from which the supposedly FAA-licensed crew had been hired, relied on its pilots' responsible attitude to their own training and proficiency checks, and that other US agencies also had flight crews over the legal age limit on their rent-a-pilot rosters. (The NTSB then recommended more stringent checks on the crews of foreign airlines flying into the United States, and on the practices of American agencies supplying contract personnel.) Now that there is, yet again, a sizeable surplus of pilots, is it not likely that over-age, keen-to-work captains come cheaper as long as their licences are not subjected to thorough scrutiny? (Arguably, there are many older fliers who would be perfectly fit to utilize their great experience – and in America the age limit may soon be extended – but illegal hiring is not the way to change the law.)

Air safety and the prevention of accidents are delicate matters: it is impossible to define precisely their cost efficiency and determine how much a company could save on the crashes that did *not* happen. Yet savings are one of the crucial lifelines available to a financially punch-drunk industry in a fiercely competitive climate.

To find a bargain – let alone get something for nothing – is attractive to us all. Should we then just enjoy the ever-cheaper tickets with no questions asked? Were the airlines so very profitable in some long-gone seven fat years that they could easily endure the current fare-warfare? Or were they so inefficient that some belt-tightening, rationalization, redundancies and voluntary wage cuts (widespread these days) could produce a sudden abundance of funds to underwrite fare-slashing and ensure the survival of the fittest?

The fact is that most airlines suffer crippling and mounting losses year after year. Dozens of them go under or go the American way into so-called 'Chapter 11' protection. (They write off or renegotiate billions of debts, lose credit facilities, and must pay cash for services and fuel, but during that debt holiday can offer bargain-basement fares, undercutting competitors who have to service their massive loans.) With too many seats on offer, the load factor is falling – on a flight I took from New York to Tampa, we the passengers were outnumbered by the cabin crew – and in 1993 IATA is 'dead worried' about the industry's three-year loss of $10 billion.

A fascinating insight can be gained by the comparison of two lists: it appears that, almost invariably, the worst losses are accumulated by those airlines that claim the greatest success in carrying the most passengers. In 1992 the following were the top ten airlines according to the number of scheduled passengers they carried (the number of millions in brackets): American Airlines (86), Delta (83.1), United (66.6), USAir (54.7), Northwest (43.5), Continental (38.4), All Nippon (35.1), Air France including Air Inter (30.1), Lufthansa (26.9) and British Airways (25.4). Of those, BA was the only one to appear on the list of the top ten profit-makers, together with Singapore, Cathay, China, Thai, Qantas, Southwest, Swissair, Air New Zealand and Malaysian Airways. Of the rest of the 'successful' ones, Continental was at the time in bankruptcy protection, and the other five American majors were listed among the top ten loss-makers. (The other main losers were Iberia, Varig, Air Canada, TAP and JAL.) Despite their leading positions, Air France and Lufthansa were also heavily in the 'red', and All Nippon had only just managed to make a profit.

Competition is fiercest on the trans-Atlantic and American domestic routes. To entice full-fare passengers (especially in first and business classes, the only consistent profit-makers) airlines must introduce more frequent flights, with special offers and extras, such as limousine service or two tickets for the price of one, finance advertising extravaganzas (the new BA ad took thirty-eight miles of film, four months and £1.8 million to produce – *Sunday Times*, 24.1.1993), sink fortunes into further fare-slashing (thus subsidising passengers for the privilege of transporting them), and lavish spending on in-flight entertainment, such as personal seatback video sets. (Emirates Airlines, the first to install these sets, spent $7500 per seat – $1.5 million for each aircraft.)

Air France is planning to sell last-minute tickets at a 75 per cent discount. When BA's much vaunted profitability took a dive, despite severe measures and pay cuts, it was not entirely surprising that, under pressure to produce results, some BA employees resorted to dirty tricks against Virgin, their main British competitor. Then in the spring of 1993, BA reduced its trans-Atlantic return fare to $380. Virgin countered the move by charging only $366 for the same. And in an apparent suicide pact, everybody followed suit.

It appears from the above list of the most successful airlines, that the more people they carry, the greater losses they chalk up. If the reader is inclined to call this crazy, nobody will argue.

The mathematics is fairly simple. Experts estimate that it costs about $250,000 to fly a Jumbo across the Atlantic and back – $625 per seat. (Cheaper only if overheads can be slashed.) Empty seats are a total loss, but if a return ticket is sold for less than the cost, the carrier still loses on every passenger. What they all hope to achieve is to force competitors who cannot last the course out of business, and then once again start to charge realistic and economically viable – i.e. soaring – fares. That daydream of the aviation industry is still many a flight year away.

Airlines must rejuvenate their fleets to remain competitive, and take advantage of the lower operating costs of modern aircraft. Recession and crippling losses force them, however, to slow down their expansion plans considerably. As a result, the aircraft manufacturers' rate of output had to be curtailed (halved in the case of the MD80 by McDonnell-Douglas) because worldwide firm orders were revoked or deferred (Northwest cancelled seventy-four orders for Airbuses in one go), and many airlines greatly reduced their leasing requirements.

The price of modern aircraft is phenomenal. Depending on specifications, a Boeing 737-400 may cost $42 million, a 747-400 up to $158 million, and the new 777 up to $140 million. Boeing has orders and options worth some $500 billion to be delivered by the year 2010, but must shed 30,000 jobs and cut output by 40 per cent because of cancellations. American Airlines is set to cancel leasing $1 billion worth of Airbuses, causing similar problems to the manufacturers. The Russians will compete with their TU204, which has still to gain airworthiness certification – being a Boeing 757 look-alike, it is already known as the '757ski' – and could undercut Airbus and the Americans by some 30 per cent. That is why smaller, poorer airlines are very interested in it.

So from where does all the money come to cover the losses and the cost of fleet rejuvenation? 'Over here,' as a Boeing executive in Seattle put it, 'banks and creditors must keep running after their money, i.e. pump more and more into the airlines, if they don't want to lose their investment. The additional loans may at least help to cover the payments of interest. Those who supply services and fuel can't afford to have defunct customers, so they keep rescheduling the payment of debts . . . Thank God,' he added after a pause. In other countries, including several European ones, where the demise of a flag-carrier would fatally dent national pride, government subsidies keep many airlines afloat. Ignoring the Treaty of Rome which forbids state aid, even Lufthansa, Air France, Alitalia, Olympic and Iberia receive cash injections on favourable terms that are not available to BA, SWISSAIR, the American carriers and many others in the private sector. The European Commission did not object to the bailing out of the endangered Sabena by a hefty Belgian government loan of £310 million because it was, allegedly, for 'restructuring'.

European governments are bent on increasing competition through legislation for the travellers' benefit. They want to follow the American example, hoping to avoid the pitfalls of deregulation and the risks of going from total control to total freedom in a single leap. In the United

States, the initial result was a vast proliferation of airlines with welcome yet suicidal fare cutting, closely followed by an avalanche of almost 200 bankruptcies, and the emergence of even bigger conglomerates that gobbled up the competitors. 'For good competition we don't need many ill-financed, tiny airlines,' said John Parr, Director General of the AUC. 'Some take-overs promote competition. Megacarriers biting into others' internal markets force them to compete.' But the AUC Annual Report of 1991 emphasized that the EC Commission must 'prevent airlines from abusing their new-found freedoms, whether to the disadvantage of consumers or by predatory behaviour towards other carriers.' Nevertheless, dozens of new, small airlines are being set up while, in the name of cutting costs, global megacarriers are emerging through take-overs and the pooling of resources to gain access to markets.

These trends are not entirely to the long-term benefit of the consumer. The crewing of Surinam Airways was an example of the risks. The Third World and the former communist states want their share of international air transport. The *Daily Telegraph* reported in 1991: 'The nice thing about East European airlines, the optimist argues, is the way it puts excitement back into air travel. Pessimists tell you to check your life insurance.' Aeroflot, the world's largest airline, has enormous problems with old, substandard equipment, fuel shortage that may ground a hundred aircraft a day, and, lately, the need to improve its hitherto secret and shoddy level of safety. The former Soviet, now autonomous, republics have given birth to forty airlines for scheduled services, amazing their domestic passengers with offers of hot coffee and biscuits – for cash.

Some new flag-carriers make do with elderly, second-hand Russian machines. China uses them extensively, but accidents revealing their poor safety record (five crashes in four months) have just started to become known internationally – and only because Western tourists were involved. (Between 1985 and 1993, thirty-five independent airlines were set up in China, and in 1992 the country suffered its worst ever safety record: three out of its four major accidents happened to the new carriers. It is only now, at last, that the government has put the brakes on to avoid spreading the pool of trained mechanics and managers too thinly. It has set minima for the number of flight attendants, ground support and managerial staff.) Ukrainian Airlines was started with a bargain deal – just $15 million for seven Ilyushin-62s and ten smaller Antonovs, offloaded by LOT, the Polish airline that found them uneconomical and unsafe. Others put their faith in new and hand-me-down Western aircraft.

If those airlines are backed with finance and expertise from major American or European carriers, they can institute a vigorous, premodernization flight and maintenance programme; if not, they may gamble on the truth of an old Hungarian saying: when the good Lord grants you a job, he'll also give you the brains to handle it. Which in the case of modern technology may be just a touch too optimistic. An aircraft of China Southern, a fast-growing Cantonese airline that operates modern B737s and 757s on lease, crashed into a 1500-foot mountain in an area where the minimum safety altitude was five times higher up. The weather was sunny and the control tower had warned the captain he was descending too fast. Were the pilots or their charts good enough? When an A320 crashed at Bangalore in 1990, a government committee criticized Indian Airlines for rushing its Airbus into operation when it was ill-equipped to fly that sophisticated, state-of-the-art machine in such large numbers with insufficient training of pilots and engineers. It failed to criticize, however, the government regulatory body that had rubber-stamped those operations. (Airbus Industrie, like other manufacturers, provides training and back-up but, ultimately, the achievement of satisfactory standards is not their responsibility.)

'Everybody would like to see high global standards,' said Carl Vogt, chairman of the US NTSB, 'but ICAO can only *recommend* standards. Advice, and all the accumulated experience is available to all, but only if they ask for it. While there're some small airlines staffed with real experts, there're unfortunately some African and Middle East countries, for instance, that remain well below average.'

Anthony Broderick, Associate Administrator of the FAA added: 'ICAO is not an enforcement agency, and no government can supervise others. But airlines operate in international service only in accordance with commercial agreements between the countries they serve. We have overcome ICAO's lack of enforcement capability by insisting, as a condition of granting commercial access to the United States, by foreign airlines, that they and their countries adhere to the international safety standards established by ICAO (which is an obligation the countries assumed when acceding to the Chicago Convention). We review other countries' standards, the rules they have, the way they license pilots and check aircraft. If they're not up to it, we demand they fix those problems – or stop flying to this country. Four hundred and seventy-five airlines from ninety countries fly to the United States, and none of them wants to lose this privilege. The program has just been finalized, and we've already had a few very difficult sessions with some countries, leading to the withdrawal of some carriers' landing rights. Belize is a good example. We discovered that it was exercising no control over an airline flying from there, and seemed to believe that all the checking would be done by us. The carrier wasn't really an airline, just a collection of airplanes and pilots and a travel agency. So we demanded they should come under the umbrella of a proper airline, operating from and overseen by another country that would impose its own standards. Some states use the excuse of the Chicago Convention, and maintain that the way others operate is none of their business. But that's not good enough. It threatens our own safety in the air and on the ground. And you take your life into your own hands when you fly with any of the substandard operators that may be tiny – or even big internationals.'

In 1993 passengers were grounded in Gambia, when the UK Department of Transport banned Air Gambia from flying into Britain. The airline then signed a contract with a British company to maintain its three old B707s. As the carrier was in bankruptcy administration at the time, it also used an Ilyushin chartered from Uzbekistan.

So how can we, the passengers, make our selection from thousands of flights with due consideration to decisive factors beyond the lure of the price tag?

OPTING FOR SAFETY – A MATTER OF CHOICE

There have been numerous attempts at drawing up comparative charts for airline safety. Although sometimes it is possible to pinpoint hazardous trends, and expose operators who show less than total dedication to safety, even the best of such efforts have a barely ephemeral validity: the available statistical sample of disasters is, touch wood, too small to be truly representative, and a single event can distort the picture. An airline that had no more than one accident in ten years, would *seem* to suffer 100 per cent deterioration in safety if it had just one more. And how would those ingenious charts take into account all the injury-free *incidents* that, by the grace of some lucky element, have *not* become fatal disasters? To escape from the whimsical vagaries of statistics, and to abide by the unwritten law of keeping mum about hazards, airlines shy away from discussing, let alone advertising, their safety record. They feel that any reference to *safety* may imply the existence of exactly the opposite. Many carriers, even those with as good a record as Cathay Pacific, simply ignore or refuse to answer questions regarding 'areas upon which the airline does not comment, such as safety'.*

There could, nevertheless, be some objective ways to discover, at the time of booking a seat, how much an airline *cares* about safety, and what exactly a passenger is buying. Captain Heino Caesar, Lufthansa's safety chief, for instance, produced a World Accident Survey in 1989. One of his startling conclusions was that airlines with fifty or more aircraft had proportionately fewer accidents than those with smaller fleets. It was 'alarming' that smaller operators, who owned altogether only 2 per cent of the world's fleet, suffered almost 40 per cent of all accidents in the sample.

The American Aviation Consumers' Action Project devised a system of great potential. Tom O'Mara, the secretary of ACAP, explained: 'Federal labelling laws could be applied to boarding passes. Nobody buys medicines without reading the label, so why should anybody board an

*Letter from TPS, a PR company handling Cathay Pacific, 16.11.1992.

airplane without knowing key factors affecting safety and security? Modern computer technology makes it possible for any airline to follow normal "full disclosure" practices used by all – except aviation. With that a boarding pass could be turned into a security information pass.

'Each aircraft is given a wing number for life. It is like a fingerprint to which all data about age and condition is attached. Information about personnel and bomb threats could also be matched to specific aircraft and flight numbers. Incidentally, the tickets fail to reveal that passengers have a penalty-free cancellation right if a flight is threatened by a criminal. Like the punctuality record of the airlines, all this data is already available on computers. Travel agents could bring it up on their screens at the touch of a button with no extra investment, and it would enable passengers to ask questions and make an informed choice.

'If we had an Airline Passengers' Bill of Rights they would have to reveal: (1) the type of aircraft, including the number of engines; (2) the age of the aircraft; (3) the number of repairs, as required by Service Bulletins and Airworthiness Directives, still outstanding on the aircraft; (4) any known bomb or other threats to a particular flight; (5) the pilots' years of experience; (6) the current financial condition – loss, profit, bankruptcy, Chapter 11 of the airline.'

'We'll get all this only when we become insistent, when parents, for instance, start asking questions before sending their children on a holiday flight,' comments Chris Witkowski, Air Safety and Health director of the US Flight Attendants' Association. 'A high-powered FAA official once told us that passengers don't give a damn. Well, they should be made to. After the death of 250 soldiers in the crash at Gander, the Defence Department began to demand safety checks on all carriers that sought contracts to carry the military. The same could be done by the FAA for everybody, and then effective public pressure would develop.'

Gerald Wilde, a Canadian psychologist, expounded the theory that 'the number of accidents occurring in any one country is – in the long term – exclusively dependent on the accident rate that the population is willing to tolerate'. With reference to that, in 1992 *System Errors in Aviation*, an excellent paper by the Aviation Department of the Swiss Reinsurance Company, argued that 'in terms of safety, only as much investment is made as necessary to maintain this tolerable level', and that 'in order to render the whole aviation system safer, no additional safety measures are required but a lower level of willingness to assume risk'. Though some of this is debatable – extra measures must deal with emerging hazards and stamp out sloppy practices – the paper illustrated its point with what had occurred in Germany: road traffic fatalities had 'continued to increase – despite a constant improvement in technical reliability and safety technology – until the situation became a political issue and the level was regarded as unacceptable. The accident rate finally dropped not as a result of technical measures or because of stricter traffic regulations, but purely because of the wide public debate . . . and a collectively lower willingness to assume risk.' The accident rate then levelled out 'at 8000 fatalities a year. Expressed bluntly: these victims are the price society is prepared to pay' for the pleasure of driving cars. The paper concluded that 'safety must – as far as possible – be detached from purely economic considerations. For instance, by rating safe flight operations as a value in itself and not simply as an addition to the service offered. For this to work, passengers must be prepared to pay a higher price for increased safety.'

Safety and economy form a vicious circle. Maximum safety would depend on minimum economy: if all possible safety measures were multiplied and built into the machine as well as its operation, no aircraft could ever take off the ground. From the dreams of 'total flight safety' either the word 'total' or 'flight' itself would have to be omitted. The fine balance between safe and economically viable air transport is in the hands of those who take the sword (of performance) and shall (sometimes) perish by that sword. Unfortunately, economic performance is more readily measurable than safety performance: far more airline managers of the highest echelons have been booted out for excessive losses than deteriorating standards. Yet those are the people we need to trust even more than the pilot who actually flies us, because only they can imbue an entire organization with the ideal of *safety first*, and introduce painful or even economically hurtful measures.

Boeing studied ten years of fatal accidents, and found that 12 per cent of the operators had over 90 per cent of the so-called 'crew-caused' accidents; 86 per cent of the operators had no such accidents. The achievement of that 86 per cent was attributed to top management emphasis on safety, usually through the good offices of a dedicated safety manager. Experienced airlines, such as United, usually have a formal written safety policy, said Jerome Lederer, one of the great gurus of air safety, at an international Human Performance symposium (Lisbon, 1991). He advocated that in the course of any accident investigation, the president of the airline involved should 'be required to describe in person their safety policies and implementation', and that airlines should introduce *risk management*, the continuous exploration of all foreseeable hazards in their infancy.

It would be hard to find a better example than the case of MALÉV. After an accident in 1968, the Hungarian airline was hit by a series of fatal disasters: Copenhagen in 1970, Kiev in 1971, Beirut in 1975, Bucharest in 1977. 'Accusations were flying in every direction, above all against the pilots, until at long last, a high-powered government committee was appointed to examine training, licensing, maintenance, recurring problems, routes, and even minor incidents,' said György Mátyásy, the current head of safety and security. 'Eventually, the root of all problems was found: management. We had incessant changes of chief executive and chief engineer – most of them professional soldiers, chosen for political reliability, who demanded more parade ground discipline than aeronautical professionalism. For example, our elderly maintenance staff had mostly been trained as *car* mechanics, and sent to the Soviet Union for two or three months of theoretical but hardly any practical conversion courses before assigning them to work on aeroplanes! They just about managed to keep our unsophisticated Russian turboprops flying. But in 1969, MALÉV received the TU-134s, the first jets to replace our Ilyushins. The urgent need to introduce new technology ought to have been obvious to all, but that was ignored or overlooked by the management that was also quite happy to take on retired fighter pilots rather than train new professionals. Due to the committee's recommendations, the soldier managers were replaced by experts, the old car mechanics were retired or transferred, new people received proper training, operations and maintenance quality controls were tightened, and as if by waving a magic wand, the airline was safe again. And that experience has never been forgotten. Before we began to modernize the fleet with Western aircraft, we first prepared for the changes.'

Deregulation, cut-throat competition and the price wars tend to force even the most safety-conscious manager to make compromises. If he *actually* compromised safety, he would be fired. But it is hard to detect when he goes just to the brink with hardly visible corner-cutting under the banner of *economizing* that may in the end erode the safety cushion protecting the aviation industry. 'In my opinion, US deregulation went too far,' says Konrad Wittorf, General Manager of SWISSAIR's Aircraft Maintenance, emphasizing that his was a strictly personal view. 'In some airlines it opened the way to the reduction of technical know-how to such an extent that a critical situation could develop. PanAm, for instance, used to operate with 200 highly qualified engineers. At the end, before going under, it had only four engineers left to check the operation of some 200 aircraft. What's more, when the mechanics are made to feel the economic pressures, they may do things that otherwise they wouldn't even contemplate. Because of built-in safety cushions, several built-in system redundancies, double checking, et cetera, no accident can happen without the opening of many gates. Some engineering slackness may not cause trouble in itself. But if the quality control, then the pilot fails to notice it, it could become critical in, say, severe weather conditions.'

Don Madole, the American aviation lawyer, also uses the PanAm example: 'Losing for decades, they tried to achieve savings on everything, even security. They used to charge five dollars of security levy on each ticket on flights to and from the United States. It was to be spent on nothing but security, but they used the accumulated $300 million mostly for advertising. No wonder they failed to introduce all the recommended security measures that might have helped to prevent the Lockerbie bombing disaster.'

Most airlines do not go as far as that, but Jerome Lederer noted some examples of cost-cutting: 'limiting fuel reserves to minimum requirements; winking at minimum equipment lists to satisfy the urgency to meet schedules; . . . turn around time on long flights has been reduced. Engineering staffs, medical departments, safety organizations have been reduced or abolished. Economic restraints have been put on maintenance' in order 'to stay in business'.*

'Non-revenue medical departments were among the first favourite targets of cost-cutters,' said Dr Frank Preston, a consultant in aviation medicine. 'The rot began in the United States. When Eastern Airlines [one of the biggest and most aggressively take-over-oriented carriers] ran into serious financial trouble, long before its total collapse, it was the first to get rid of its specialists. TWA used to have an excellent medical department. Then the work was contracted out because it was cheaper. United and American resisted the trend, but Northwest, Delta and others followed suit. What they lose is in-house dedication, personal knowledge and confidence of individual pilots, the chance to gather valuable information over a drink with patients, the facility of seeing a patient as a whole person, in his natural habitat, instead of meeting him for a brief consultation by appointment with a doctor who may be a good practitioner but without airline experience.'

Thanks to those durable safety cushions, such measures, even the decimation or liquidation of dedicated safety departments, do not manifest themselves directly through any increase in fatal accidents – though the proliferation of minor, potentially dangerous incidents could be significant. So does one need to worry about booking with an airline that is losing year in, year out? 'Hard to take a strong view,' says Rick van Woerkom of the NTSB in Washington. 'Take the Eastern Airlines saga. They lost billions, reduced their safety department to almost nothing, there were allegations about poor maintenance and shoddy operations, yet they suffered no big accident in their last few years.'

Others feel that the writing is often on the wall – if only people bothered to read it. 'The trouble is,' says Madole, 'that the old, safety-conscious, professional aviators at the top are much too often replaced by bookkeepers, lawyers, green Harvard graduates, who understand the needs of advertising more than the needs of flying. And of course, unlike pilots and engineers, managers are not licensed. Anybody is entitled to run an airline.'

*Sixth Annual International Aircraft Cabin Safety Symposium, Southern California Safety Institute, 1989.

The British Cork Committee report in 1982 had some invaluable thoughts about incompetent directors. It recommended that the limitation of their personal liability should be withdrawn retrospectively if they were shown to have caused their companies to trade wrongfully, and if they were proved unfit to manage a company. Yet, to this day, Britain has 'still no entry or training requirements, and discipline by the threat of disqualification' because 'mere incompetence will not suffice', and it is difficult as well as costly to prove *total incompetence* or *reckless disregard*. 'One solution would be for directors to be regulated by a professional body, controlling entry requirements and continuing education . . . Insurance cover against wrongful trading' might also help to control directors because insurers would require 'health checks'* – safety audits for airlines, advocated by the Flight Safety Foundation, and practised by some insurance specialists, such as Peter Spooner of Willis Corroon. Aviation lawyer Malcolm Keogh, of Pannone and Partners, sees a good chance for suing airline managers for criminal negligence in certain cases: 'If a car driver kills someone, it may be due to some momentary distraction. But if he drives at a hundred miles per hour along a street, it's a deliberate, criminal act. Similarly, a mechanic may make some genuine mistake, but if it happens due to risky or thoughtless management decisions, criminal negligence could be proven.'

The regulatory authorities can bring some pressures on directors, but only in extreme cases. Mike Willett, Safety Regulations Director of the British CAA: 'We issue AOC's [Air Operator's Certificates], and check every stage of a carrier's operation, its expertise in safety, management structure, training and maintenance set-up, as well as finances. We know only too well that a manager can over-pressurize a mechanic, for instance, to let an aircraft fly, and we risked libel cases when we said that XYZ was unsuitable and should be removed. But ultimately, safety is vested in the operations manager or director whose practices may endanger the airline's vital AOC.'

Likewise, the American FAA monitors the safety of airlines. Joe DelBalzo, executive director of Systems Operations, assures us: 'Cost reductions often affect the invisible "nice-to-do" items but must not violate the safety minima. If they abolish the safety department, we demand to see how they conduct their safety surveillance in its place. Most of their mistakes are unintentional, but we impose fines, demand corrective action, and monitor it. If their finances are unhealthy, they get more attention to see if there's a risk. A US airline in Chapter 11 is actually one of our safest carriers to fly today. Why? Because as soon as we see economic problems – say, they start paying bills sixty instead of thirty days late, or delay the payment of wages – we increase the frequency and depth of unannounced inspections, check their data,

*C. Williams and A. McGee, *Research Report 30* by ACCA (*The Times*, 15.10.1992).

monitor performance, and so on. A carrier in Chapter 11 is talking about paying off its debts at two cents a dollar. Its creditors may feel that two cents is better than none, for if it's forced into Chapter 9 or 7, the debtor goes out of business. Competitors may feel that carriers in bankruptcy protection have an unfair advantage, but while they're safe to fly, we don't interfere.

'True, we license pilots and engineers, not managers. Anybody with money can be president or chairman of an airline, but a vice-president of operations or engineering must show expertise and the right track record. When I worked in the Eastern Region, I personally disapproved – forced out, to be precise – some managers. Admittedly, they ran small airlines.'

Such examples are, however, few and far between. Greater control of managers could perhaps be accompanied by government help to financially troubled airlines – not a subsidy, but hard cash that the passengers themselves have forked out specifically for their own increased safety. ACAP's first international conference, supported by the Air Disaster Groups, revealed that some countries have Aviation Trust Funds to pay for the elimination of bombs from commercial flights. The accumulated American Aviation Tax Fund, collected for the improvement of security and safety, holds some $6.5 billion, yet it is used for disguising – on paper – the national deficit rather than for financing extra safety of airports and loss-making airlines.

Regarding government control of airline management in states still permeated by communist-style political appointments, and in Third World countries where bribes, tribal affiliations or loyalty to an absolute ruler or dictator may decide who gets what job, the problem grows even more complicated. 'Air safety is a worldwide goal. When one buys a ticket, one shouldn't have to worry about the integrity of the operation being affected by some local political or social conflict,' said John Enders, vice chairman of the Flight Safety Foundation. 'Yet we come across cases like, for instance, the well-trained and qualified aircraft mechanic having international experience but being denied employment as a mechanic in his home country because he belonged to the tribal group currently out of power. This situation occasionally extends to religious differences, or to circumstances where bribes or family connections "buy" licences or managerial jobs. We hope that, as high aviation standards become increasingly globalized, these practices will steadily be abandoned in favour of seeking the very best people qualified for critical jobs in aviation.'

So when we buy that extraordinarily cheap ticket to the sun, some probing questions ought to be asked.

5

Charters: Living Down a Certain Reputation

- It was a flight that had everything to offer: an abundance of legroom, the pilot's personal attention, free and unlimited alcohol. To the lone, somewhat jittery passenger's chagrin, there was, however, a minor drawback: virtually all that free booze was being consumed steadily by the pilot himself.

  This was a charter flight – the best I could find in a bar in Perth, Australia, to fly me to Kalgoorlie, a boom town (well, a dusty street lined by brothels and a pub) during the Australian nickel-prospecting bonanza in the 1970s.

- In 1992, fifty lorries were lined up expecting to move a vast amount of concert equipment from Stansted airport for Michael Jackson's British and European tour. There was, however, a slight hitch: all of the rock singer's electronic paraphernalia was to arrive aboard a chartered Russian Antonov 124. The aircraft had been used extensively to ferry beef to starving Muscovites under an operation certificate that satisfied the Russian military, but not the civilian safety standards. Following CAA advice, it was banned from British airspace.

Though the pitfalls of such individual charters will never become a widespread experience, the words 'charter flight' may still carry certain disenchanting, if not unnerving, connotations. For in the not-too-distant past these words would conjure up images of elderly aircraft, crammed to the brim, flying to dodgy airports, offering sufficient legroom for people below four-foot-six, survival rations that tasted like cardboard at their best and, above all, worse than average safety margins due to excessive economizing, sometimes illegal corner-cutting, with pressure on pilots to exceed their duty times and land, whatever the weather, at their destinations.

That uncalled for generalization, condemning the best with the rest, was propped up by facts. In America, post-war 'nonskeds' (non-scheduled airlines) mushroomed. Many of them were built around a couple of cheap, clapped-out, surplus machines, but the authorities trod cautiously on the tightrope of anti-monopoly principles and showed some leniency towards those poorer brethren's safety standards. In Britain, such double standards transpired when a Board of Trade investigation admitted that the small, independents' record was inferior to that of the corporations because of 'shortcomings of the flight crew, the airline and airworthiness'. But in a few years the number of 'nonskeds' dwindled from 400 to thirteen, and more than half of the British independents went out of business – some were merged, liquidated or bought out, while a fifth of them lost their operator's certificate for failure to maintain the safety minima.*

Since then, charter flights have changed beyond recognition to grow into the mainstay of the mass holiday travel explosion. They save on marketing and advertising because instead of going direct to the public, they sell big blocks or entire flights to tour operators who may also own some charter airlines. But the key factor of their success remains that they cut the fares to the bare bones, safe in the knowledge that virtually all seats will be sold – still a pipe-dream for everyone else. (Laker Airways used to make just 15 pence profit on each transatlantic passenger. Sir Freddie Laker, who collected £5 million in an anti-trust settlement when the big ones forced him out of business, now plans to make a comeback with cut-price holidays in the Bahamas.) Numerous dedicated charter airlines fall victim to the fare-wars, collapse, have their aircraft impounded for non-payment of landing fees, seek bankruptcy protection or accept take-over bids, but others flourish and sometimes resort to calling themselves 'leisure airlines' – a euphemism designed to eradicate the old image.

'Gone are the days of dubious service and bare minimum maintenance,' said Richard Hedges of Britannia, Britain's number two operator, and the world's biggest charter airline, carrying some 7 million people to more than 100 leisure destinations. 'Charters are a bulk business mainly for winter and summer holidays. With our tight profit margins, we depend on very high utilization of aircraft – each of our planes flies almost 4000 hours a year. To achieve this we must have top-notch preventive maintenance because we can't afford to have an aircraft stranded on, say, a Greek island where we would have to put a planeload of people in hotels, fly out parts or an engine or another aircraft to ferry everybody home, and suffer the knock-on effect on the entire schedule. Our aim is that less than one flight in a hundred will be delayed more than five minutes by technical problems – most airlines allow fifteen minutes for this "technical despatch reliability" measure.'

An added advantage of charters is that there is hardly ever any bumping, for there is no overbooking in the ordinary way. Whereas a

*Aircrash Detective, by Stephen Barlay (Hamish Hamilton, 1969).

scheduled departure can be cancelled because of technical or air traffic problems or even shortage of bookings (transferring passengers to another flight of the same or another airline), charters cannot call off a flight, except in extreme cases, without first trying to lease a substitute aircraft. Because of the overriding need for technical despatch reliability, the larger, profitable charter carriers also tend to run younger fleets. (The worldwide average age of jets in service is about eleven years. BA's Britannia's and Airtours's average is one, five and nine years below that respectively. Dan Air's fleet was above the world average before the take-over by BA. It must be said, however, that sometimes the extreme youth of a fleet only shows that the carrier is brand new.) In-flight food and entertainment, particularly on long-haul, have become comparable to those on scheduled flights, and charters also compete in the family-friendly attitudes to children and the nervous flier.

On the negative side, there is still the lack of flexibility (once booked, the ticket cannot be changed), and the old problem with legroom. Some charters continue to 'cram them in', and even the best can do no better than provide one or two vital inches less space than the scheduled carriers. (This is because the seat pitch, the longitudinal distance from headrest to headrest, must be kept to a minimum for the sake of full cabin utilization. BA would have 112 seats in two-class configuration on a B737 – the same aircraft in Britannia service would take 130 people.)

Delays and, not infrequently, *very long* delays, particularly on the return leg of the journey, remain the bane of the charters. Though airports deny it, they tend to put charters and the smaller airlines that have less muscle to the back of the queue when there is serious traffic congestion – and which European summer is free of that? The ensuing pressure on the pilots could be enormous: after all, they are loyal company men as well as dedicated fliers. The RAF Institute of Medicine, which ran a strictly confidential human factors incident reporting pro-gramme, received a note from a pilot who, in 1985, had suffered a heart attack while his charter plane was on the tarmac, ready to depart. Trusting his guaranteed anonymity, he confessed that he had chosen to carry on and fly to Spain rather than lose his take-off slot, cause great inconvenience to his passengers and a massive loss to his employers.

The CAA's punctuality charts of departures show a steady improve-ment at all British airports, but there are still startling differences between charters and scheduled flights. The 1989–1991 average delay for charters was (scheduled carriers' data in brackets) 43 (18) minutes at Gatwick; 41 (9) minutes at Manchester; 38 (13) minutes at Birmingham; and 42 (22) minutes at Luton. The differences between airports can often be explained by the differences in service types and the desti-nations served, as well as in the routes and the airlines themselves.

The cheap-flight-to-the-sun bonanza reaches its pinnacle with last-minute deals. A tour operator who took, say, a fifty-seat block on an aircraft but could sell only forty packages, would flog at least the surplus seats below cost to cover some of its losses. In June 1992, tour operators tried to clear 400,000 packages, offering up to 60 per cent price cuts. Charles Newbold, Managing Director of Thomson Holidays, was quoted as saying, 'We are seeing an undignified scramble for the patronage of the late-booking holiday-maker,' and, 'We'll sell all the holidays on offer for whatever we can get for them . . . It's collective madness but something has got to give.'

The patient, the adaptable and the gambler, who may not get away on a given date or to the chosen destination, may pick up fantastic bargains, but if at the very last minute that block of packages is sold after all, it may be the individual who gets bumped. Another pitfall is that a popular resort may be so overcrowded that virtually no accommodation can be found. In 1992, for instance, fearful of the effects of recession, some Cyprus hoteliers double-booked their rooms to be sure of occupation, while British tour operators sold 900,000 charter seats – 50 per cent more than the island's hotel capacity – many with 'hotel vouchers' of no value, purely to satisfy the law. So Cyprus set an example that may be followed by others if need be: it fined every airline £170 for each passenger brought in without guaranteed accommodation.

Those readers who have by now become convinced that there is much to be said for asking questions and finding out *who* on *what* aircraft will carry them, could be in for a pleasant or not-so-pleasant surprise. Some tour operators devote a full page in their brochures to the praises of their charter carriers' aircraft, services, catering and in-flight entertainment; but, sometimes, the meaningless name of the 'holiday airline' (for example, Condor, not exactly a household name outside Germany) hides the welcome fact that it is an integral part of a major, international organization (Lufthansa, in this case). In such situations, it is a reassuring discovery that the good name of a well-known carrier is on the line as far as safety is concerned. (A classic example of clashing attitudes occurred once at Heathrow. A small tour operator, who had wet-leased a KLM aircraft – complete with flight crew, that is – insisted that the pilot should take on extra passengers rather than extra above-the-legal-minimum amount of fuel. 'I don't like the weather reports,' answered the captain, 'and I want to have that extra safety margin of fuel in case we have to hold, divert and hold again. It's none of my business if you save on legroom or serve stale old sandwiches. But otherwise the flight is a KLM operation, and in this respect the decision is mine.')

On the other hand, answers to persistent questions can come as a shock if it transpires that the aircraft is geriatric, certified by a country of inferior technical reputation, and crewed by people who have just a smattering of English – not a great advantage in an emergency. When tour operators and charter airlines (those, above all, that create capacity 'on demand' rather than pre-planned services) need to lease an aircraft in a hurry for some unexpected reason, they may take the most readily available and cheapest one. Britannia, for instance, has a clearly defined list of companies – and countries! – that it will use or that it will not approach under any circumstances. Others may be less choosy.

The small, so-called *feeder, commuter* and *taxi* airlines – the latter a fast-growing industry that carries almost 30 million Americans a year – have inherited the old charters' mantle of ill-repute. Some of them are prepared to resort to the 'where there's a will . . . ' principle: one such airline, having already had a fatal crash, still saw certain crew regulations as 'an unwarranted economic hardship' which could be circumvented. 'The company ran both scheduled and so-called "on demand" charters, using small twin-engined aircraft with fixed landing gear. Flight 901 was to be a scheduled run carrying eight passengers, baggage and cargo. The available twenty-one-year-old pilot was qualified to take an "on demand" flight but *not* a scheduled one. So, using the excuse that "too many passengers had booked in for one aircraft", an *additional* "on demand" Flight 901A was created – on paper. In fact, the original Flight 901 was cancelled and substituted by the same plane with different documentation.

'The rest of the drama was an inevitable sequence of doom. The flight was 12 per cent over the permitted gross weight. The pilot taxied to the gas pump, and put in an extra 30 gallons of fuel. He forgot to drain the water from the fuel system. Soon after take-off, one engine went dead due to its water-contaminated fuel. In the developing emergency, the pilot then failed to follow the proper procedures which would have saved his life. At the root of all these mistakes was the fact that the FAA had never put an end to the management's habit of cutting corners. The operator's licence was now rescinded, but nine people had already been killed.'*

In 1987, a British holiday charter company ran short of seats and wet-leased aircraft from Tarom, the Romanian carrier with cautionary tales to its name. (One of its old TU-154s, for instance, took off from Sweden without its pilots noticing the 'door unsecured' warning light. The door flew open at 1800 feet. Had a former world champion wrestler not been among the passengers, people and seats might have been sucked out. He wedged his body into the gap, and struggled to shut the door until the aircraft managed to land. The Swedish investigators concluded that the aircraft 'should have never left the ground' because among other shortcomings, many seatbelts and life-jackets were missing.) The British authorities were obliged to issue temporary licences because the leased aircraft and crew from Tarom were under Romanian control according to the Chicago Convention. After a while, the operator wanted to make both aircraft and crews British-registered. For that the pilots had to take

*_The Final Call_ by Stephen Barlay (Sinclair-Stevenson, 1991).

46

the more stringent British tests – and four out of five failed them. Eventually, a compromise solution was found, but a rightly disgruntled government official told this author: 'That episode lifted the veil, but what we saw was not much more than a drop in a dirty ocean . . . Training in Romania was totally antiquated by our standards . . . When British passengers book seats on British charter flights, they ought to be told who and what aircraft will fly them.' In 1992, there were some objections when another charter company wanted to wet-lease a Bulgarian Airbus and two elderly B727s from Yugoslavia, claiming that no British aircraft was available. Finally, the licence was issued on the promise that the aircraft would be maintained at their British bases, and it would be ensured that flight deck and cabin crew spoke good English.

Since then, new EC regulations have come into force. Following the American example, Europe could thus be able to impose stricter controls. The emphasis is on the words 'could be able', for the rules are not sufficiently specific to eliminate the risk of flying under 'flags of convenience'. Like in shipping, it is not impossible to indulge in 'flagging out', i.e. to operate under the flag of a poor but accommodating country that for profit turns a blind eye towards irregularities, rubber-stamps unacceptable standards, and issues licences and airworthiness certificates on receipt of a bribe (even Italian pilots were found to have false qualifications). And, of course, the ruling does not apply to the many Third World countries that allow leasing for cut-price charter operations, with no questions asked, under the umbrella of the Chicago Convention that guarantees the freedom of the air for all, thwarting the right of international inspections and enforcement in the name of mutual trust. 'Flagging out' could result in considerable savings at the expense of safety. Though many people dismiss the likelihood of such practices with righteous consternation, some, like Captain de Silva, safety chief of Singapore Airlines, believe it *could* happen, and others are convinced that it does already happen in various guises, because it only takes a shrewd entrepreneur who knows that some questions of aviation law are hard to answer.

Take this minor incident at Frankfurt. It involved a DC8, owned by Gabon, flown by the Swiss BalAir, with an LH number, because the shipment of its cargo was booked with Lufthansa, making it a German flight. So who was the real operator? And whose safety standards applied when a British charter company filled up aeroplanes that were owned by French banks, leased to a Luxembourg airline, serviced in Paris or Amsterdam, and sub-leased, flight by flight, to a Caribbean state, whichever island the destination happened to be. The interlocking responsibilities never reached the ears of the charter passengers enjoying a half-price vacation.

6

Embarking on Adventure

A drunken vagrant created a rumpus; a young woman locked herself in a lavatory, refusing to set eyes on the husband her family had chosen for her, and demanding to be returned to Kashmir; there was a false security alert, and another one due to rumours about the unannounced arrival of the Duchess of York; a child who spoke no identifiable language had to be rescued from a luggage carousel; and there was some rowdy celebration or a drowning of sorrows (nobody knew which) by Italian football fans; 137 Japanese computer specialists, determined to check in at the wrong counter, blocked a gate – the time was 6.45 a.m., and the day had just begun at Heathrow.

Airports are a magnet for everything there is to human life, people converging from all corners of the globe, mingling, passing by, sensing without sharing the others' joy, grief, anxiety, expectations, aggravation, yearning and fulfilment. You have asked an airline *fly me (and preferably, my luggage, too) to the moon*, or a Spanish Costa or whatever exotic destination you have chosen, and your wish is about to come true.

That airport cavalcade can baffle or startle the inexperienced passenger – the person who does not jet daily from country to country or Concorde routinely across the Atlantic to bask in the sunroof of yet another limousine, and savour the stunning sights of yet another boardroom. Feeling and looking bewildered can be embarrassing. Laden with suitcase and packages, calm and rational people grow uptight, defensive with aggression, fail to allow time to familiarize themselves with the layout or study the free guide books to terminals,* become unable to read and follow signs or listen to the (frequently unintelligible) announcements, shy away from asking questions, develop tunnel vision, and

---

*Information in a freely distributed Heathrow guide, for instance, ranges from the general to the seemingly trivial that may, however, come in extremely handy at times: in Terminal 2, 'If you are departing from Gates 17, 18 or 19, the last toilets are in the departure lounge. For Gates 2 to 9 there is *an accessible toilet* by Gate 5 which although *through the door to the ladies* toilet is in fact unisex.' (My emphasis.)

with the pretence of the true jet-setter's self-assurance – hurry off in the wrong direction.

In principle, nothing could be simpler. The words 'All thine ego abandon, ye who enter here' ought to be emblazoned (with apologies to Dante) on the gates of Schiphol, Changi, Kloten and all other mysteriously named airports of the world, and with that, the exhilarating *Divina Commedia* of travelling hopefully could begin. From then on, you are centrestage, and the script, the procedural art of moving masses every which way, takes charge of your life. For once through the first door, you will be sorted, directed, lined up, checked, processed, labelled, licensed with a pass, urged on, stopped, told to queue and queue again, filtered, double-checked and carried on the crest of multitudes, only to be tinned, finally, in a winged can. Yet people resist regimentation, fight to retain their individuality, and wander about blindly. For even those who would never venture into the back streets of a strange city without a map, arrive at airports, those ever-changing towns that never sleep, without a clue as to where to park, turn, go, and wait and wait above all.

There could be no doubt about it: airports are towns in their own right. Take Heathrow, the number one crossroads of the world. Spread out on some 3000 acres – with forty miles of roads, its own police, fire department, standby power station (designed to restrict the duration of an electrical breakdown to one second), places of worship, restaurants, shopping arcades, nurseries, medical, business and car service facilities, banks, post office, and quarantine for animals – it is a workplace for some 60,000 people, accommodating 45 million passengers a year.* (On 21 April 1990, 12,837 people passed through it in one hour and in a single autumn day in the same year it handled a record 153,722 passengers.) It uses some 600 million gallons of water, and 350 million kW of electricity per annum. On its busiest ever day, Heathrow saw 1232 take-offs and landings. It has 10,000 trolleys, and two miles of moving walkways. (It is estimated that passengers at Washington's Dulles airport each year walk enough to make twenty-three trips to the moon.)

When the quality and performance of airports is compared in travel magazines from the passengers' point of view, numerous factors come into play, including the speed of checking in (a seasonal nightmare at Heathrow's old Terminal 2), the efficiency of passport control, customs clearance, luggage retrieval, and the availability of shops, duty-free and other facilities. In 1992, the annual readers' poll of *Business Traveller* voted Singapore, Amsterdam, London Heathrow, Zurich, London Gatwick, Atlanta, Dubai, Copenhagen, Frankfurt and Geneva (in that

*Heathrow is number one, followed by Frankfurt, Paris and Amsterdam, but only in international traffic. American airports are capable of handling far more aircraft movements and passengers – Chicago O'Hare with 65 million, Dallas, Los Angeles, and Atlanta top the list – but the traffic at US airports is mainly 'domestic' whereas most passengers who use European airports are on international flights.

order) the overall best in the world. Singapore and Zurich topped the list for quick luggage retrieval (with Gatwick beating Heathrow), and Singapore was also the winner in customs clearance (Heathrow getting its revenge on Gatwick).

The worst rush-hour conditions at any airport can develop when there is a congestion of international arrivals. In slowness of customs and passport checks, American airports seem to excel – their reputation is even worse than Moscow's and Bombay's in that respect. Kennedy airport occupies an area half the size of Manhattan Island. Its international traffic is barely one half of Heathrow's but, like Miami, it is notorious for its hold-ups on arrival. Hopefully, the newly installed fifty-two immigration control booths will reduce the long delays that may run up to ninety minutes. The new $400 million Terminal 5 at Chicago's O'Hare will have sixty-eight inspector positions to help deal with 4000 arrivals. (BA passengers will have speedier entry with the company's special ID card and a 'bio-metric reader' measuring the bearer's hand.)

SHOPPING

with abandon is a most peculiar airport phenomenon. Purse strings are loosened perhaps because people have time to kill, and the temptation increases in foreign countries where prices and money appear to be a little meaningless. Add to this that beyond passport control, in the departure areas, goods are sold tax-free, and the combination helps us to forget that most of the airport shops sell top-of-the-range (i.e. expensive) wares, creating an urge to buy something we never needed, spend the leftover currency in the last moment, and obtain the present/ souvenir we had forgotten to pick up locally at half the price.

The vast expansion of airport shopping (British airports have half as many shops as Oxford Street) is justified by surveys, such as the one conducted at Kennedy, which concluded that 'international travellers today spend more time at airports and *want* to spend that extra time shopping, particularly for more expensive, high-quality products' (*my emphasis*). That 'extra time' is not a testament to the efficiency of air transportation, but that apart, such findings reveal nothing except the limitation of choice that seems to suit the Japanese and the Swedes who are considered to be the keenest airport customers, with Bally selling more shoes per square foot at Heathrow than in any other of its British shops. Admittedly, the higher the price, the greater the apparent tax saving – very considerable, indeed, on Beluga caviar, Johnny Walker Blue Label at £180 a bottle or Davidoff cigars – but has anybody ever succeeded in finding a good but cheap watch, lighter, pen or scarf tax-free at an airport?

Duty-free goodies are always tempting, but beware of the price variations. Athens, Amsterdam (probably with the widest choice) and Brussels are among the cheapest in Europe, but the greatest bargains are to be found in Abu Dhabi, Dubai and Singapore where a bottle of perfume may cost half as much as in London or Frankfurt. American duty-free shops are usually cramped, offering a minimum choice. Similarly, but more understandably, the duty-free selection in the air tends to be meagre as well as more expensive than on the ground, and cabin crew sell most of the stock to panic-buyers near the end of the flight.

The booming business shops generate is stunning: they produce more than half the airports' income! At Heathrow, the revenue from cargo, retail and duty-free concessions is creeping up towards 70 per cent of the overall profit, as if the runways and all those flying machines that congregate there – such an expensive and noisy nuisance – were only of secondary importance. Landing charges vary with the location, time of the day and the number of passengers. Africa is the cheapest for landing an aircraft. For an A-300 they charge $277 in Lagos, $634 in Accra, and $813 in Nairobi. At Heathrow, the summer landing and parking of a Jumbo with 298 passengers between six and eleven in the morning or five and seven in the evening costs £6031 – not considered to be expensive worldwide, though Kennedy would charge less than half that much, and Lagos less than a tenth. Half-empty flights, landing in low season at off-peak time, enjoy a massive discount, and another 10 per cent reduction for Chapter 3 type – most modern, least noisy – aircraft.

THE MAYOR OF AIRPORT CITY

is the duty manager. Having spent two days with two such Mayors (one at Heathrow, one at Dulles International) it appears that the job calls for a born schizophrenic. 'Well, you don't have to be one, but it helps,' said Peter Edmunds at Heathrow, 'for we can get rather busy.' It was a beautifully British understatement. The neatness of his office revealed nothing about the nature of the work. His activities did. While we talked, he kept an eye on the small computer screen (he could call up all sorts of data as well as pictures of every nook and cranny of the airport), signed some papers that kept dropping on his desk, and listened incessantly to all the news (builder fell off some scaffolding, traffic jam at the tunnel, some commotion in Terminal 3, a flock of birds reported near a runway) crackling out of his portable. He answered my questions and those on the telephone simultaneously with the unperturbable cool of thirty years' airport service behind him.

'Here at least we don't need to cope with the tricky situations that may crop up at places like the Middle East, where almighty rulers can make life difficult,' he said. 'I used to have problems with a certain ruler's uncle there who would arrive with a convoy of limousines, stroll through the airport and security without anyone daring to stop him or ask about minor technicalities such as the possession of a ticket. He and his retinue would climb into the only aircraft on the tarmac, and issue a stiff order:

"To Paris!" That the plane was London-bound made no difference to him. As he couldn't be told to get out, we'd let the passengers board, then announce that the aircraft was 'unserviceable', and let everybody disembark. He'd storm off, back into his Rolls-Royce, and we'd wait for the departure of the convoy. Then we'd apologise for the *technical delay*, and ask people to board again.'

The anecdote was peppered, of course, with bits of dialogue between the Mayor and his portable. A disembarking African had had an epileptic fit. Queue-busters needed in Terminal 2. (They would comb the longest queues to pick out pregnant women, families with small children, late passengers whose flights were about to board.)

'77 in Terminal One.'*

'Keep me posted.'

Edmunds knew that the response was in hand, controlled by the Terminal Communication Centre where, with the help of a bank of TV screens showing key areas, they constantly monitor what is going on, spot developing congestion/commotion caused by a lack of trolleys, or, as in this case, supervise the partial evacuation of Terminal 1. Whenever an alarm is sounded, lights on a huge wall-chart pinpoint a fire, the stoppage of a lift or the unauthorized opening of a security door. The Centre also acts as a glorified caretaker with two mobile duty officers who may be the first to help anyone who is taken ill, and provide privacy for a police officer who may bear bad news for an arriving passenger. (The British Airport Authority and BA also finance a social service that may assist passengers who have run out of cash, and even feed vagrants, some of whom shelter at the airport, though no begging is permitted.)

Justifiable schizophrenia? Not by half. For the Mayor's duties do not end with this incomplete extract of his 'landside' responsibilities. As we move into his other office, his car, to tour his 'airside' empire, he displays six pairs of eyes to dodge traffic, some of it Jumbo-sized, without missing a word from the ever-chattering portable that, of course, comes too. 'Let's stop here for a moment – and watch a Concorde taking off.' Years of service have not blunted his enthusiasm.

To control life on 'airside' he has an Operations Centre where they play a giant chess game with aircraft. The 'board' is the entire tarmac, and a 'game' takes some 1200 moves a day. A massive computer holds all events (expected arrivals, likely length of stay and departure of aircraft), and is modified all the time. When an aircraft lands, it cuts a radar beam, its transponder identifies the flight, and the Centre's computer feeds the arrival/departure monitors in the terminals. At the Centre, they also listen in on the conversation between pilots and air traffic control because

---

*Not the actual figures. The digital codes simplify radio communications. This one signalled the finding of some unattended luggage, and triggered a set response procedure of checking: would police or even bomb squad assistance be needed?

from the moment of touch-down, everything is in the Operations Controllers' hands. They can monitor the vast amount of computer data, and all the sights of the airport (some of them several miles away) on their five dozen screens. Every flight arrival involves some ten ground movements – first of all to an allocated stand for disembarkation or unloading of cargo. The allocation takes into account special security requirements – Israeli aircraft and other potential terrorist targets are positioned with that in mind – and also the likely length of the visit: after a long flight, the aircraft will be parked, whereas a short-haul flight will need a quick turnaround. Airlines and handlers extract the relevant computer data, so that the aircraft can be met by a convoy of vehicles and an army to unload and load luggage, carry out maintenance, tidy up the cockpit, the galley and the cabin, clean ashtrays and all windows, replenish everything from seatback literature to toilet rolls, after-shave lotion, toys, nappies, baby food, newspapers, flowers for first class, bring fresh pillow cases and blankets, load water (some 300 gallons for a Jumbo), clear out the toilets (done by a special vehicle known as the 'honey wagon'), while tyres and essential controls are checked, and fresh food and drink supplies arrive – all in about an hour.

At Heathrow nothing can move on the ground without the Operations Centre's knowledge. With all that electronic paraphernalia around, it is almost incomprehensible how it all worked – not very long ago – when marshals used to walk backwards in front of aircraft, signalling with discs 'a bit to the left, now to the right'. An incoming pilot is now guided by maps and yellow lines: facing finally his allocated stand, he watches two vertical green bars on the wall; if he deviates from his centre line, those bars, seen from an angle, turn red. The Centre monitors security, can stop all traffic, even the underground, and tannoy instructions if there is a fire. At night, when flying stops, it answers enquiries about anything from arrival times to the 'last bus to Manchester'.

As opposed to three or more at US airports, Heathrow has only two main parallel runways (and a smaller one for adverse wind conditions). They stay virtually dry even in a rainstorm, for its rough, porous surface (ten inches of asphalt on a concrete base) lets water seep through or run off it. The Mayor's runway patrols constantly check the lights, collect rubbish and broken off bits of aircraft, and spot heavy tyre marks and defects to be repaired overnight. (When a US President arrives, his men insist on checking out everything themselves, but they need the patrols' help, for without familiarity with the runways they would not recognize if anything was wrong.)

If visibility falls below 1500 metres, it is monitored by the transmissometer: two yellow funnels, as if borrowed from an old steamer, a cricket pitch apart, one containing a light, the other a mirror; a computer compares the loss of light intensity between the two, and works out the density of the fog. (Sometimes visibility is zero, but if dense fog just sits on the ground, pilots may have unrestricted vision above it. There is also an automated, all-weather microwave landing system now tested by a single B757.) Although a heavy snowfall could interfere with traffic, Heathrow has closed down only once in twenty years, when a strong northerly wind blew back ten inches of snow as fast as the sweepers could push it aside. Edmunds points out a small, red shack (it had housed the airport's one and only steam-age radar), a concrete pad (an Air Traffic Control caravan used to stand there for 'talking down' flights) and a plaque, set into a remote area of the tarmac, saying, 'The River Longford used to pass through here' (it now runs diverted, like the Duke of Northumberland river, through underground pipes).

It seems almost incredible how young the great airports of the world are. Heathrow began to take shape only in 1950, when it was envisaged that an astounding 130,000 passengers would pass through it. 'Not all that long ago all this used to be an orchard, and the last wolf in England was seen here,' said Edmunds. 'But we still have quite a bit of wildlife in the grass around the runways. That's why the first runway inspection is always for birds that can cause a great deal of damage when they crash into windscreens or get ingested by the jet engines. The patrols use loudspeakers to play recorded bird distress calls to frighten them away. Our balancing reservoir for runway drainage was a favourite of swans that enjoyed landing parallel to aircraft. Now we have lines across, like swimming lanes in pools, to keep them out.'

Flocks of starlings, pigeons, gulls, lapwings, ducks, swans and, particularly, the massive Canada geese create a difficult and expensive problem for most airports. It calls for special measures to keep the runways bird-free. After a South African Jumbo had been badly damaged, and all flying had to be suspended on several occasions, Tony Sayers, the chief of bird patrols, had an ingenious idea: the grass all round is now cut to exactly nine inches; if it is higher, birds feed and breed in it; mow it shorter, and it becomes an ideal landing strip.

NOISE ABATEMENT

is another serious headache for airports. Everybody likes to have airports close at hand – with the proviso of the NIMBY (Not in My Back Yard) factor.

Speed and altitude are the cushions of air safety. Noise abatement procedures require banking and turning as well as throttling back (reducing power) at relatively low altitude and speed, often in clouds, so there are some hard feelings about the law that protects the eardrums of Sally-at-the-end-of-the-runway, as American pilots call the inhabitants in the vicinity of airports.

'We're glad that control of aircraft noise is not our direct responsibility in Aerodrome Standards,' says Trevor Ward, the head of that CAA department. 'It's an environmental "hot potato". Left to his own devices, no pilot would choose to throttle back and execute the prescribed manoeuvres. After airports are established, settlements tend to spring up around them, but that doesn't mean the newcomers do not complain and press for significant changes. London City Airport was different, it was established in an existing densely populated area, and strict environmental rules were part of the original planning permission.'

Stansted, London's new airport, was a typical example. It was built in an open area, but as it begins to generate work, a town will grow up fast around it, and the new inhabitants may soon complain bitterly, and justifiably, about the noise and the potential danger on the ground. (The Israeli cargo flight crashing into blocks of flats on the outskirts of Amsterdam in 1992 was the worst example.) Hongkong and Japan have created off-shore airports, linked to six-lane highways and bullet trains, but most towns cannot find the space for such special solutions.

Noise levels are monitored at all airports, quotas govern the number of permitted movements, and a strict night curfew is operated – except for emergencies – according to the season. Excesses and infringements are penalized, even if the too early or too late arrival of a long-haul flight is due to a delay in its departure. Airports make surcharges for 'Chapter 2 type' (older, noisier) aircraft such as Concorde, BAC 1-11. The early versions of 737 and 747 – Amsterdam even penalizes overflights – and the 707s that have not been 'hush-kitted' may be banned. 'Chapter 2 types' – 95 per cent of the air traffic at Manchester – are to be phased out by 2002. British Airways sponsors some noise research to eliminate the irksome problem.

At Heathrow, blast screens are set up in certain areas, and at three o'clock every afternoon they alternate the direction of landing and take-off on the two runways, to even out the inconvenience to people in the neighbourhood. In the New York area, where the assault on everybody's eardrums is the greatest, new regulations have been brought into force – flights could minimize the noise by taking just a ninety-second detour.

Though the regulations are understandable from Sally's point of view (supersonic flights are barred overland), they can lead to bureaucratic bungling. As William Heller, a vastly experienced, retired airline captain and Colonel of the US Air Force, recalls in his book *Airline Safety, A View From The Cockpit*, San Franciscans once sued their airport for the noise they suffered, and were awarded $750 each by a judge who was reportedly up for re-election. 'A non-stop flight from Alaska to Hongkong was just north of Tokyo when a male passenger suffered cardiac arrest,' Heller recounts. Flight attendants administered first aid, and the captain asked for permission to make an unscheduled, emergency landing at Haneda International. The local time was 6.30 a.m. The airport was under curfew until 7 a.m. The captain decided to land anyway, and radioed for an ambulance to be waiting. He and the airline were fined for noise curfew violation.

GROWING AIR TRAFFIC

and bigger aircraft create an ever-increasing demand for airport expansion, but apart from space and noise, outmoded air traffic control, terminal capacity, and surface access to airports impose severe limitations. (At Heathrow, all road traffic to Terminals 1, 2 and 3 must enter through a single two-lane tunnel. Terminal 4 was built to avoid that Achilles heel of the airport. Better access will be one of the advantages of Terminal 5, planned to cost a £1 billion and open by 2002, but serious environmental objections will first have to be overcome.) Congestion in the air is costly: stacked aircraft waste a fortune as they wait for a slot to land, burning up fuel worth billions of dollars, each year. Congestion on the roads around and into airports can cause safety problems as well as inconvenience: emergency planning needs to count on some outside help, and in some cases rely on it entirely.

PESSIMISM PAYS

The coordination of emergency plans is yet another duty that weighs heavily on the Mayors of Airport City. Four out of every five accidents happen on or within a thousand metres of the runways during landing or take-off. The main reason is simple: the chief protection of flying is a combination of speed and height. Near airports, flights lose or are about to gather both. Inadequate preparedness can turn a mishap into a disaster.

'Prevention, a non-productive service, always seems too expensive: it is often in danger of losing out to the "low benefit v. cost" considerations,' says Bernard Brown, the head of CAA International Services. The ICAO *Annex 14* aims to set worldwide standards for preparedness and training, but whilst international standards and recommendations are published, there is no international supervision. The requirements for firefighting agents, manpower, equipment and medical facilities are governed by the largest aircraft using an airport, but if the number of air movements falls below a certain level, the airport can be downgraded by remission, and that is open to misuse. (The UK has standards higher than those of ICAO, and Brown is pleased that the hazardous 'remission factor' will be eliminated everywhere – though not until 2003.) Several Asian, African and South American countries plead poverty when failing to invest in equipment (a modern fire engine, to discharge thousands of gallons of foam at a prescribed rate, costs some £300,000) and claim that the infrequent arrival of large aircraft does not justify resident medical units. But even they cannot find excuses for their lack of emergency plans, or for allowing their plans, such as they are, to gather dust on a shelf without anybody practising their implementation. (At most good airports, an expensive, simulated full-scale emergency practice must be held at least once every two years, with desk-top exercises in between.)

In 1990 the Indian Passengers' Association accused the government of a 'casual' attitude to inadequate emergency services (*Flight International*, September 1990). When an Air India A320 airbus had a tragic crash at Bangalore, the airport licence was twenty-nine years out of date, there was no emergency plan, rescue vehicles got bogged down in a marsh, firemen had no key to the security fence, and there was a shortage of foam. At Bogota, Colombia, fire and rescue services were, it seemed to some, not quite up to 'rubbish standards'. Cairo, Dominica, numerous African and Asian airports have 'dodgy' equipment as well as poor access facilities. At Tangier, after an Air Maroc flight suffered a gear collapse in 1986, the fire service arrived twenty-five minutes late. Since a Tristar tragedy in 1980, Riyadh has been over-equipped with stocks of firefighting agents, exceeding twenty times the necessary levels, but maintenance and training are inadequate.

Despite frequent inspections, 'potential risks can go unnoticed for years,' said Anthony Broderick, Associate Administrator of the FAA, illustrating that gaps can be found in the preparedness of some airports even in rich, advanced countries. 'At Kennedy we've discovered that at some locations, the nearest fire hydrants were 3000 feet away. This was more an environmental problem than a matter of life or death, because the fire engines carry enough foam and water to save lives, but it could make the difference between a twenty- and an eighty-minute fire.'

Captain Vic Hewes, who ran the US airline pilots' Accident Survival Committee revealed that 'The training of American firefighters varies too much. In some states firemen cut the grass, but know nothing about opening emergency exits, and many localities prohibit "hot" fire drills [actual use of foam] for environmental reasons.' His colleague, Captain McBride of the Canadian Pilots' Association, complained that 'Transport Canada fails to meet international standards. The money goes on fancy tenders, operated by just one man who wouldn't have the chance, with the best will in the world, to deal with a door that fails to open.' At Pisa, after a minor 'flat tyre' incident, a pilot witnessed an Italian comedy of errors that featured some dangerous practices: the arrival of fifty-year-old fire trucks ten minutes after the event (one pushing the other which could not be started), the splitting of a hose as soon as foam was applied as a purely preventive measure, a man running with a bucket of water, and the closure of the airport with the firing of two red flares that came down in dry grass, starting a huge conflagration. At Manchester, in 1985, the fire service was not responsible for the extent of the tragedy (see page 220), but a hydrant – disconnected for repairs without informing the firemen – ran dry during the emergency. 'Although four times the quantity of foam and water recommended by ICAO was available, nobody knew at the time how to deal effectively with free-flowing, running fuel, because firemen had only been trained to suppress fuel burning on the ground,' said Bernard Brown. 'Since then, the CAA has developed a successful technique.'

Certain characteristics and shortcomings of airports can contribute to causing accidents and aggravating tragedies. Usually, the failings do not constitute a serious enough hazard to ban all flights there (though Australian pilots, for instance, once boycotted Jakarta), but Greek and Spanish air traffic controllers had to strike repeatedly for better equipment. The airlines themselves could bring much more determined pressure for improvements. Their argument that 'If *we* stop flying there, somebody else will take our place' is somewhat feeble. As the risks are widely known, airline pilots make their approach to some airports with extra caution every time, for only fools rush in . . .

WHERE ANGELS FEAR TO TREAD

'Airport certification is a very complex, strictly controlled affair,' said Trevor Ward, head of the CAA Aerodrome Standards Department. 'We check all physical characteristics, the layout, cleanliness, lighting and all markings of runways, potential obstructions and overrun areas. The latter are sometimes questionable in certain countries. In Britain, where some of our aerodromes pre-date the international standards, we have sometimes had to insist on compensatory measures where overruns are inadequate. Such measures can include reducing the declared distances available or removing significant obstructions. At one major airport with a steep drop into a river valley after the overrun, the airport authority has provided, on CAA advice, a special arrester bed that would help to halt an aircraft that failed to stop on the runway.'

Yet again, there is an infinite variation in worldwide standards. The following is just a brief, random selection culled from surveys as well as individual interviews and confidential reports submitted to pilots' organizations.

The three major *Nigerian* airports have problems with power supplies, communication and navigational standards. *Romanian* navigational facilities need serious upgrading. Markings had to be improved at *Frankfurt* after an Air Gabon aircraft had taken off accidentally from a taxiway. *Madrid* can be deceptive when pilots are landing. *Tenerife's* landing aids and communications (often in Spanish, defying the law that makes English the language of the air) have been criticized in accident reports. *Corfu*: pilots claim it is a classic example of airlines flying there only because others do too. *Athens?* 'Would hate to divert there. They keep closing the alternative airports. There's radio and traffic congestion, limited radar, bad runways surface, often contaminated.' *Cyprus* is a problem because Turks and Greeks who control adjoining airspace will not hand over flights to each other, so pilots themselves must talk to each in turn. *Tehran* may not answer radio calls if the pilot is a woman;

'unreliable beacons lead into a U-turn over hills; high degree of human inefficiency'. (A British pilot delayed take-off for forty-five minutes because it took him that long to find out exactly how much runway was available during repairs.) *Jakarta* has short runways with bad surface and unreliable landing aids. *Manila's* radar and electricity supplies are unreliable; the emergency service is patchy. *Rhodes* has dangerous wind conditions; the construction of a new airport, suggested by IFALPA, has remained a recommendation ever since the 1970s. Landing aids at *Tripoli*, in Libya, are frequently inoperative. The runway at *Rio de Janeiro* is liable to flood. Several American airports (including *Atlanta, Charleston, Columbus, New York's Kennedy* and *La Guardia*) have dangerous overrun areas.

The American Airline Pilots' *Guide For Airport Standards* once concluded that 'throughout the history of commercial aviation the airport has been treated almost as a stepchild ... In far too many cases, development motivation has been slanted towards the terminal area because it is a virtual extension of the community's image – as well as being a ready source of income.' The demands of growing traffic are still more readily answered with palatial and more glamorous terminals than additional, better controlled and extra-long runways (larger, heavier aircraft require longer runways, particularly in a hot climate and high above sea level).

LOST AT SPAGHETTI JUNCTION

On 3 December 1990, Flight 299, a B727 of Northwest Airlines (NWA), was scheduled to depart at 12.10 from Detroit Metropolitan/ Wayne Country airport (DTW) but boarding was delayed. The captain was given instructions on how to reach runway 3C/21 for take-off. The visibility was a quarter of a mile – deteriorating.

Meanwhile, Flight 1482, a DC9 of NWA (Detroit is a hub of the airline), followed ground control instructions for taxiing in the maze pilots call 'spaghetti junction'. Its Cockpit Voice Recorder (CVR) was preserving the conversation between the captain and the first officer. Had anybody listened in on it, it would have transpired that the captain, who had been off flying for medical reasons, was under the impression that his co-pilot was familiar with DTW, and allowed him to make the decisions. At 13.36, they were searching for the yellow taxi line.

'Just kinda stay on the ramp here.'

'OK.'

Reaching the 0-6 (Oscar Six) intersection, they took the wrong turning. The sign there had no arrows pointing the way, and might have aggravated their mistake of moving without any reference to their compass. (At some point they thought they were travelling eastwards when it should have been obvious from the map that on that particular

The fateful route taken by Flight 1482 at Detroit Metropolitan/Wayne Country Airport

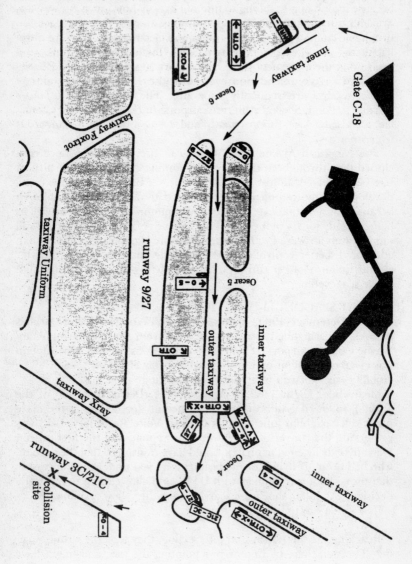

taxiway that was impossible.) At 13.40, the first officer admitted, 'OK, I think we might have missed Oscar Six . . . Think we're on Foxtrot now,' but the captain still failed to realize that they were lost. The instructions they did get might have helped to confuse them, and they did not stop to ask for more precise guidance from ground control.

By now the pilots had given up trying to follow their airport diagram, and relied on the airfield signs and markings – seen through the thickening fog. At 13.42 they were approaching the Oscar Four intersection.

'This, this is a right turn here?'

'Yeah, that way,' and after a twenty-one-second pause: 'Well, wait a minute. Oh#[expletive] this uh ah [eight seconds pause] I think we're on ah, X-Ray here now . . .'

It began to look like an active runway. (The runway centre lights ought to but might not have been on maximum intensity because the tower had a rickety switch with crayon markings.)

At 13.43, the B727 pilots were about to complete their take-off checklist. They would begin to roll in ninety-six seconds. Visibility had worsened, but they had an adequate view of the centre line markings.

'This is a runway,' said the captain of the DC9. 'Yeah, turn left over there. Nah, that's a runway, too.' Twenty seconds after 13.44, the captain stopped, set the parking brake, and called ground control, but on the wrong frequency. Eleven seconds were wasted. The gist of the conversation, based on the CVR transcript, went like this:

> CAPTAIN TO GROUND: Hey, ground, 1482. We're . . . stu . . . we can't see anything out here . . .
> GROUND CONTROL: Northwest 1482, just to verify, you're proceeding southbound on X-Ray now and you're across nine two seven [the runway that intersects Runway 3C/21C]
> CAPTAIN TO GROUND: Ah, we're not sure, it's so foggy out here we're completely stuck here.
> GROUND CONTROL: OK, ah, you're on a ru— taxiway or on a runway? . . .
> CAPTAIN TO GROUND: Yeah, it looks like we're on 21 Centre here.
> CAPTAIN OR FIRST OFFICER: #[Expletive]
> *Ten-second pause.*
> GROUND CONTROL: Northwest 1482, y'say you are on 21 Centre?
> CAPTAIN TO GROUND: I believe we are, we're not sure.
> FIRST OFFICER TO CAPTAIN: Yes we are.
> *Another five-second pause.*
> GROUND CONTROL: Northwest 1482 roger, if you're on 21 Centre exit that runway immediately, sir.

In the tower, there was cause for concern. Some of the ground controller's instructions had been imprecise. Now it took him just five seconds to warn his colleagues. The supervisor was aware of the bad visibility, the worst in her experience, but during that midday period had had a relatively low workload and had been attending to some administrative duties. She now ordered all traffic to stop at once. The local controller in charge of departures was convinced that the B727 was already airborne. (He did not check that on the radar, and had cleared, in fact, yet another aircraft into take-off position before the B727 began to roll.)

Seven seconds after the last exchange between ground control and Flight 1482, the DC9 captain heard the roar, then saw the lights of the B727 bearing down on him. Instinctively, he ducked. The Boeing was travelling at 211 feet per second. In the poor visibility, nobody had a chance to take evasive action. The wing-tip of the B727 tore into the side of the DC9 along the fuselage, and broke when it sheared off an engine. Eight people were killed aboard the DC9, 190 people escaped with serious or minor injuries. The DC9 was destroyed by the collision and subsequent ground fire. The repairs to the B727 were estimated to cost $5 million.

No aviation accident can happen without the interplay of numerous coinciding factors, and this case was no exception. Imprecise communications, less-than-helpful signs leading to an active runway, bad weather, inexperience and role-reversal in the cockpit added up to a painful reminder of the hazard of runway incursions – the bane of modern airports under ground control that had failed to keep up in sophistication with the increased traffic. Despite hundreds of such incursions by maintenance and snow-clearing vehicles as well as aircraft, many airports economize on ground radars, proper markings and runway lights.

Some airports live on their luck (Phnom Penh in Cambodia may now get a $3 million loan to renew runway lights and equipment that had been purchased from the former Soviet Union twenty years ago, and are 'on the blink' or out of order most of the time), while others must take the responsibility for needless slaughter: in 1991, a Nigerian BAC-111, operated by a private company, circled in the air for an hour, waiting for the runway lights to be switched on; running out of fuel, it finally made an emergency landing near the city of Sokoto, killing three people outright, and injuring another two dozen. Pilots need all the help they can get even at the best of times, for it is easy to feel adrift on a bewildering sea of coded signposts and multicoloured lights.

'Britain' says Trevor Ward, 'has a high degree of standardization to help pilots' navigation on the ground with visual signing of airports, to tell them where they are, lights, signs, paint marks showing taxiway exits, parking areas, et cetera. Despite forty years of efforts to achieve harmonization and standardization there is still a lot of variation around the world in terms of provisions with regard to surface movement guidance information. Obviously in some cases it's a matter of cost but the main problem has been a failure to recognize the positive safety advantages that can come from presenting pilots with consistent and unambiguous messages. We really do have to grasp this message and give it effect out on the aerodrome.'

The biggest ever air disaster, in terms of fatality, happened on the ground, and its cause was a runway incursion. In 1977, after an explosion and another bomb threat at Las Palmas in the Canary Islands, all flights, including two Jumbos, had been diverted to Tenerife's Los Rodeos airport where the runway centre lights were out of order yet again, the runway intersections were not lit or even marked properly, and the weather played its treacherous tricks (a local speciality with drifting fog and sudden changes of visibility). Everybody was under pressure, all pilots were anxious to deliver their passengers to their destination with minimum delay, some crews were running out of permissible duty time, and the radio communication channels were as overcrowded as the runways and taxiways, creating some confusion. The Dutch pilot of a KLM Jumbo *thought* he had received take-off clearance. A PanAm Jumbo captain, equipped with only a small map of Los Rodeos he had never intended to use, missed an unmarked turn-off. Lost and worried, he tried to warn the Dutchman directly. That caused a temporary blocking of the frequency with a four-second squeal. He could see no threat in the fog, but sensed the danger.

'Let's get the hell out of here!'

His co-pilot joked: 'Yeah, he's anxious, isn't he?'

A few seconds later, the captain saw something: 'There he is . . . look at him . . . goddam . . . that son of a bitch is coming!'

He tried to turn his aircraft out of the way of the KLM Jumbo charging down the runway. The Dutch pilot now spotted the obstruction. Desperate to get airborne, and fly over it, he yanked at the wheel. The nose lifted, but that was not enough. Neither man had more than two seconds, far from enough to avert the collision. A horrific crash was followed by an inferno with almost 100,000 gallons of fuel gushing from the ruptured tanks. Once again, 'inadequate language', ready acceptance of non-standard instructions, bad markings, weather – the combined force of all the old culprits – took their toll: 583 deaths, 67 badly injured survivors.

The thorough investigation of all accidents (including the apparently insignificant incidents) and learning the lessons the findings can teach are the mainstay of air safety. But the acquisition of such knowledge does not always guarantee a satisfactory follow-up. After Tenerife, everybody thought the hazards on the ground would soon be eradicated. They were to be proven over-optimistic.

In 1986, a special NTSB study produced scores of chilling examples of serious incursions even at the busiest, and often best, American airports, including Chicago, Austin, Houston, Kansas City and Washington. In

March 1990, Dr John Lauber, a member of the NTSB board, testified at a Congressional investigation, and referred to Tenerife: 'I cannot help but believe that had this accident occurred on US soil – and might well have – the FAA would have given more attention to the runway incursion hazard during the past decade . . . We are relying too heavily on perfect human performance combined with a bit of luck to assure safety of landing and departing traffic.' He quoted many tragic instances and lucky escapes, incursions caused by controller errors, pilot deviations, inattention, and misinterpreted clearances. Following the NTSB's recommendations, the FAA had taken some preventive measures, but the incursions continued: 382 in 1987, 212 in 1989. In 1990, US airports with control towers handled 64 million aircraft movements. By the year 2000, the annual average was forecast to rise to 80 million. The introduction of surface surveillance radars that could alert controllers to risks was expected to bring 'tangible benefits' but not much before the end of the century. Runway incursions would thus remain 'one of the most significant hazards to aviation today'.

Lauber's words turned out to be prophetic. The accident at Detroit, preceded by many other less disastrous incursions, happened just nine months later. The post-Detroit preventive actions were regarded by some people as no more than a distribution of rubber gloves against leaking fountain pens. But such measures, if taken to heart by all concerned, could still prevent inky fingers, save lives, and help to ensure that the air passengers' greatest concern will remain how to cope with customs, immigration, language, taxis and transfer to hotels – the old vagaries of arrival at a strange airport, where a waiting friend is said to be worth two anywhere else.

7

The Art of Self-Defence

In Copenhagen, a poster in an airline's office offered the solemn promise to 'take your bags and send them in all directions'. While that might have been just a routine assault on the Queen's English,* it was only half in jest when a seasoned traveller was overheard in Prague asking for 'a ticket to wherever my bag was going'.

Going by the travel specialists' advice and the principles of 'Defensive Flying', compiled by the Consumer Affairs Office of the US Department of Transportation, much of the time-consuming inconvenience, and the annoyance that can ruin happy trips by air, can be avoided.

If you drive to the airport, the first step of self-defence ought to be taken in the car park: hide your parking ticket or keep it with you. If thieves see the ticket on the dashboard, they can break into the car, pay the parking fee, and drive away safe in the knowledge that no one would report the car missing while you are away on business or holiday. Admittedly, a professional would know that if he tried to take your limousine out of the car park without a ticket he would be asked for proof of ownership, and may, therefore, drive his own, probably stolen, banger into the car park, take his pick, and use his own ticket for exit. (Alarms are all too often ignored, but thieves who plan to use their time for respraying and exporting the vehicle, will go in the direction of the least resistance, and usually not bother trying to get past immobilizing devices.)

Early arrival at the airport reduces the risk of tunnel vision, what some psychologists call the 'airport syndrome' that causes stressful confusion. (The 'Jerusalem syndrome' causes an overdose of religious fervour and crazy acts such as the destruction of Madonnas and altars. First-timers in

---

*One of the examples collected by an EC survey (*Wall Street Journal*, 1992). Others included notices in a Japanese hotel ('You are invited to take advantage of the chambermaid'), in Acapulco ('The manager has personally passed all the water served here'), in the Budapest zoo ('Do not feed the animals. If you have any suitable food, give it to the guard on duty'), and the exhortation in the window of a Roman laundry ('Ladies! Leave your clothes here, and spend the afternoon having a good time').

Florence may suffer from the 'Stendhal syndrome', falling in love with, and trying to pinch, great works of art.)

A high point of defensive flying is the check-in. As said before, late-comers are more likely to be bumped, and very late-comers may be denied boarding with the resultant loss of the ticket unless a full scheduled fare had been paid. Those who sit back, waiting for the evaporation of check-in queues, also stand a chance of having their luggage lost or misrouted in the helpful hurry of the check-in clerk. Britain is at the forefront of speeding up the check-in procedure: the 'smart' airline ticket-cum-boarding pass with a magnetic strip – to be used initially for business- and first-class passengers – could save twelve seconds per person . . . a considerable advantage if hundreds are to board a fully booked Jumbo.

When people are asked to choose their seats, they tend to give preference to those 'with a view', at the windows. Aisle seats are often shunned (would you prefer to trouble and climb over others or be troubled every time someone wants to get out?), forgetting that at the outer end there might be extra legroom in the aisle itself, and no competition with neighbours for at least one arm-rest. Serious addicts, who are anxious to get a seat in the smoking section (if there is one) had better be early because the few available seats can be snapped up. Smoking is never permitted in the aisles or toilets – an important safety regulation, routinely flouted by some Third World airlines.

You can ask for a seat next to an exit (suitable for passengers with babies because of the extra legroom) but your physique must be sufficient to open the door or overwing hatch in an emergency if the assigned cabin attendant is unavailable or incapacitated. Many people believe that seats at the back of the aircraft are safer, but that does not seem to be supported by accident investigators' findings.

Finally, having checked in during a peak period when flights may suffer long delays, it can be detrimental to be in too much of a hurry to get airside (beyond passport and security controls), where space may be at a premium, causing havoc at the bar and other facilities, and offer only standing room in the waiting areas.

A SUITABLE CASE FOR (ROUGH) TREATMENT

The *Business Traveller* (March, 1991) revealed that country and wes-tern singer Dolly Parton travels only with Louis Vuitton luggage that she puts into other bags – for protection. A BA official told the magazine that the pretty (and pretty expensive) make gets damaged too easily and 'isn't really suited to airline travel'. Airport luggage handlers admit that baggage does not receive the gentlest possible treatment, as it is tossed on to conveyor belts, travels a quarter of a mile from check-in to carts, and tumbles around first in cargo compartments and, finally, on carousels. Handlers recommend aluminium or hard-shell cases, preferably with retractable wheels and handles. They also warn against over-packing: you may shut a case by sitting on it, but the locks can fly open under the slightest provocation.

Prominent markers on cases help to prevent mistakes by others who, perhaps in a hurry on arrival, pick up someone else's luggage and then go on to a connecting flight. It is no solace that it had been their fault, and that it had caused annoyance to them too. Everybody agrees that each piece of luggage should be tagged for identification, but some American advice to use labels with name, telephone number and home address could be dangerous: burglars have often received tip-offs from handlers, and a night phone call can double-check that a home is indeed empty. Some airlines hand out privacy tags but these conceal the data only from innocent passers-by. Security experts want all such information (unless it is an office address) on a card *inside* each suitcase (if the bag is lost or misrouted, it will be opened by airline officials who carry skeleton keys), but the greatest help to airlines is a tag outside with the destination address.

Airlines and airports are constantly trying to combat pilferage of luggage, but no amount of control will ever stamp out the risk completely. 'It becomes significant when there's a big ring in operation,' said Hoyte Decker, Assistant Director of Consumer Affairs in the US DoT. 'The big gateway airports are usually their best hunting ground. It has happened at Miami and Kennedy, and it's bound to happen elsewhere. Passengers who keep that in mind could do a great deal for their own protection.'

At Heathrow, 3 million pieces of luggage are checked through each week with under two dozen complaints regarding theft or missing items. In 1992, when the airport had just about lived down its nickname Thiefrow, large-scale baggage thefts – this time by security guards! – were recorded by secret video cameras. The alleged technique was simple: when X-ray machines, installed against bombs, revealed expensive gifts, cameras, cash or high-tech equipment in a suitcase, the guards carried out a dutiful hand-search – and helped themselves to the valuables. The bags were then re-locked, and sent to a wrong destination to mislead passengers and investigators who would suspect that the theft had occurred somewhere else en route.

Never pack fragile, perishable items, valuables (cash, jewellery, irreplaceable documents, securities, etc.), cameras, essential medicines, liquids or objects that are of sentimental value in checked-in luggage, and anything that could be considered a weapon, such as scissors and knives, in carry-on hand luggage. Your ticket lists the banned, hazardous items. Aerosols, corrosives, flammables – including paints, thinners, lighter fluid – explosives, flares, fireworks, radioactive materials, compressed gases, and certain electrical equipment come into this category. During the flight, always check with the cabin crew before attempting to use devices with built-in receivers or transmitters, such as radios, TV sets, remote control toys, mobile phones and certain computers, that can interfere with the aircraft electronics for navigation and communications. Violations could cost, in America for instance, up to $25,000 in penalties, and up to five years in jail.

'It's quite unbelievable how careless or even stupid people can be,' said György Mátyásy, the security chief of MALÉV. 'Among lost luggage we've come across vast sums, works of art and fine jewellery packed in rucksacks and hold-alls that were secured only by a zip with no lock.'

If, despite better judgement, you pack items that exceed the compensation rates printed on your ticket, you must declare them at check-in, and pay the charge for additional insurance, though airlines usually refuse to insure cash, manuscripts, musical instruments, and various other objects of great value that ought to fly with you in the cabin.

Always pack in your hand luggage some essentials (toiletries, change of underwear, etc.) for the first twenty-four hours. The aircraft may be diverted because of bad weather or you may be separated temporarily from your luggage, and even if the airline will eventually pay for emergency necessities, the inconvenience may ruin an important meeting or the first days of a holiday.

Concern about thieving, and the extra weight of durable suitcases, aggravate the old problem of baggage allowance and the amount that can be carried into the cabin. The overall weight permitted varies with the type of ticket and flight (long-haul, short-haul, charter). European carriers tend to insist on weight limitations while Americans focus on the two bags maximum irrespective of weight. (To entice customers, US-bound flights by European lines fall in with the American two-bag custom. This practice, and the differences, can cause confusion and disappointment when one changes flights.)

The excess weight regulation is less rigid than it sounds: airlines are disinclined to publicize the fact that they often turn a blind eye to the scales if the flight is not full because charging can cause hold-ups, unpleasantness, and more bother than it is worth. If the excess is charged, the bill can be substantial. (BA charges £50 per 70 pounds overweight, and as *IAPA World*, the magazine of the International Airline Passengers' Association, disclosed, 'European carriers insist on charging weight fractions based on first-class fares for overweight luggage.')

The international ruling for cabin or hand luggage is made crystal-clear by all airline tickets: one piece only. Experience makes it equally crystal-clear that you take pot luck every time you board an aircraft. Bags of duty-frees are exempted – they are good business – even though glass bottles could be a hazard. Suit-carriers are a grey area. Regardless of weight (though in principle it should not exceed five kilos), hand luggage is governed by size: it must fit into an overhead bin or under a seat. 'Many airports have by now introduced measuring bins but fail to use them,' said Chris Witkowski of the US Flight Attendants' Association. 'Cabin crew are pressurized by claims that other airlines on previous flights did not object to this or that, so why do they? Passengers who fought for non-smoking aircraft to protect their health, will endanger everybody's safety when boarding with heavy objects and bottles – stowing them overhead without a care.' (In 1989, for instance, when a British Midland B737-400 crashed on to the embankment of the M1 motorway, overhead bins tore away on impact, and the heavy contents injured numerous passengers.)

The idea of measuring bins is simple: if a bag does not fit in, it must go into the hold. (The size is 18 by 12 by 9 inches.) In Paris, at Charles de Gaulle airport, this author had the misfortune of a long delay, with the opportunity to watch (and envy) passengers boarding fourteen flights. Measuring bins were available at the gates – not once were they used. Stewardesses were most obliging to passengers: they helped them lift large pieces of hand luggage over the bins.

If luggage is damaged (see Chapter 27) it may cause inconvenience and a justifiable claim against the airline, but if it is separated from the passenger – be it deliberately misrouted and forwarded when unaccompanied – it may become a serious hazard to air safety. Against loss, passengers can watch the actions of the check-in clerk, ensuring that the right tag is attached to their luggage, that the weight is not understated (compensation will depend on it), and that the check slip is attached to their tickets. Without the slip they have no right to retrieve their bags – even though no airport seems to pay any attention to that – and cannot make a valid compensation claim for loss or damage.

In the check-in phase, the most vital element of defensive flying concerns the safety of the journey: passengers can do a great deal for themselves by full cooperation with the time-consuming and *apparently* meddlesome security procedures that precede boarding.

8

The Archways to the Sky

Some, seemingly unconnected, events occurred in November 1987. First, international terrorist organizations issued an open threat to disrupt the Olympic Games soon to be held in Seoul, South Korea. Then a disenchanted, Libyan-trained Japanese Red Army terrorist's confession was published in Tokyo: beware of attacks on airliners. Some governments took notice, many others did not. Four days later, a South Korean KAL B707 took off from Baghdad. After a scheduled stop-over in Abu Dhabi, it continued the flight to Seoul. At Bahrain, airport police, acting on a tip-off, stopped two Japanese passport holders, a young, fragile beauty and a septuagenarian man. Both asked for permission to smoke. They bit on their cigarettes, and collapsed. The man was dead. The girl was only unconscious, for an alert guard had snatched the cigarette out of her teeth. While she was treated against cyanide poisoning, the KAL flight disappeared from the radar screens over Burma.

It transpired that the 707 had exploded in the air, and crashed. Bahrain had not been on its route, but there *was* a connection with the suspects: they had disembarked at Abu Dhabi to fly on to Bahrain. Extradited to Seoul, the girl confessed to sabotage – a story of skulduggery and blunders.

Her real name was Kim Hyun Hui. A former child actress, she had been recruited by North Korean communist intelligence in 1985, at the age of twenty-two. For almost three years she was trained in China and Macao as a secret agent. She still looked fragile, but was, by then, a martial arts and firearms expert. In 1987, she was paired with the old agent and sent to Belgrade, a notorious lair of terrorists. In the Metropolitan Hotel they collected a transistor radio and a bottle of 'duty-free whisky' concealing a bomb and additional liquid explosive. Emplaning for Baghdad, to connect with the KAL 707, their hand-luggage was just waved through by Yugoslav security. Only a stewardess spotted the radio on board. The batteries would have to be removed for safekeeping until the landing in Baghdad.

Twenty minutes before boarding the KAL 707, the timer was fixed to detonate the bomb nine hours later, long after the Abu Dhabi stop-over. Going through Baghdad security, they were asked about the radio. The old man switched on the set to demonstrate its innocence. (Kim thought the Iraqis 'acted as if they were sorry' for troubling them, as if they knew what sort of a radio it was.) The bomb was stored in an overhead bin, and left behind when the pair disembarked at Abu Dhabi. It duly exploded over Burma, killing 115 people.

But the story did not end with Kim's confession. Sentenced to death by hanging, she repented, received a Presidential pardon, turned into a political propaganda asset, got herself hired as a senior security adviser to South Korean intelligence, published her memoirs (*Now, I Want to Become A Woman*), and earned royalties in excess of a million dollars. In many ways, Kim's was a classic case. Apart from the security blunders at Belgrade and Baghdad (if, indeed, Baghdad was a mere slip-up), it demonstrated that a criminal might be allowed to enjoy the fruits of her murders.

Security and the main purpose of airports – fast and easy access to aircraft – are in a natural conflict. Nobody likes to see searchlights and gun-towers around airports (undue laxity tends to follow periods of red alert with tanks and troops), but the threats of bombs and skyjacking is too great to let the flying public remain a soft target.

Against determined, expert and well-financed terrorists, *total* security is impossible without closing the airport – just like total air safety cannot be achieved without keeping all aircraft on the ground. 'We have five and a half miles of runways and numerous buildings around the vast expanse of tarmac to protect,' said Alastair Widdup, Heathrow's Deputy Security Manager. 'We put a ring of steel around it all, with almost fourteen miles of perimeter fencing, but we realize that people got through even the Iron Curtain. We have a strict system of limited access for all staff, including cleaners and people wandering about with tool boxes, and their ID cards restrict them to certain zones. Yellow ID cards, for instance, are only for terminal buildings, and very few people hold red ones that afford access to all areas. The guard on duty looks at the photo, inserts the card into the machine that gives a green light if it's valid for crossing an entry point, a red one if it's the wrong zone, and flashes if the card is about to expire. Collusion is, of course, a risk, so everybody is subject to physical checks and search. Mobile patrols operate everywhere, and a team of inspectors test the guards with rogue ID cards and devices.

'With almost 50,000 staff to control, we must retain an element of trust, but guards are sponsored and referenced back twenty years or to the age of fifteen. Some security people would like to see fingerprinting, and with modern machines it is claimed they could analyse the seventeen identifiable features, but staff would resent that. The new type of ID card for the future may not have a photograph but when it is swiped through the reader machine, it would call up the bearer's picture on a screen from the central computer. There's also some research into voice and retina identification.

'Cargo areas that adjoin and overlap the apron are particularly hard to police though we make them restricted zones. We have 1990s security requirements for airports designed in the 1940s. When an aircraft is parked, it becomes a temporary restricted zone. It's the airline that must ensure that access is limited to their aircraft which must be searched by them because it's a flag-carrier, and therefore a sovereign territory.'

The best airports and most cautious airlines begin passenger screening even before the check-in. Europeans tend to concentrate on certain nationalities and inbound flights originating from countries that are considered to be a risk. Americans question everybody, but that is time-consuming. Northwest Airlines plans to use an Automated Profiling System that would reduce the size of the haystack where they look for bad needles. When passengers are questioned, the sophisticated data base would flag the risk revealed by answers and behaviour. It is a closely guarded secret what sort of responses would trigger the flags. Passengers, milling around Heathrow, are profiled quietly by watchful eyes. Alastair Widdup is understandably reticent about giving details, but claims they can spot those who may carry dangerous items. They look for nervous passengers, obvious signs such as a big heavy coat worn on a hot day, people who ask others to carry or mind their bags. Australia may soon introduce a system containing information from Interpol: at passport control, it will photograph everybody, compare the picture with fourteen variants of the image in its data base, and so identify faces despite any recent changes, such as a newly grown beard.

In their own interest, passengers are expected to put up with the inconvenience of questions (Where and when did you buy your ticket? Did you pay cash? Did you yourself pack your bags? Are you carrying gifts or anything for somebody else?), and the early check-in for security reasons. (El Al has an extra-long procedure, but the much threatened carrier's security has not yet been compromised. That is how they caught a wretched, pregnant girl who unknowingly carried a bomb in the false bottom of her suitcase, a gift from her Arab fiancé for the trip to Israel.) Full and willing cooperation with security is essential even if mistakes may lead to unpleasant situations. In 1991, for instance, a Syrian gave unsatisfactory answers to six routine questions before boarding in Milan for New York; he was taken into custody when an additional screening found 'a device' on him; it looked like a bomb component – but turned out to be an anti-theft briefcase alarm.

Some captains of industry and other so-called VIPs are reputedly the least cooperative passengers. 'They often *expect* to be recognized rather than stopped at check-points,' said Wilfred Knight, security consultant, who protected three Government Ministers and visiting heads of state when he served as a senior police officer. (He used to warn his charges that there was no total protection, but promised jokingly that if they got killed, a hit team would make sure that the assassin was buried with them.) 'Pop stars are often indignant if questioned. And what does an inexperienced guard do if someone says he's a Lord of the Realm? He should, but will he always demand proof of identity? Chairmen of multinationals are sometimes the worst offenders, believing that if they flash a plastic card, that should be enough. One of them thought it was a big joke that he entered VIP lounges every time with a card bearing his dog's photograph. Yet the risk is serious, particularly if the face is familiar, and the tie on the white shirt has an airline logo – what if the man was sacked the day before, and he is now up to some mischief?' (That is how in December 1987 a disgruntled American airline employee boarded a flight with a Magnum, and shot his boss, a fellow passenger, then both pilots of the BAe 146 commuter jet. All forty-three people were killed in the dive that followed.)

THE BIG BANG

Not all that long ago, when anybody could buy insurance for any passenger from airport vending machines, mothers, spouses, friends were disposed of by the would-be beneficiaries who had kindly volunteered to pack a passenger's luggage. (In 1988, a South African thought he had invented the perfect crime: he managed to kill seventeen people, but the insurance fraud was detected. A year later, a Ukrainian sought a lucrative divorce from his wife. His bomb was found in time, but he was granted a lengthy separation – in a Siberian labour camp.)

Some charitable fraudsters used to blow themselves out of the sky for their family's benefit, but modern political saboteurs seek *glory* rather than suicide or profit by stealth. They prefer the big bang. The more spectacular the better – images associated all too readily with the horror of Lockerbie, the media triumph of murderers that demonstrated yet again that a small bomb, strategically placed, can tear an aircraft apart. Since then, aircraft manufacturers and a British defence company have been developing safer structure designs and materials that might, some day in the distant future, soak up or vent the force of an explosion out of the cargo hold through flaps in the fuselage.

'Terrorists take advantage of malleable plastic explosives that can be finger-sculpted into any shape,' said accident investigator Eric Newton, the foremost expert on air sabotage. 'We've seen bombs in the shape of toys and electronic components, a modified commercial catalogue, a carrier bag, even a domestic soapflake box. The timer and detonator can similarly be disguised, and concealed in everyday objects, biscuit tins, washbags, cosmetics or baby food.' (In 1989, warnings were circulated that a look-alike of Halawi, a Middle Eastern marzipan paste, might in fact be made of Semtex – both are odourless substances of similar colour, with the only difference being that the explosive does not taste sweet.)

One of the most crucial tasks of the battle against bombs is to prevent the separation of passengers and their checked-in luggage. A new, sophisticated bar coding, like that in supermarkets, now helps to ensure that the passenger and his luggage are on the same flight. If the passenger fails to board after loading, hours can be wasted because *all* the luggage must come off, and everybody must disembark for individual luggage identification. Against that, modern airports put every bag in a known, specific container so that the missing passengers' luggage can be easily located. Passengers transferring from one flight to the next are a special problem (yet another echo of Lockerbie) but even at better airports, only about a third of their luggage is searched. At older terminals, arriving and transfer passengers must mingle with departing ones, who are already beyond security controls, and if the incoming people's point of embarkation was one of the numerous scantily protected airports, there is a risk that weapons or bomb components might be handed over. (New measures are being designed for segregation like those at Heathrow's Terminal 4.) Airlines are not allowed to carry unaccompanied luggage unless they are fully satisfied that it is truly innocent. But how complete is full satisfaction?

X-ray examination/metal detection and random search of suitcases are the main methods in use, but both can be erratic. The UK government wants to have *everything* that goes into the cargo hold searched, but that may bring airports to a halt, and create long queues all the way out of the terminals – another soft target for terrorists. Some carriers use strategically positioned equipment for speedy customer service. (At Heathrow, United has an X-ray machine under the floor of the concourse, American Airlines has one built into the check-in desk – only security men, who watch the screen, can clear the luggage and press the button that moves the conveyor belt.)

Bomb detection is hardly ever as easy as it was at Sao Paolo in 1991: 307 people, including Pele, Socrates and other soccer stars, were boarding when a ticking noise was heard coming from a suitcase about to be loaded on to the aircraft. More often than not, the cause is a rechargeable razor (I frightened a MALÉV stewardess out of her wits when this happened to me), but in Brazil a bomb *was* found, and its Japanese carrier detained.

Semtex (manufactured by the former Czechoslovakia, and sold in large quantities to many countries, such as Libya, that finance terrorism) is the most difficult explosive to detect. In Prague, sniffer dogs were trained to find it. There is more hope, however, for the long-delayed introduction of mechanical sniffers. Makers of IONSCAN, a portable appliance, claim to need only five seconds to detect explosives. EGIS, another product, takes twenty-eight seconds to vacuum a sample and analyse it (a potential cause for long hold-ups). Envisaged to be a back-up if X-rays have already spotted something suspicious, it is now tested or used at some twenty airports, including Detroit, New York, Miami, Heathrow, Gatwick, Tokyo, Hongkong, Jakarta, Bali, Zurich and Frankfurt, in a dozen countries. (Originally a large, six-ton installation, there is now a portable version of EGIS which works like a vacuum cleaner, sucking in and analysing air samples of the aura of people and luggage to detect nitrogen vapours emitted even by traces of explosives.) This sniffing technique is known as Thermal Neutron Analysis (TNA). Its false alarm rate is claimed to be one in a hundred. With 3 million people flying every day, the delays caused by false alarms can still be considerable, because the bag must be searched, while its owner is found and questioned.

'A piece of equipment tested at Gatwick,' says Alastair Widdup, 'could detect an explosive, and handle roughly 600 bags an hour. But it occupied a lot of floor space that needed underpinning because of its weight. Just because the machine detects the presence of explosives, it doesn't necessarily mean you have a bomb because many military people and quarry engineers, for instance, can never wash themselves totally clean of legitimate contamination, and partly because the machine detects minute quantities.' (False alarms may also be caused by the detection of some nitrogen in passengers' winter woollies.)

An American Presidential Commission was very critical of PanAm's security as well as the FAA that failed 'to enforce its own regulations' before, and for nine months after, Lockerbie. The TNA machines may well be the best for bomb detection, but at $1.5 million each, their widespread introduction is very costly. So who should pay for it? Airlines claim that terrorists threaten entire nations, therefore governments should foot the bill. The counter-argument is why should granny pay for rich, frequent fliers' security?

The squabbling seems obscene in the light of past experience. In 1988 Lockerbie was a horrid landmark and, hopefully, its impact on security will never fade, but what blind penny-pinching inexcusable carelessness let us ignore all that had gone before it? Take the Air India disaster, barely three years earlier: 329 people perished as the Jumbo crashed into the ocean 110 miles west of Ireland. The accident investigation was exceptionally complicated (most of the wreckage was never recovered from the bottom of the sea), and the Indian authorities handled it in an unprofessional manner, jumping to conclusions on the basis of genuinely feasible theories that were supported by a simultaneous attack against a second Air India Jumbo. Both flights originated from Canada, where investigators uncovered startling security loopholes.

On 20 June 1985, a man in Vancouver made two reservations by telephone. One was for a single ticket for a Jaswand Singh, who would take a Canadian flight to Toronto where he would transfer to an Air

India flight to Delhi via Montreal and Heathrow. The other was a return for Mohinderbel Singh, who would take a Canadian flight to Tokyo where he would transfer to an Air India flight to Bangkok. A few hours later in Vancouver, an Indian man paid $3005 in cash for the two tickets but made some changes to the reservations: both passengers would remain named as Singh, but one would now be a Mr M. Singh, and the other a Mr L. Singh, who would not take the return flight.

Confusing? Yes, but the ticket clerk was unperturbed. Many Asians live in that area, and both aircraft would carry mostly Indians (coyly described by the investigators as 'members of one of our visible minorities'), with two dozen Singhs, the most common Sikh name, on each flight. As rebellious Sikhs had made political threats to Air India, a special alert was in force, but not an eyebrow was raised by the changed initials.

On the day of the flights, M. Singh telephoned to confirm his reservation, and asked for his suitcase to be checked right through to Delhi. As he was only wait-listed on standby from Toronto onwards, that was refused. Three hours later, checking in for Toronto, he repeated his request, created a scene, held up a long queue, and the passenger agent relented: the luggage was tagged through all the way to Delhi. Half an hour later, M. Singh was not in his assigned seat, but the flight was allowed to depart! At Toronto, his suitcase was duly transferred to the Air India flight: presumably, by then it was treated as unaccompanied cargo. During the stop-over at Montreal, a long delay occurred.

Meanwhile, L. Singh checked in for Bangkok via Tokyo. His luggage was tagged to be transferred at Tokyo and flown all the way to Bangkok. When the flight departed, L. Singh was not on board. In Tokyo, the following morning, the cart carrying transfer luggage from Vancouver suffered an explosion. Two people were killed, four were injured.

Conceivably, something like that might have been planned to happen at Heathrow, to coincide with the Tokyo bombing, but due to the delay Air India 182 was still over the Atlantic when it should already have landed in London.

All this does not, however, constitute hard evidence that there *was* a bomb aboard AI 182, but the likelihood of such a scenario increased when, in addition to the luggage separation, numerous other blunders came to light: some airport security staff were untrained, air crews were not subjected to security checks, the baggage X-ray worked only intermittently, and the transfer baggage at Toronto was not X-rayed because it was presumed that it had already been screened at Vancouver.*

---

*A detailed account of the investigation can be found in *The Final Call* by Stephen Barlay (Sinclair Stevenson, 1991). A Scottish type 'not proven' verdict would have been more appropriate. Inderjit Singh Rejat was convicted of manslaughter by making or helping to make a bomb that had killed baggage handlers in Tokyo. He was jailed in 1991 for ten years.

More sabotage cases ensued in quick succession. Urged by the NTSB, a Congressional inquiry then found that the US airport weapon screening system for carry-on baggage was only 80 per cent effective – with a failure rate of 60 per cent at Phoenix, Arizona – an unacceptably low standard that was still considerably higher than that in the Third World and many parts of Europe.

The AUC is concerned 'that security standards vary dramatically from one country to another' (*Annual Report for 1991*). This is partly because the implementation of the standards set by ICAO is 'a matter for individual states. The Committee expects the UK to press foreign governments to exercise the same care and maintain the same standards as we are entitled to see from our own . . . ' In the same year, at a Civil Aviation Conference, it was claimed that some European airports, such as Charles de Gaulle and Frankfurt, were a major worry, and the standards ranged from very good to barely existing. The Third World security budgets were found to be virtually non-existent. This was illustrated within a few months: though it was not a *bomb* which killed 233 people in the Lauda Air B767 crash in 1991, it transpired that passengers, boarding at Bangkok, had only their hand luggage screened or searched because the high alert imposed during the Gulf War had been lifted. (See pages 87 and 223.)

ARCHWAYS AND X-RAYS

Watching the screen as the conveyor belt carries hand luggage through the X-ray machine must surely qualify as one of the most vitally responsible, tiring and unspeakably boring jobs in the world. Isaac Yeffet, former security chief of El Al once revealed that virtually all American carriers hired the lowest bidder for security guards who were insufficiently trained. Two years before Lockerbie he had surveyed PanAm, and warned that it was highly vulnerable to attack, but his recommendations were not implemented because PanAm, like most airlines, held that the extra inconvenience would drive passengers away. The guards were – and in many countries, still are – as badly paid as trained, and many airports have a 100 per cent annual staff turnover.

'Search by TV is perhaps the worst invention,' said Eric Newton. The *show* is soul-destroying, and it is an almost impossible task to keep watching it. In many parts of the world, its role is just cosmetic. Buzzers and flashing lights will not fool anyone. Carrying a radio/cassette recorder, this author was simply waved through a Spanish airport when such devices were the number one security suspects. The guards, with their backs to the screen, missed it as it went through the X-ray, and would not examine it even when it was called to their attention. Security specialists frequently carry electronic equipment, but some guards fail to question them about it. They find 'Italian security very slack, with Greek and some other Mediterranean security just a joke. Some people refuse to board aircraft that had a prior stopover in Athens.' With such refusals and general complaints, *passengers could do a great deal more for their own security*. Even in Britain and America, inspectors who test the system often succeed in getting through with guns and other weapons.

'In Britain, the carefully vetted security guards receive eight and a half days' classroom training, then work forty hours under supervision,' said Alastair Widdup. 'There's also an annual refresher training and "on the job" practice throughout the year. We know that people's attention span is limited, so they must not spend more than twenty minutes on the X-ray screen. Then they must be on other duties for at least forty minutes to keep them alert, because machines spot nothing – only humans do. Frisking passengers is also a challenge. Initially, most guards have a natural reluctance to lay hands on strangers, feel their pockets and rummage in their bags. They must learn that not only bombs but also potential bomb components must be found, and if we get it wrong, the customer may not come back. Most people can't imagine how tiring that frisking job is: we never keep anybody on that duty for more than thirty minutes at a stretch. Staff must be polite and courteous, but the security principle is that the passenger may be guilty until proven innocent. And if any guard doubted the importance of the job, passengers would soon alert them to it. We have quite a range of items people must not carry on board, and we take things such as knives, teargas sprays, off passengers every four or five minutes. It's incredible what people carry in handbags and pockets. We found antidote for mustard gas, large batches of razor blades, nuts and bolts on African and Middle Eastern traders, cans of paint, even a car engine as cabin luggage.'

It is not commonly known that all passengers may rightfully refuse to submit to frisking on, say, religious grounds. The guards will always respect their wishes – but then may deny permission for boarding.

Men tend to set off the detector arches' alarm more often than women because they carry more metal objects in their pockets. At some airports, you are asked to put keys, coins or electronic diaries into a basket before stepping through. If there was a written sign to that effect, the process could be speeded up. UK regulations, however, go the opposite way: if a buzzer is activated, the passenger is asked to empty his pockets, and then may be subjected to a random search. But those who take out metal objects without being told to do so will *always* be searched because the archways are tuned to accept a certain small amount of metals, and a terrorist may try to reduce the amount he is carrying to the barest minimum. Some experts suspect that archways for charter flights are calibrated to a much higher level, as if package tourists were less likely to commit criminal acts beyond getting drunk.

Another anomaly concerns knives. Small penknives may be carried. The acceptable blade length varies from country to country, and Widdup would like to see the introduction of a global standard. Ordinary cutlery, such as a sample of the set you intend to buy on your next trip, will be confiscated or taken for safekeeping if found in cabin luggage. Yet because of customer service and marketing considerations, your meal on board will these days be served with steel cutlery even though such a knife, held to a pilot's throat, could cause problems.

Gifts and souvenirs are confiscated if they look dangerous. Some people are given to naïve complaints that the replica of a Colt is 'just a toy', but if a stewardess is threatened with it, who would have the nerve to ask for a demonstration before complying with the toy-gunman's demands? A man, leaving Washington, carried a defused hand-grenade that was meant to be a paper-weight. It became a memento on the Dulles airport manager's desk. Another one, mounted on a wooden plinth with a brass plaque – 'If you're having a bad day, pull the pin' – now decorates Widdup's office.

'It's hard to say what is and what isn't a weapon,' said Widdup. 'An aircraft was once diverted because the hijacker had a banana in his pocket, and nobody risked demanding to see the "gun". Terrorists don't need a bomb for such purposes. Holding a detonator to the pilot's ear would be bad enough. That's why we also look for potential bomb components.'

If you are the jocular type – *beware*. For cracking the little joke of 'Watch it, I have a bomb in that bag' you could be arrested, and you would certainly be held long enough to miss your flight. Yet hundreds of people cannot resist being *witty*. A British higher education minister was greatly embarrassed by publicity after his remark that his case was 'full of explosives'. A Spanish businessman was detained and fined £600 for the same jest. 'Threats are an even more serious matter for security because their number runs to double figures at major airports every day,' said Knight, 'and it's difficult to evaluate whether it's something serious or just a stupid hoax. Some people find it hilarious that they can delay a flight or induce an airport evacuation by a single telephone call, that may come from a disgruntled employee – or a terrorist.'

In November 1992 a threat was faxed to United's Chicago office claiming that there was a bomb on board a Los Angeles to New York flight, and that it would blow up at 10,000 feet or on landing unless $600,000 was paid. Feasible? Certainly. Detonators that are timed or triggered by reaching a chosen level of barometric pressure can be constructed. So was it an attempted extortion or a hoax? The aircraft was searched. Nothing was found, but that was no guarantee of safety. So what was there to do? Pay up? Risk calling the bluff? The dilemma was aggravated by a probably far-fetched but not impossible suspicion: just a few hours before the departure of that flight, the airline had switched its security guard contract from one company to another. What if a disgruntled former employee was trying to prove the new guards' inefficiency? The flight survived without any incident. Commendably, it has never been published whether there was a bomb on board or if the airline negotiated with the would-be extortionist. But two days later a man, unconnected with any of the security companies, was arrested on a tip-off to the FBI. The happy ending did not diminish the toll taken by the terrifying hours when the decision-makers had to choose the path to follow. The case served as a reminder of a question everyone would prefer to sweep under the carpet: should we tell the passengers? ACAP and IADG, the association of International Air Disaster Groups, believe that the answer should be 'yes'. They demand that people should be told at the boarding gate 'when there is a high degree of probability that their flight is threatened by terrorists or criminals'.

Since Lockerbie, much but far from enough has been done for airport and air security. Passenger-baggage reconciliation is still incomplete even in countries where it has become compulsory. The installation of state-of-the-art technology, the implementation of many essential recommendations for higher world standards in prevention, and the introduction of better paid, better trained, more tightly supervised security guards are still patchy.

In May 1992, the American government, pilots and carriers put their faith in the lure of the dollar: they offered up to $4 million, plus a new life and identity with US citizenship, for inside information that would help to prevent a terrorist attack. But ultimately, only the unfailing detection and severe punishment of perpetrators can greatly reduce or stamp out air terrorism. Piracy on the high seas had been eradicated (well, almost), only in the wake of worldwide condemnation and inevitable extraditions. Similar measures went a long way towards the elimination of political skyjacking, the bane of air traffic in the 1970s when passengers were killed or held to ransom, stewing in aircraft under the desert sun of the Middle East. Governments sometimes had to make painful decisions: communist defectors, with whom they sympathized, had to be jailed if they had skyjacked flights and endangered lives. This was why the counter-measures worked. These days, skyjacking is limited mostly to cranks, extortionists, and less secure areas like South America and the Middle East, the political turmoil of the former Soviet Union, and to airports, such as Frankfurt (where the Lockerbie disaster began), that seem to have learned little from past experience. (In February 1993, an Ethiopian student managed to board in Frankfurt with a starting pistol, and forced the Lufthansa aircraft to fly to New York. Five days later, a .38 Smith & Weston revolver in a Frankfurt duty-free bag was found in a rubbish bin at Birmingham airport. The German pilots' association complained about the 'considerable defects' of Frankfurt security.)

There is, however, no room for complacency. The bombing and skyjacking of aircraft come in recurrent waves of flavour-of-the-day fads. Whatever fortunes are offered as rewards, the menace will not go away as long as governments, like in Korea, capitalize on the conversion of potential or actual murderers, and refuse, like Libya, the extradition of suspected terrorists.

9

The Mystery of Flying

Hold one end of a sheet of paper to your chin. Blow hard and evenly over the loosely hanging sheet. Instead of going down, it will begin to rise.

If you are one of those to whom the lift-off of big, heavy aeroplanes will always seem miraculous – rejoice. You have just recreated that miracle, called the *lift*. For that is how kites fly. And aeroplanes, too. Admittedly, it takes some engineering wizardry, and a few bits of electronic, hydraulic and technological gadgetry to turn an aluminium tube into a flying machine, but the principle is the same.

Needless to say, aeronautical boffins might be horrified by such simplistic explanations, but the blushes might have been their own, had they been among the throng in a room at Farnborough on a sunny day some five decades ago. The debate had been going on for hours. Thick pipe and cigarette smoke clouded the blackboard on which somebody had sketched a most peculiar design that looked like anything but an aeroplane. Expert opinion began to sway towards the 'it'll never fly' verdict, when a young scientist rose to his feet at the far end of the room. He threw a hastily folded school-kid's paper dart, exclaiming, 'Like hell it won't!' The dart skimmed in level flight the pates of wise heads, and scored a bull's-eye on the blackboard. A simplistic demonstration, surely, that could not have been the decisive factor – but Concorde, the first supersonic airliner was born. And it looked nothing like any other aircraft.

Galileo Galilei, the great sixteenth-century physicist, was convinced that man must emulate birds in order to fly.* Leonardo da Vinci and others agreed with him. They thought if wings of minimal weight were attached to our body, we could lift off. But they failed to realize that the power output of human arms (or even legs) would be too small to achieve that. For compared to birds, we are weaklings. The flight

---

*Those who wish to gain a comprehensive insight into the science of flying will find Peter P. Wegner's book, *What Makes Airplanes Fly*, an excellent source.

muscles of stronger birds constitute up to a quarter of their total body weight. The tiny hummingbird weighs as much as a small coin, but 30 per cent of that is flying muscle. The power it can generate is ten times that produced by a champion cyclist, and will keep it in flight for some 1500 miles without a pause. A nightingale needs only one gram of fat for 'fuel' to power it across the Sahara. Birds can also hover, and the hummingbird can even move backwards in the air.

Men who tried (and to this day still try) to fly took a running start to create an airflow over their wings and to lift off like our sheet of paper. Knowing not what they did, with that they added forward propulsion (legs for an engine) to their separate lifting surfaces – the essentials of the great breakthrough in thinking that came in the nineteenth century with Sir George Cayley, the father of a new science, who set down the mathematical principles of flying. The first to use models for research, he gave his brainchildren fixed wings plus vertical and horizontal tail surfaces. He also achieved a series of other firsts, starting with the glider that carried the first human, a ten-year-old boy, aloft in a heavier-than-air craft, at Brompton Hall near Scarborough in Yorkshire. The first adult in the air was his coachman, who promptly resigned his job: 'Please, Sir George, I was hired to drive not to fly!' Sailplanes could emulate birds in gliding and soaring on rising air, but they lacked the initial forward propulsion and had to be catapulted for lift-off. (Cayley's boy pilot flew after dozens of men had towed the craft down a hillside.)

To replace leg-power, there were experiments with engines driven by steam, oil, gas or guncotton. Research continued, and the first wind tunnel was built by Wenham for the Aeronautical Society of Great Britain in 1871. The German Lilienthal, who believed that the ultimate answer would be bird-like wing-flapping, published a pioneering textbook, got airborne with running starts to fly record-breaking distances, and died crashing one of his gliders. The American Langley built fine petrol-engined models, but his full-scale machines and their pilots just dipped into the Potomac river. The Wright brothers' first powered, sustained flight in 1903 followed in the wake of Langley's flops – and the rest, with millions of people hopping on an aircraft to Australia as if they were taking a bus downtown, is history.

NOW WE ARE FLYING

On their way to the boarding gates, passengers might catch sight of a pilot walking around the aircraft for a final visual check before joining his colleague in the cockpit. Subsequently, the pilots go through long checklists that leave nothing to chance or the fallibility of human memory: the rigorous drill for every take-off and landing is that one pilot must read out the list, down to the no smoking and seatbelts signs 'on', and each item must be checked and confirmed by the other. The latest weather reports and operational data are noted, and the route to be flown is fed into the autopilot: once it has received the exact geographical location of the parked aircraft, it can do the flying halfway round the world, to any chosen destination.

The pilots wait for clearances to start the engines, taxi to the runway, and begin their take-off run. Like a child pulling a kite, 'run' is the operative word, for that is what creates that seemingly mysterious upward force – the *lift* to the skies.

Propulsion, the role once played by Lilienthal's muscular legs, comes from the engines. Their number (one, two, three or four) depends on the size and power requirement of the aircraft. Two may be mounted on the sides of the aft of the fuselage, with a third, if necessary, atop at the foot of the fin. Two or four engines may be hung on pylons under the wings.

Propellers, driven by piston engines, are rarely seen these days in airline service. Since the 1950s, they have been replaced rapidly by the jets. Turbojet engines suck in the air, compress it, add fuel, and burn the mixture that explodes in a white-hot jet of gas at the rear, creating *thrust*. The driving force of that continuous explosion is so huge that four such engines can produce the speed to ease a fully laden Jumbo, some 900,000 pounds, off the ground, and keep propelling it forward in the air. Some of the exhaust works the windmilling blades of a turbine that, in turn, operates fans and the compressor to run the engine. (Turbofans use a large fan at the front of the engine; turboprops drive propellers on smaller aircraft; the new propfans spin large propeller-like blades at very high speeds, and resemble the turboprops.)

Racing down the runway, the aircraft generates high pressure below and low pressure above the cambered profile of the wing. That pressure difference increases with acceleration – a risk to cars, but a must for flying. What matters more than the actual groundspeed is the *airspeed* that measures in knots how fast the aircraft is going relative to the air surrounding it. Running into headwind, for instance, gives a bonus: at a groundspeed of 100 m.p.h., a 20 m.p.h. headwind creates a 120 m.p.h. airspeed. To achieve sufficient acceleration, i.e. lift, the runway length may need to be up to 10,000 feet, commensurate to the weight (aircraft plus fuel, passengers and cargo) about to leave the ground. It must also allow for the prevailing wind, temperature, humidity, as well as the altitude, slope and surface of the runway. (In the tropics, and at airports high above sea level, the air is thinner, so more speed, hence a longer runway, is needed.)

When the aircraft reaches a certain point at a precalculated speed (V_1 for 'velocity one'), it is decision time for the pilots. If a klaxon or flashing light indicates a systems failure, they can safely abort take-off by following a set procedure. If all is well at V_1, the aircraft continues to accelerate to V_r ('velocity rotate'), when the pilot must *rotate*, i.e. lift the nose of the aircraft. V_r is the point of no return – beyond which, whatever goes wrong, it is usually safer to take off and land again than to try stopping on what is left of the runway ahead. Even if an engine fails at or beyond that critical moment, the pilot can continue the climb-out, fly a circuit, dispose of the fuel (maximum landing weight is far below that permitted for take-off), and still land safely with an engine out.

V_2 is then reached: that is the minimum safe flying speed that must be maintained even with an engine failure. After a steep initial climb-out, the V_2 is usually reduced to satisfy noise abatement regulations. Eventually, the aircraft settles at its assigned cruising height where an equilibrium of weight and lift prevails, and the thrust of the engines exceeds the drag caused by the resistance of the air. (The engines have far more power than that needed to keep the craft in the air, so the pilot has much in hand, and can keep flying with half his power-plants out of action.)

Most jets have swept wings (not perpendicular to the fuselage, angled towards the rear) because that design increases efficiency at high speed at high altitude where modern aircraft operate most economically. For supersonic flight they use delta wings.

FLIGHT CONTROL

The flight control surfaces are relatively small compared to the wings and tail section. At the pilot's or autopilot's command, they move up or down or sideways, changing their relative position to the main structures, deflecting the airflow over the aircraft, and so rendering the three-dimensional freedom of flying controllable.

The *flaps*, extendable parts of the wings along the trailing edge, and the *slats*, mounted on the leading edge of the wings, are used for take-off and landing, to increase the lifting capability at relatively low speeds.

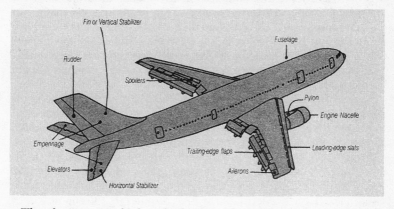

The *elevators*, attached to the horizontal stabilizers (the small wings, called the empennage, at the back), control *pitch*, making the nose point up- or downwards.

The *rudder*, a vertical moving surface, forms the rear end of the fin, the vertical stabilizer. It initiates *yaw*, to turn the aircraft left or right.

Ailerons are mounted near the tips of the wing trailing edges. Their position can increase or decrease the amount of lift one or the other wing produces. That makes a turning aircraft *roll* like a cornering cyclist.

Spoilers are panels that can rise out of the upper surfaces of the wings. Their role is to spoil the lift and act as speed brakes when the aircraft descends and lands.

The basic principles of flying are clearly defined, but their practical application, and their execution with a sufficient safety margin, can be affected by a multitude of minute details. Paper darts may never fail, but despite the amount of calculations and testing, a new aircraft always needs to be . . .

CERTIFIED TO FLY

Each country is supposed to examine and approve every detail of a new design, but in practice that hardly ever amounts to much more than rubber-stamping the original – mostly American, British or French – certificate issued by an aeronautically advanced state of manufacture. That initial airworthiness certification is an arduous process. The controlling authorities, however, lack the financial and manpower resources to duplicate and double-check everything done by the manufacturers, and much is taken on trust. Ultimately, both manufacturers and governments rely on and benefit from the experience of users to iron out snags, and introduce further, chiefly safety-oriented, refinements through issuing advice and warnings (SBs and ADs) of a varying degree of urgency. In order to avoid duplication of work and different standards (including additional requirements that can result in costly changes of design requirements), the FAA and the JAA, the Joint Aviation Authorities of Europe, have been trying since 1983 to achieve common international certification procedures, but little progress has been made. Variations persist even in Europe, and a new strategic plan has still not been devised for quick results.

Critics of aircraft and engine certification have plenty of scope for disapproval. Aviation lawyer Don Madole, who is currently chairing a combined US government and National Academy of Sciences appraisal of the certification process and principles, would like to see more thorough checking of the work done by foreign authorities. He claims that 'the FAA has no one who has ever built or designed an aircraft, needs outside expertise, and relies too heavily on the manufacturers' assurances'. Tony Broderick of the FAA disputes that strenuously, and quotes examples, such as having the former head of structures of McDonnell-Douglas on the FAA staff, but nobody denies that it would be impossible for an authority to duplicate absolutely every test by manufacturers without a vastly inflated budget for extra thousands of inspectors, delaying each certification for up to a decade.

The limitations are recognized, and to some extent catered for, by the British CAA which is always under pressure to reduce costs because it is financed by the industry it must police. 'We can't design a new aircraft yet again, but we can validate what has been done by the manufacturers,' said Michael Willett, the Safety Regulation Group Director. 'We work with the industry, monitor its progress, and use a check-sheet system. Occasionally we investigate certain design aspects in depth if we see serious potential problems, particularly when new technology, such as flying by wire, is introduced.'

When despite worldwide certification a new aircraft or engine comes to grief, the critics have a field day with the crucial question: was the mishap *unforeseeable* (the key criterion of what can truly be regarded as an accident) or was it just *unforeseen* (an oversight or slip-up by the manufacturers, airlines and regulatory authorities)? The disastrous sequence of events that led to the Kegworth disaster (a British Midland B737-400 in 1989) had started with a flutter and resultant fan blade failure in the new, powerful high bypass turbofan engine. Flutter was not a new problem. Scientists had warned against it and, ultimately, the pilots could have averted the tragedy. But could it have been prevented by further studies of flutter and more thorough certification by France, Britain and America? 'With hindsight, it's easy to say that the answer is yes, more could have been done,' said Dr Bernard Loeb, Director of the NTSB Office of Research and Engineering. 'But was it an oversight, was it some degree of negligence, was it something that someone just *might* have foreseen, and above all, had I been involved in the design or certification, can I honestly say that I would have demanded and forced through more research?'

In the same year, a DC-10 crashed at Sioux City, killing 112 people. The NTSB investigation blamed maintenance for overlooking a crack in a turbine disc, and criticized the FAA for certifying the design that had left the hydraulic lines vulnerable to uncontained engine failure.

Another classic example occurred two years later. A B767 of an Austrian airline run by Niki Lauda, the former Formula One World champion driver, was climbing out of Bangkok towards its cruising height when it disappeared from the radar screens. It broke up in the air. One of its wings landed twelve miles from the main crash site where 223 people were killed. After the mostly media-led flurry of speculation had subsided, and sabotage theories had been eliminated despite slack Thai security (as seen), it was found that an unintentional engine thrust reversal had caused the accident.

Reverse thrust is used for slowing down aircraft on the ground. Did it not occur to anyone that it could happen accidentally in the air? Did nobody think of the potentially disastrous consequences? 'Of course they thought about it,' said Bud Laynor, the Deputy Head of the NTSB Investigation Division. 'Certification tests, carried out to see if such a reversal could cause aerodynamic problems, proved that the engine could be brought back to idle, and demonstrated that the aircraft could be landed safely. *After* the Lauda accident, further research uncovered that the premise on which the certification had been based was not sound, because during the original trials, the reverse had been deployed only at much lower airspeed and thrust. The post-accident testing now pinpointed the problem: if reverse thrust occurred at high airspeed and thrust, such as during the doomed flight over Thailand, it would affect the airflow over the wings, create an uncontrollable aerodynamic problem, and that would not be tolerated by the aircraft structure. The reverse system was then altered, and the snag was cured. Some people believe that more and different tests *could* have been done during certification. But who can be certain that they *ought* to have been done?'

Mike Willett concurs: 'There's no limit of what else could be done. The possibilities are endless. So the line must be drawn somewhere at a reasonable level. Even when investigators work backwards from a failure, there's a one in ten million random element.'

The certification of a new design can never be entirely free of worries and soul-searching: is it reasonable, in fact *essential*, to ask even more probing questions, and test and test ad infinitum? Is our current knowledge, the state of the art, sufficient to let a new aircraft or engine fly?

THE MORE THE MERRIER?

Not all that long ago, engines gave pilots frequent headaches, illustrated by the story of Lord Hives, a great engineer and ex-chairman of Rolls-Royce aeroengines. When he was asked what would constitute a really safe aeroplane, he said, 'If during a flight the co-pilot reported that "We've lost our number twenty-nine engine, sir," and the captain could ask, in turn, "Twenty-nine, you said? Which side?" I'd feel happier.'

Engine technology has improved beyond recognition since then, which is why new, long-range aircraft with only two engines could be certified for transoceanic flights. Apart from various additional safety measures, the key criteria concerned the determination of how far a twin-engined aircraft should be from the nearest airport to which it may have to divert if an engine fails and must be shut down. The acronym EROPS (Extended Range OperationS) was quickly translated by the four-engine devotees as 'Engines Running Or Passengers Swimming.' EROPS became ETOPS (Extended-range Twin-engine OperationS), a more truthful reference, but queries about the practice are still raised in the flying community. Regulatory authorities, manufacturers and airlines (that enjoy a huge financial benefit from flying more frequent long-range services with smaller aircraft they can fill) believe firmly in the safety of ETOPS. They emphasize that many *extras*, the frilly safety features of operations and maintenance, are now compulsory by law and airline self-regulation; that no aircraft is certified for ETOPS without proving its ability to fly and land safely on just one of the two engines, and that the record of modern engine and systems reliability speaks for itself: Britannia Airways, for instance, suffered only two IFSDs (In-Flight engine Shut-Downs) in 280,000 hours of flying B767s.* (Rolls-Royce has claimed a world record for an RB211 engine flying in four years 10.45 million miles, the equivalent of twenty-one return trips to the moon, on a Delta TriStar without a hitch.)

For large twins, the maximum acceptable distance from the nearest available diversion airport grew from 90 to 120 to 180 minutes' flying time on just one engine. This means that they will be allowed to fly to any destination, subject to individual operations licensing and additional airworthiness requirements. More twins than four-engine aircraft are already flying over the Atlantic. There has not been a single case of double engine shut-down, and with the reliability of the latest generation engines, it is considered to be even less likely to happen than a four-engine failure on a Jumbo.

So is it unreasonable, exaggerated caution that inspires the doubting Thomases' persistent questions? 'What would happen if an engine must be shut down over the Bay of Bengal, a long way off an alternate, where pilots may be left to their own devices because airport radio operators in the area might say, as they often do, that they're too busy to answer calls?' asks an experienced Jumbo pilot. Others query the suitability of some of the alternate airports that are surrounded by high terrain, exposed to frequent low visibility, fog and lightning. These days, the potential need of ditching an aircraft in the sea is regarded as a negligible risk of one in a billion. The last time it happened to an airliner, a DC9, was in 1970. But some pilots complain that the twins have not even been tested for the survivability of such an unlikely event. (Scale models of UK-built aircraft must undergo vigorous trials in a test tank, but that does not apply to the Airbus series or any of the American products.) The crews of twins do not receive any additional ditching training. 'Airlines do not consider it necessary,' said a pilot, 'and even if they did, they'd regard it as an admission of some extra hazard.'

At a Moscow trade show in 1992, Ben Cosgrove, Senior Vice President of Boeing, illustrated the reliability record with the case of the B767: in seven years, '99.8 per cent of B767 ETOPS flights reached their intended destination without turnback or diversion', discounting diversions caused by weather. Only six in-flight shut-downs occurred during

An Airline's View, paper by P. Webber, Navigation Manager, Performance and Planning, Britannia Airways, 1992.

the ETOPS phase of the flights – and of those, four happened in 1985, during the first five months of ETOPS operations by 767s.

It is claimed that over the Atlantic, the twins suffer fewer turn-backs than three- or four-engine jets – and the cause is more likely to be a blocked toilet than engine trouble. The data is impressive, but its validity raises many queries. The performance monitoring is carried out by 'interested parties' (the manufacturers and the licensing authorities), and IFALPA, the International Federation of Air Line Pilots' Associations, was unhappy because it could not obtain *raw* data of incidents. 'Until now we have seen only rather scrappy statistics,' said Captain Steve Last, chairman of the IFALPA Aircraft Design and Operations Committee. 'When we asked for details, we were told that those were confidential, commercial information. ICAO was to set up a study group, but apparently it could not find the resources for it, and the idea was abandoned. Now, at last, the manufacturers' attitude is changing, and they have promised us access to data we need to see.' (When, allegedly, a 767 suffered an uncontained engine failure, with some debris penetrating the other engine, no details were revealed, so the pilots could not make their own evaluation even though such events are very significant, and not only regarding the 767s.)

'The most important question is: are *all* engine shut-downs fully reported? It's now up to the regulatory authorities' judgement whether an event becomes significant. The operational pilots' view may be different. We, pilots, ought to be part of the judgement equation.

'The next generation of twins, the B777 and the A-330, are designed to enter ETOPS operations straight from the drawing board. The engine-airframe combination will be entirely new. Though there will be extended certification tests using airline personnel, there will be no proving period to iron out problems in actual airline service. We can only hope that they get it right first time.'

Confidential information from American sources has been circulated, alleging that 'One engine fails on ETOPS flights each week,' and that some airlines had issued verbal instructions to pilots to throttle back – rather than shut down – engines that are not performing adequately, because in that way, the event would not show up in ETOPS engineering records.

Finally, the most profound worries concern the secondary ETOPS carriers. The first to use twins for extended range flights were some of the best and safest airlines in the world. Not only that, they were under the strict supervision of the aeronautically most advanced countries' authorities, but they also introduced their own high standards. Lately, however, the massive financial advantages have attracted airlines to ETOPS everywhere. 'Icelandair, for instance, is one of the majority of carriers that follow the manufacturers' specific requirements for ETOPS to the letter,' said John Enders, vice chairman of the Flight Safety

Foundation in Washington. 'On the other hand, there are a few operations in various parts of the world, where ETOPS rigor is not practised, and some authorities may not perceive the vital importance of ensuring that the redundancies and other back-ups necessary for safe ETOPS operations are provided.'

'Oasis, a small Spanish charter airline wanted to start flying the Atlantic routes,' said Konrad Wittorf, General Manager of SWISSAIR Aircraft Maintenance. 'The Spanish authorities said no, your technical knowledge and staff are no guarantee for sufficient backing for ETOPS as yet. So now we have a Swiss team working for about a year with the airline to help them to fulfil all requirements and achieve the necessary reliability and despatchability. The Spanish authority acted with due caution. But many countries have serious problems. Even in Switzerland, where we have good, qualified people, the regulatory authority is not large enough to re-invent every rule for ETOPS certification. So they adopt and then enforce the rules of the FAA and JAA whose combined expertise nobody can match. I wish every country did the same.'

Captain Hal Sprogis, an American aviation safety consultant of great experience, goes even further: speaking at a meeting of the British Air Safety Group in 1992, he reported that there were signs of eroding ETOPS standards laid down by the authorities, and predicted that further erosion was inevitable.

And Captain Roger Hoyle wrote in *The Log*, the magazine of BALPA: 'Sooner or later an ETOPS aircraft could well go down in circumstances where a three- or four-engined aircraft could have been able to continue to a safe landing. Whilst one naturally hopes there will never be cause to say, "I told you so," nagging doubts remain.' So despite all the apparently convincing evidence presented to us, should those doubts be sounded more vociferously, and should more tests and more post-certification research be conducted now, before anything untoward could happen? Whether the answer is yes or no, the aviation fraternity must find ways to introduce, monitor and enforce global standards.

10

Frightening Non-Events

Forty-one thousand feet above some clouds in the blue skies of California, a China Airways Jumbo was cruising peacefully. Approaching the end of an eleven-hour boring flight, 274 passengers and crew looked forward to landing at San Francisco. There was some buffeting – attributed to clear air turbulence – and the 'seatbelts' sign was switched on. Then the number 4 engine 'flamed out'. Flying on three engines should have been no problem, but the aircraft began to decelerate and roll slightly. The Chinese captain was preoccupied with airspeed, and to avoid stalling put the nose down without disconnecting the autopilot. Then the remaining three engines stopped, and the 747 went into a dive. As it rolled out of control left and right, G-forces pinned everybody to the back of the seats and people could not even lift their arms. Those who had failed to fasten their seatbelts hit the ceiling, popping like corks from champagne bottles. A flight attendant and a passenger suffered serious injuries as 440,000 pounds of flesh and metal tore through clouds, hurtling towards the ground. The captain, losing the horizon, became spatially disoriented, and the altimeters went haywire. Aural overspeed warnings and a stall-warning from the stickshaker went unheeded.

Coming out of the clouds at 11,000 feet, the captain at last began to see which way up he was. The dive had to be stopped somehow, but the risk was that the aircraft would simply break up from the clash between human effort and vast aerodynamic forces. The captain needed the co-pilot's assistance as he tried pulling back the yoke. After the 32,000-feet dive, the aircraft began to obey, and the engines restarted without any trouble. The landing was smooth, but it was obvious that a miracle had happened. The wings were cracked and bent upwards, key sections of the controls and structure were twisted and broken. The investigation by the US National Transportation Safety Board, using data from the Cockpit Voice Recorder and the Digital Flight Data Recorder, revealed that the Jumbo had actually *rolled over* without the pilot realizing it. The engines had not failed – only the crew had in their diagnosis, in taking the wrong decisions, and in deviating from the instructions of the flight manual.

The case was a magnificent testimony to the strength of a modern jet. 'The way that aircraft was handled, it had no god-given right not to break up and kill everybody on board,' said Geoffrey Wilkinson, a former head of the British Air Accident Investigation Branch.

A non-event? Far from it. But, as Carl Vogt, the NTSB chairman puts it, a passenger would have to take a scheduled flight every day for 4000 years before the likelihood of experiencing anything like that or being in a fatal accident – and even then they would have a fifty-fifty chance of survival.

What justifiably frightens thousands of the 3 million people who fly safely every day is ignorance – the misunderstanding of noises, sights and petty occurrences that are an apparent threat to the uninitiated but a mere routine of flying.

- *Whirring of motors under the floor* – the APU (Auxiliary Power Unit) is switched on to provide power, air conditioning and pressurization.
- *Whirr-and-buzz* is heard – motors run, systems are checked.
- *Cracks and gaps in the wings* noticed – leading-edge slats, trailing-edge flaps, ailerons and spoilers . . . aerodynamically essential mobile parts to control flight (see page 85).
- *A tongue of flame shoots out of the engine* – such torching may occur when the engine is started up. It looks terrifying but is perfectly innocuous. (When the engine is shut down after a flight, it windmills to a halt, and the fuel it still contains usually evaporates in the exhaust, but if some cold residual fuel is left in the jet pipe, the engine will subsequently make a 'wet start', it may not fire at once – such as when a car engine is flooded – and torching may briefly occur. It is not a risk as it is burning at a low temperature, and helps, in fact, to ensure safety.)
- *Sudden vibration* – the engine is running but the aircraft is still stationary.
- *Cabin lights are dimmed* – a routine for take-off by many airlines, *not* a power failure. This may upset the nervous passenger as it happens just as the engine noise increases.
- *Thump . . . thump . . . thump* – wheel noise on uneven runway surface.
- *A bang like the firing of a shotgun* – a tyre blow-out. Not an immediate hazard, though it does call for precautions. In June 1992, for instance, an Air-UK B737 with 108 passengers had to return to Manchester after bursting a tyre on take-off. The emergency services were alerted, but the landing was uneventful.
- *The roar of the engines suddenly subsides soon after take-off, as if about to stop, and the aural phenomenon is accompanied by a slight negative g – weightlessness felt in the stomach.* The pilot applies maximum power for take-off and the steep climb out, then does a 'push over', reducing the angle to

use less power, conserve fuel, lengthen engine life, give a more comfortable ride as the aircraft gathers speed, and above all, to comply with noise abatement regulations. (As seen in Chapter 6.) The momentary sensation of falling back to earth can be quite intense on Concorde.

- *Rumbling below the floor followed by a heavy chunk and clank* – the undercarriage is retracted. The rumble is caused by the wheels that are still spinning; the thumps by the locking of the undercarriage for safe storage.
- *Renewed whirring* – the flaps, extended for added lift on take-off, are retracted. This is when most passengers near the wings notice the holes.
- *A winding down sound* – a compressor pack is shut down to let another one come on and supply air to the cabin. It is audible particularly in some seats halfway down the aisle on Jumbos, and the cabin crew may have to reassure passengers that, no, the engines are not stopping.
- *Bumps and jolts* – from air pockets. Some pilots call it 'cobblestoning'. A car needs shock absorbers to avoid breaking its axles when hitting a rough road or a stone. The 'flimsy' aircraft structure, that could be badly damaged if it is just bumped by a loading vehicle, can withstand very severe turbulence – or even dives. Roy Humphreyson, a pilot and editor of *Focus*, the journal of Britain's Flight Safety Committee, puts turbulence in four grades: 'the smooth (just an *oops*), the humblies, the grumblies, and the rumblies that shake the aircraft, and you really feel it.' (See Chapter 23 on ogres.)
- *Thunderstorms* – with radar and ground guidance, modern jets can almost always avoid them. If lightning happens to strike, it is a truly terrifying experience, but it passes through the cabin harmlessly (aircraft are well prepared for it), and passengers will live to dine out on the tale.
- *The wings seem to be flapping* – if they were not flexible, they would break off. When a fully laden B52 bomber sits on the ground, the wing tips move sixteen feet vertically to take the strain of lifting off and getting airborne.
- *Water dripping from the ceiling* – The aircraft is not leaking: it is condensation, mostly prior to take-off and landing, due to the difference in the temperature outside and inside. On Tupolevs, flown by many Third World and former communist countries, 'If water is dripping, the insulation needs to be repaired,' said Sándor Herpai, chief engineer of MALÉV. 'In the vicinity of crew seats, water droplets may appear around the exits where there's no heat insulation. We also had to make substantial refurbishing for comfort and internal noise reduction because the Tupolev flap motors are noisy, though much of that is absorbed when the aircraft is full.'

- *Sudden frantic activities in the cabin, an exchange of glances between purser and his staff* – somebody has forgotten about the captain's cuppa!
- *Something flying off the aircraft* – though passengers would rarely notice this frightening occurrence, it does sometimes happen, without endangering the flight. How people on the ground may feel about it is another matter. (An A-320 Airbus of the French Air-Inter had to return to Orly after an engine cover flew off during take-off in 1992. Safety was not compromised. BA subjected all its seven Concordes to strict examination after three rudder incidents in the early 1990s, one of which involved the loss of a 6 by 4 foot section of the tail-plane. The vibration it caused while flying at 1400 m.p.h. over the Atlantic worried not only the passengers but also the crew who knew nothing about the damage, and thought they had an engine problem. The investigation exonerated all engines. Corrective action was introduced.
- *UFOs passing by* – after every 'UFO buzzes jet' headline, sightings increase. Not only UFO fanatics, but also pilots and sober passengers report them. They might have seen balloons on the loose, or even plasma bodies (a recently identified meteorological phenomenon) that seem to be glowing objects tracking an aircraft only to disappear into the blue yonder. In the 1960s, alarm bells rang when several passengers spotted a UFO flying in close formation with their aircraft. The authorities' concern grew even more when the same report came from another flight. The jets in both cases were of an identical type. So a similar one was flown with cool-headed observers – and, lo and behold, they made the same sighting. It transpired, however, that in certain light conditions, a diffraction would make a UFO 'materialize' outside the windows every time.
- *Renewed whirr and buzz* – the flaps are lowered to increase the lift as the aircraft slows down for landing.
- *Heavy clunk and, possibly, a jolt making the airframe shudder* – the undercarriage is released and locked down. In larger aircraft the action is hardly noticeable.
- *The ground comes up menacingly* – as height and speed are being reduced, the aircraft seems to be floating precariously. The sight of the ground subjects many people to the 'Exocet syndrome': 'Once you can see it, you can do bugger all about it!' The runway comes into view . . . it appears that the pilot has missed it. Wrong. He is making a safety landing a thousand feet beyond the threshold of the runway. He has plenty of concrete left for touching down and stopping safely, though a thousand feet may appear to be an awful lot of missed ground.
- *A whistle and yet another, sometimes shuddering, thump* – after the main wheels, the nose-wheel settles on the runway: most aircraft are designed to land in a nose up attitude. The noise is accompanied by

the spoilers emerging from the wing, as if its skin is peeling off. If the thump is unusually loud, particularly on a wet runway, it may reveal a controlled heavy landing that was required to avoid aquaplaning, break the film of water and ensure a firm grip by the tyres. Truly hard landings are rare; they are evidenced by the flight recorders, and a full inspection will follow every time. The pilots are then asked to answer some uncomfortable questions.

- *A thunderous roar, the most frightening of them all, accompanied by the strong sensation of deceleration* – like changing down gears in a car to arrest speed, the reverse thrust of the jet engines is safer and more effective than the mere hammering of the brakes.
- *Engine power sounds louder on one side than on the other* – not an engine failure: the pilot is using differential thrust to help steer the aircraft on the ground.
- *The sight of frost on the wings* – not a great surprise, having just come down from an altitude where the temperature outside might have been −50° or −60° Celsius.

Those embarrassed by their worries should remember that many stewards and stewardesses admit it took them a number of flights to grow completely indifferent to what at first seemed the unexpected. They are taught to ask questions every time they feel concerned, and seek more senior colleagues' advice and reassurance. Passengers can do likewise, without losing face. More than just allaying their fears, passengers' questions help to keep airlines on their toes, and remind them that the public have the right to expect attention to every detail at all times – including faultless maintenance to ensure that the aircraft will always be as safe as technologically and humanly possible.

11

89 Bolts from the Blue

'Mayday mayday – London this is the Speedbird five three nine zero mayday mayd—'

The emergency call of BA's scheduled Birmingham to Malaga flight (callsign Speedbird 5390) came through to LATCC (London Air Traffic Control Centre) at 0733 on 10 June 1990. The call was acknowledged, 'mayday' was repeated, and 5390 reported that it was descending fast from 17,000 to 1100 feet because of 'emergency depressurization'. It did not sound as if disaster was imminent. Radio reception problems caused some confusion, and other flights in the area offered to relay messages, but the exchanges remained remarkably calm and polite, peppered with 'good morning sir' and 'thank you sir'. (In transcripts of recordings there is never any punctuation.) Six long minutes passed, and nobody knew that the pilot could not hear properly because of loud airflow noise in the cockpit. He now requested radar assistance to the nearest airfield.

At 0743, having accepted Southampton, with which he was unfamiliar, the pilot said, 'I'm afraid er we have some debris in the flight deck.' Ninety seconds later, he requested 'You shepherd me on to the runway please.'

Southampton told him 'We have been advised that it's pressurization failure is that your only problem.'

'Er negative sir er captain is half sucked out of the aeroplane I understand I believe he is dead.'

'Roger that is copied,' came the cool acknowledgement of the stunning announcement.

'Er flight attendant's holding on to him but er requesting emergency facilities for the captain I . . . I . . . I think he's dead.'

The flight was not just shepherded but nursed and talked down gently all the way. Twenty minutes after the first 'mayday', it landed smoothly. The captain's windscreen was missing. He was hanging halfway out of the cockpit. Though he was badly bruised and in shock with severe frostbite, broken arm, wrist and thumb, he was alive and rushed to hospital. Apart from a steward (bruised arm), nobody else was hurt.

A quick evacuation followed, and only then did the full drama in the air unfold. Soon after take-off, just as breakfast was about to be served, there was a bang, the door to the flight deck blew out, and the cabin filled with condensation mist. A steward rushed forward, and found the flight deck in a mess. The captain – flying the aircraft with his shoulder harness off and his lap-strap loosened – had been sucked out through the missing windscreen aperture. His leg was caught by part of the cockpit structure, and that alone was holding him. The steward grabbed him by the waist, and tried to hang on to him, but frostbite and bruising impeded his effort. Inch by inch he was losing the captain, who was still breathing but could do nothing for himself. Meanwhile, with admirable presence of mind and airmanship, the co-pilot took over the controls, and despite suffering a degree of disorientation, initiated an immediate descent. The purser arrived, and now the two men tried to pull the captain back in, but the strength of the slipstream outside was too great. Another steward strapped himself into the jumpseat behind, grabbed the by-then unconscious, doomed man's ankles, and held them until the aircraft had landed.

Apart from design and infinite precautions, air safety derives from the thorough investigation of not only disasters, but even the seemingly most insignificant incidents, treated as 'accidents that did not quite happen', from which invaluable lessons are learned. The British AAIB (Air Accident Investigation Branch), outside America the most experienced body of outstanding specialists, and BA's own experts swung into action. The windscreen design was not the plug type (when cabin pressure helps to retain it), but it seemed virtually impossible that the ninety bolts securing it should have failed. Yet only *one* had remained in place.

Tests and examinations revealed a shocking saga. Because of air safety philosophy, no aviation accident can occur without a series of coincidences, each of which opens a chink in the numerous layers of protection. This mishap was no exception. It transpired that twenty-seven hours before the flight, the left windscreen had been replaced; of the ninety bolts, eighty-four were 0.026 of an inch in diameter below specification, six were 0.1 of an inch too short; all were incorrectly tightened; the task was not classified as a safety 'Vital Point' (so the work was carried out without supervision) and many available cues were missed, weakening the built-in safety net; the very experienced Shift Safety Manager needed corrective glasses to read small print but did not use them on this occasion, which might have contributed to the choice of the wrong bolts; the quality of his work 'was eroded by his inadequate care, poor trade practices, failure to adhere to company standards, and the use of unsuitable equipment, which were judged [by investigators] symptomatic of a longer term failure by him to observe the [company's] promulgated procedures'; BA's local managers of 'Product Samples and

Quality Audits had not detected the existence of inadequate standards employed by the Shift Maintenance Manager because they [and the superficial supervisory visits by the CAA] did not monitor directly' his working practices. The report and detailed recommendations took two years to complete, but BA and the CAA accepted the findings, and, in fact, the company introduced stricter safety measures long before that to prevent similar mistakes.

Aircraft maintenance is the cornerstone of air transport. As it must ensure the availability of safe flying machines on time, it is such a strictly regulated, vastly expensive, precisely planned and closely monitored operation, that engineering misadventures are responsible for less than 4 per cent of all accidents. In excess of the manufacturers' requirements, a BA Jumbo would have a transit check before each flight, a daily ramp 1 check by four engineers, then a progression of more thorough ramp checks by a growing number of engineers, increasingly detailed service checks every 1060, 2000 and 3875 flying hours by up to fifty engineers taking five shifts to complete them, an inter check 1 after 5750 flying hours by an army of 160 engineers, and a D-check (major service) every five years or 24,000 flying hours, when the aircraft is virtually dismantled, repaired and rebuilt in just about a month (see Chapter 24 on so-called geriatric aircraft). In addition to service hours, the number of cycles (take-offs and landings) flown determines the routine because it is the pressurization–depressurization that exposes airliners to the greatest stress, and the structure grows permanently stretched like a balloon that has been blown up repeatedly. Short- to medium-haul aircraft, such as the Airbus 320, may take off and land eight times while a DC10 completes just one cycle, so the servicing schedule is even tighter.

Because of the complexity of the tasks performed by the thousands of engineers of each major airline, the risks are fully appreciated and catered for. There are, however, constant reminders that there is no room for complacency.

Though BA's terrible slip-up might seem quite incredible in the face of meticulous precautions, it was not unique. In 1992, for instance, Transavia, a Dutch charter airline, had a major emergency en route to Greece because a fitter had only hand-tightened two bolts, i.e. guessed the necessary torque, to hold two turbine discs together. In 1983, an Eastern Airlines Tristar suffered a near-catastrophe at Miami because somebody had fitted a wrong O-ring, a few pence-worth of washer, to the hydraulic system, and oil pressure was lost, rendering the engines inoperable in flight. That case was yet another illustration of the maxim that *every single disaster has its forerunners in incidents from which the lessons are allowed to go unheeded*: it was the twelfth occasion that wrong or missing O-rings had caused unscheduled landings. More than anybody else, the aviation industry is aware of Murphy's Law (if anything can go wrong it will go wrong), and therefore not only double- and treble-checks are operated, but planemakers also prepare for such eventualities with duplication and triplication of systems to satisfy the fail-safe principle, and design out potential maintenance snags. (For example, since a British military accident in the early 1950s, valves that control the direction of fuel flow have different threads at both ends to ensure that never again will they accidentally be fitted the wrong way round.)

Ironically jets built, rather crudely, by the former Soviet Union seem to be 'non-sensitive to weather or even unsatisfactory maintenance,' said Sándor Herpai of MALÉV. 'They were designed for remote areas that can be reached only by air in the heart of the taiga or deserts where the maintenance bases are rather primitive, and engineers have not grown up with flying traditions. The maximum speed of a marching army is determined by the slowest man. Similarly, Soviet aircraft were designed to cater for the worst maintenance conditions.

'Maintenance mistakes are not only dangerous but also very expensive because an aircraft on the ground earns no revenue. We average 98 per cent despatch availability of aircraft, and if there is a delay, we look for the reasons. On the engines we do regular diagnostic checks even if there are no complaints from the pilots. In that way we can prevent the development of faults that may lead to shut-downs or costly, flight-delaying repairs away from our home base.'

At an international conference in 1990, Ben Cosgrove, Boeing's Vice-President, Engineering, sounded a note of concern: 'Airplanes are designed to be rugged and forgiving. But, as with any piece of machinery, safety and reliability depend on proper care and attention. Business conditions change. It is common practice to lease airplanes and contract their maintenance. Airplanes are transferred to, and operated by, developing countries and smaller operators with less experience. Maintenance and inspection skills have been diluted by the retirement of experienced personnel, and by the increased need for inspection of older aircraft. We are concerned about these trends, and work to counter them . . .'

Aeronautically less advanced countries, poorer companies and Third World airlines are run on a shoestring and cannot perform top-notch maintenance because of a lack of funds and expertise. An African jet has long been flying with an engineer on board to do running repairs after each landing. Every country wants to fly its flag, dozens of entrepreneurs want to make a quick buck, but many seem to believe that buying a state-of-the-art aircraft is a 'one-off' expenditure. (When China can buy elderly Soviet aircraft only by barter – an Ilyushin 28 for 200 railway truckloads of mango juice, another for rice – one wonders if they plan to maintain them with chopsticks.) Apart from major airlines, a fast-increasing number of specialist companies offer high-quality maintenance services at competitive rates to carriers that cannot afford (or do not find it economical) to run their own engineering support. The

International Civil Aviation Organization spends a great deal on helping Third World countries improve and match ICAO standards in maintenance, certification, training, supervision and all other essential aspects of flying in the jet age (ATC, airport facilities, aviation English, etc.). The long list of beneficiaries ranges from Argentina to Bangladesh, Romania, Nepal, Rwanda, Vietnam and Zambia.

Excessive competition, and the penny-pinching that ensues, may lead to corner-cutting, especially when top management fails to exercise tight controls or pressurizes engineers to 'get on with it' and make aircraft available, when annual losses amount to billions of dollars, or when a carrier is on the brink of bankruptcy and its philosophy does not grade safety as an absolute priority. In December 1992, a B727 of Libyan Arab Airlines crashed killing 157 people. Colonel Gaddafi's deputy delivered a furious outburst in Tripoli, and blamed the embargo imposed by the West since the Lockerbie bombing disaster: 'Every day there are dozens of flights [in Libya] on which passengers are in danger because of the lack of spare parts and maintenance. This is mass murder.' It could be, but by whom? Has it occurred to the politicians and the airline that in such circumstances they ought to stop flying? Besides, the embargo is on new aircraft and their spares. The trade in parts for 727s, of which almost 2000 were sold until production ceased some ten years ago, is unstoppable by any embargo in the open market.

The American FAA has fifty specialists to check some 900 flights a day from ninety-four countries, but the US General Accounting Service recommended that the effort should be intensified because several visiting airlines have dubious safety records due to the lack of airworthiness inspectors, technical expertise, regulation handbooks, etc., in their own countries. The FAA sometimes grounded unsafe foreign aircraft, but failed to check others in the same fleet. It found extensive corrosion of wings, rivets missing, structural deficiencies, even parts that were held in position with 'speed' tape (*Flight International*, 20.1.1993). When, following an incident, Canada suspended all in-bound B727 operations by TAESA, the FAA delayed informing its field offices for two months, during which time the same Mexican carrier suffered four serious take-off incidents in the US, twice almost over-running the runway in New York. (Boeing and the FAA have since helped TAESA to improve its maintenance and training routines.)

Mistakes, oversights or sharp practices may also go unnoticed in the Western world, but will, sooner or later, attract heavy fines. When federal agents raided a California factory, and discovered falsified test results, the reworking of failed parts, and violation of customer specifications that amounted to fifteen years of fraud, 'Voi-Shan, the world's largest supplier of fasteners to the aerospace industry, agreed to pay $18 million in fines, costs and damages' (*Flight International*, 23.5.1990). Two former Voi-Shan managers admitted to charges of conspiracy to defraud, and the company's quality-control system was completely over-hauled. Similarly, Delta Airlines replaced some top managers and took thoroughly corrective steps after FAA inspectors discovered some five dozen maintenance rule violations. As none of those endangered the safety of aircraft, and the management demonstrated the right attitude, three-quarters of the $2 million fine was suspended. 'If flying Delta were not safe,' Anthony Broderick, Associate Administrator of the FAA, told me, 'they wouldn't be paying a fine, they wouldn't be allowed to fly airplanes.' Typically, some struggling, near bankrupt airlines in their financial death throes, were most likely to cut corners and face crippling fines for condoning malpractices, the use of substandard parts and other safety violations.

Some specialists criticize not only the erring airlines but also the regulatory bodies. Don Madole, a leading American aviation lawyer told me, 'No question about it – the FAA inspectors ought to do more unexpected maintenance checks without giving anyone a chance to clean up shop before a visit and cover up for unseen rubber stamping. If carriers can't be as thorough as United, they shouldn't fly.' Harold Marthinsen, accident investigation director of the American Airline Pilots' Association, echoes the sentiment: 'All right, there may be a shortage of FAA inspectors, but why do they inspect only paperwork during their *surprise* visits? Why not look at aircraft? Many of the unreported defects and service difficulties would come to light.'*

Britain's 'CAA is not a police force,' says Mike Willett, the Safety Regulations Group director. 'We don't conduct snap inspections of maintenance shops, but keep up a supervisory presence and close relationship with airlines that must bear the responsibility for their safety. All major companies will do whatever is necessary, but we carry out unannounced ramp checks, inspect licences as well as technical logs and defect levels.' Inspectors also visit foreign airports served by UK airlines to ensure that sufficient stores and the latest information are available to maintenance engineers. The CAA monitors manufacturing standards, and by contract advises numerous Third World governments on whose behalf they may do inspections and investigate defects. UK standards are highly respected everywhere, but as Tony Ingham, head of the CAA Aircraft Maintenance Standards Department, points out, 'It would be unrealistic to impose those requirements on a country whose airlines are unable to afford the latest technology aircraft and mainte-nance facilities. Our job is to ensure that their aircraft are safe to operate even if the full extent of UK requirements have not been satisfied.'

*The sale of bogus, counterfeit, substandard spare parts is a growing global problem because, as always, there are people who try to make a quick buck through outright fraud or, in their naïvety, hope that their product will be just as good as the original. Regulatory authorities combat the practice, but the ultimate responsibility is with the airlines.

The gap between the carriers of the rich and poor, advanced and developing countries, is likely to grow. Europe is making great efforts to introduce a high level of continent-wide standards by the turn of the century. The creation of a Joint Aviation Authority has been a major step in that direction. But the biggest gap is already apparent in the application of the latest complex and costly preventive maintenance technology. In that respect, the leading airlines already live in the future. They use sophisticated techniques to spot cracks and corrosion with penetrative dyes, ultrasonic and X-ray examinations and, lately, thermal imaging which was pioneered by British Airways. Above all, they have begun to employ electronic devices that monitor trends and performance, predict faults, and improve safety. Many aircraft components have predetermined life limits when they must be replaced or overhauled. Monitoring identifies defects in their infancy or gives various parts a clean bill of health, and so introduces the new philosophy of 'on condition maintenance' (doing the job only when truly necessary rather than when it is due theoretically). This largely removes or extends the fixed safe 'lives' of parts, and the savings are enormous. SWISSAIR, for instance, found additional safety, reliability and considerable savings using the ADAS system developed by McDonnell-Douglas for the MD-11.

Recently, a flight was almost halfway across the Pacific when suddenly the aircraft was recalled. Back at the airline's base, a computer had examined the trend-monitoring flight recorders and detected some irregularity in the engine performance. Instead of risking an engine shut-down en route – or the need to fly an engine and a gang of technicians out to Japan where the passengers booked for the return flight could be long delayed – the carrier recalled the aircraft: the cheapest way to do the repairs with the least inconvenience.

'The devices can monitor all electronic systems, and store the non-critical information on board. Alternatively, they can transmit findings to a ground station, so that the right spares and personnel would be waiting to cure developing faults, and eliminate or reduce delays,' says Eddie White, a director of the Flight Data Company at Heathrow. 'Concerning modern aircraft, the great debate is where the potentially vast amount of data should be analysed: in flight or on the ground?

'It is argued that a two-man crew on modern aircraft can hardly spare the time and energy to look at massive amounts of data. It is impossible to thrust upon them an analytical investigation. If there is an indication of a fault somewhere, all they want to know is whether it is serious enough to demand a diversion or any change in the operation. In particular, engines are so reliable these days that they are very unlikely to become unserviceable in flight.'

Several airlines use plug-in type Quick Access Recorders (QARs) with cartridges that can be read and replaced with blanks on arrival. The

QARs speed up the work of engineers on the ground, revealing, for instance, that the 'vibration' which caused concern to the pilots was only spurious, perhaps due to turbulence, and required no repairs. 'The anomaly is,' said Eddie White, 'that the poorest operators, flying the oldest types with the least reliable engines, would need monitoring the most. But the installation of a device could cost some £15,000, the computer to do the read-out on the ground more than twice that, plus the expertise of highly qualified personnel – an investment they can't afford. Besides, older aircraft are not geared to produce and supply the suitable electronic data, whereas a state-of-the-art fly-by-wire machine can generate thousands of parameters (sensors turn physical events into signals) circulating on an electronic highway via a digital data bus* . . . the greatest technological revolution in recording systems for a long time.'

On the ground, the mass of data can be filtered and compared to the model in the computer to detect differences. The result is presented to the engineer who may choose no more than a dozen selected items of information. The ultimate goal is probably to transmit data in real time to the ground for analysis. This is already happening, mostly in the United States, where the ARINC Communications Addressing and Reporting Systems (ACARS) is well developed with hundreds of ground stations. Air Canada makes tremendous use of that. In Europe, there is SITA, a kind of Telex network, to transmit short messages to the ground. These may give the engineers the red or green light, but not the full diagnosis which would need a QAR to pinpoint the cause.

Whatever such futuristic developments may lead to, preventive aircraft maintenance will have to remain dependent on the traditional forte of the industry: an unrestricted exchange of incident information. All airlines are in agreement to reveal every occurrence without fear or delay so that others can learn from it – and most of them do just that. They notify IATA, and some publish freely distributed reports. The problem is, yet again, that the smaller, poorer airlines have no safety specialists to examine that endless flow of data, select the relevant items, and call their colleagues' attention to them.

Some airlines are virtually uninsurable unless they take certain safety precautions. When Peter Spooner, of Aviation Risk Management at Willis Corroon, conducts a detailed 'safety audit' and examines a carrier's

---

Data bus is the current buzz-word. It is based on the idea of multiplexing. Whereas each electronic signal used to require a separate pair of wires, it is now encoded, chopped up and interwoven with others, and carried – like people on a paternoster – on a single pair of wires that replaces huge bundles just as in a modern telephone network. Though each coded signal will be perceived to be continuous when tapped, it will, in fact, reappear only every tenth or fiftieth of a second. If ten thousand parameters were carried, each signal would have only a millisecond to itself. The decoders would select and sample those the pilot or the engineer is interested in. Eventually, even that one pair of wires may be substituted by fibre optics that are interference-free. Those are already used in military aircraft.

record, managers will often be convinced that their minor incidents can be the forerunners of accidents, that a full-time safety officer could help to cut delays, aircraft unserviceability and the cost of mishaps, and that a change of attitude would enhance profits as well as safety. (Many 'minor' incidents are not covered by insurance because, like cars, aircraft are subject to an excess clause. A Jumbo may carry a million-dollar excess, a B737 or DC9 half that.)

BASIS, a new computer programme developed by BA, may revolutionize this global incident investigation and reporting system. Cutting out the mountains of paper, it will carry all accident/incident reports (e.g. engine problems) in a classified form, produce trend graphs, alert to anomalies, with the ability to break down data from fleet to aircraft type, routes, phase of operations (e.g. landings), engineering, human factors, etc. It would highlight problems that require the greatest, immediate management effort: for example, why do we have more incidents with DC9s than with others? As a minor 'tail-scrape on the runway' may ground an aeroplane for a day or two, the prevention of such an incident alone would probably pay for the programme.

The news of any single mishap is supposed to reach the aircraft manufacturers. (Unfortunately, this is not always the case.) They may then deem it necessary to publish an SB (Service Bulletin) that has only an advisory status, and action on it is at the carriers' discretion. In more serious or repetitive cases, an AD (Airworthiness Directive) for certain compulsory repairs would be rushed out. But when it comes to the evaluation of a problem, nothing is straightforward. Sometimes it is debatable whether an SB rather than an AD will suffice. There is a Minimum Equipment List for each aircraft type and operation (nothing should fly if any of its MEL items is faulty), and Allowable Deferred Defects which an airline may carry for a while. But, as seen earlier, some companies are more conscientious in this respect than others, who stretch the limits of so-called allowable deficiencies. Even if an AD is issued, the compliance date may vary a great deal.

On 4 October 1992, an El Al B747 cargo flight departed from Amsterdam's Schiphol Airport at 18.21. Six minutes later the pilot declared 'mayday', reported engine problems and tried to return to land. He never made it. Having lost two engines, he crashed into an apartment complex, killing the four people on board, and dozens on the ground. The aircraft was totally destroyed by the impact and severe fire.

Was it a double engine failure? Was the aircraft overloaded? Or was the disaster a carbon copy of another in Taiwan nine months earlier? There were alarming similarities between the two cases, though the evidence was inconclusive as not all the essential parts of the China Airways Jumbo had been recovered. However, even the preliminary findings indicated that on both planes the fuse pins that attach engines to the wings had failed because of corrosion and metal fatigue. (They are designed to snap when certain malfunctions occur so that one engine can break free without damaging the wing itself, and allow the flight to continue safely on the remaining ones.) Both aircraft lost two engines in flight. As the fuse pins had been suspect for some time, and Boeing had issued an SB and an AD, China Airways had installed the new style pins (and crashed despite of that), but this work had not been done on the Israeli aircraft.

After a 'walk round' inspection had discovered a severed fuse pin on an Argentinian Aerolineas Jumbo, a letter from Boeing advised airlines that another SB, and an AD, would soon be issued, but meanwhile the pins should be subjected to visual and ultrasonic inspections. The day after Amsterdam, the SB was issued. It addressed the new style fuse pins, such as those on the Chinese aircraft, but not the ones retained on the Israeli one. Then an AD by the FAA made inspections compulsory within thirty days, to be followed by recurrent checks. (The NTSB believed that the required frequency was unsatisfactory.) The compliance date also varied from country to country as well as airline to airline. Japan Airlines found 118 rusty pins, 38 of which were damaged so seriously that they could not be cleaned with sandpaper alone. BA and Virgin decided to change all fuse pins regardless. 'We found just two corroded bolts on two of our five 747s,' says Konrad Wittorf, the head of SWISSAIR's maintenance, 'but we saw small traces of cracks, too, and to us the operational risk was too great. Because a full check would take at least eight hours on each of the two aircraft, we cancelled two flights to America.' It was found that the corrosion could be cleaned up, and the pins did not need to be changed, but such cancellations are a blow to finances: grounding a Jumbo for just one day may cost $100,000 in lost revenue. A month later, in November, the FAA ordered that all fuse pins must be replaced. At a considerable cost, it would affect some 700 of the 946 Jumbos in service, excluding the 747-400, the latest version.

Meanwhile, cracked fuse pins were found on the newer, popular twin-engine B757s. The cause was different – stress rather than corrosion – but it gave rise to equal concern even though no actual accident had been attributed to it. New pins were designed but failed to solve the problem, SBs alerted the users, inspection schedules were tightened, and finally ADs were issued for the engines that power the 757. But the AD for Rolls-Royce engines, for instance, concerning more than 200 aircraft, became fully effective only a year later, in December 1993.

El Al criticized Boeing, and claimed that the manufacturer's reaction was too slow and half-hearted after the Taiwan crash. Boeing argued that hard evidence had been obtained too late to help prevent the El Al catastrophe. Some American aviation lawyers thought Boeing ought to be sued to clear up whether the second disaster was unforeseen or merely unforeseeable.

'It's a complex affair,' said Anthony Broderick of the FAA. 'Some aircraft are known to have flown with a broken fuse pin without trouble. Why did others crash? Boeing is now researching a completely new concept that will eliminate the concern over the fuse pins altogether. It is always a hard decision how far regulatory agencies should go. It would be wrong to be rash, ground aircraft, and threaten to bankrupt some carriers, unnecessarily.'*

'ADs can damage a manufacturer's image, but crashes can almost ruin it,' said Harold Marthinsen. 'Remember the effect of the Turkish DC10 (Ermenonville) tragedy on McDonnell-Douglas's image. Then there's the question: is an AD enough or is it necessary to ground a whole fleet? Remember the Comet accidents. The first investigation seemed to have found the answer, the grounding order of the type was revoked, but then another crash – and only then was the real cause found.'

Whichever way one looks at it, Taiwan and Amsterdam highlighted once again the quagmire of varying, sometimes too liberal, dates of compliance with SBs and ADs. Investigative agencies, such as the NTSB and the AAIB, have fought endless battles with the industry and the regulatory bodies to speed up action on their findings and there has been a great deal of improvement in that respect. Rick van Woerkom, chief of the NTSB Safety Recommendation Division, points out that 'The FAA must respond to our recommendations within ninety days (they do now, on average, in sixty-eight days), and the acceptance rate has risen to more than four-fifths, but a case is *closed* only when action is taken. That takes an average two years and nine months, and sometimes we have to repeat urging them again and again. When we suggest an Airworthiness Directive, its issue may take six to eight months, and then airlines may get a compliance limit of another six or eight months or until the next annual inspection. Luckily, and unlike the FAA, we investigators need not pay any regard to commercial considerations. True, a demand for immediate major repairs might amount to a virtual grounding order with, admittedly, near-disastrous losses of revenue to some carriers, and so the regulatory agencies must walk a tightrope. But to my mind, air safety should come above all, and the speed with which the better airlines act upon even a routine Service Bulletin, tells a lot about their management. And in that respect, safety statistics are meaningless. One accident is one too many.' In 1993, a Lufthansa Airbus suffered a fatal runway over-run accident at Warsaw. An undercarriage modification that might have prevented it had been available since 1991. Lufthansa flew thirty-three such A-320s but until then only nine had been fitted with the modified gear.

---

*The new design, a kind of belt-and-braces modification, will call for up to three weeks' work on each aircraft. The worldwide cost, about $100 million, will be shared by Boeing and its customers.

12

Demi-gods or Sky Cabbies

When classy, costly products are advertised, pilots are often portrayed as their lucky owners. They can, indeed, afford the luxuries (a senior airline captain may earn up to £100,000 a year), and the job *is* glamorous. Pilots visit exotic destinations as a routine and, like surgeons, tend to be placed on the pedestal reserved for demi-gods: who would want to put their lives in the hands of some lesser being?

The early glamour of those brave, magnificent men, looping the loop in their leather helmets and goggles, has never waned. And brave indeed they had to be only six decades ago, when fatal crashes took an annual toll of one in every four commercial pilots. By the 1960s, the ratio was one in 1600, and the safety trend continued to improve sufficiently to convince some insurers that these days life cover should cost no more to an airline captain than it does to us ordinary mortals.

The demi-god image was eroded further with automation, computers, and a vast array of helpful devices. The job itself has become more mundane over the years (millions of people fly to the four corners of the globe), and passengers have come to regard pilots as glorified cab drivers in the sky. After all, the cockpit used to be crowded with three pilots, an engineer, a navigator, and a radio officer, whereas now just two pilots sit there up front, which lends some justification to the joke: *So what's the next step? The answer is obvious: only one pilot and a Rottweiler . . . The pilot to feed the dog, and the dog to make sure that the captain doesn't touch a damned thing on his precious electronic control panel.*

The demi-god and cabbie status are equally false. As usual, the truth is somewhere in between. Pilots are real professionals who form a part of the system that consists of human and technological elements. If something goes wrong, it is a system failure in most cases. (As we shall see later, the investigation of accidents and incidents aims to find the causal sequence rather than the opportunity to apportion blame.)

The relatively high remuneration of pilots must be commensurate with the huge responsibility they carry and never forget. (In 1991 a BA pilot came in too low, did not respond to a red warning light for seventeen seconds, and flew so close to crashing into Heathrow's Penta Hotel that it triggered car alarms in the car park. For the first time ever in Britain, there was a prosecution, and the pilot was fined for acting 'in a manner likely to endanger' 255 lives on board as well as others on the ground. He resigned and, haunted by nightmares, killed himself three years later.) Pilots' pay also accounts for their shorter working lives (the usual retirement age is fifty-five), and for the frequent ups and downs of the industry. (During the US deregulation bonanza, major operators creamed off all available personnel, and the minors promoted relative youngsters to captain. But the recent reversal of fortunes has now lengthened the dole queues: Delta laid off 600 pilots in 1993, and others, who fly for various US carriers, had to accept pay cuts; in Britain, there are about a thousand pilots without a job, and some 300 flying school graduates work as cabin crew or outside the industry.)

In the course of an investigation into pay, an American congressman was astonished to hear how much pilots earned, and asked if some serious reduction would be in order. An airline president told him that would be perfectly feasible, but suggested that 'Next time the weather is bad in Washington, you ought to consider coming by train, sir.'

Captain William Heller freely admitted in his book* that every pilot 'has one time or another earned his entire annual salary in one super-scared, puckered-up minute,' when he would have traded 'every cent of his pay for a 10,000-foot dry runway, the sun at his back and a nice headwind right down the runway'. It is with such rare moments of crises in mind that the industry seeks out people who have what it takes to be a captain.

Sometimes it must be a split-second decision. The aircraft is racing down the runway. The point of no return is reached. Then a bang. Was it just a blown tyre or something more sinister? Or a red light warns about a vital system failure. Is it the real McCoy or just a faulty instrument? Is it safer to carry on, take off, sort out the problem and land or to abort and probably overrun? No time for second guesses.

'Pilots are trained for such eventualities,' says Harold Marthinsen of ALPA, 'but reaction to a stimulus, such as stopping a car when a child runs in front, takes time. If an engine fails during take-off, the pilot hits the brake within seconds. But how long will it take him to recognize that engine failure? Is he below or above V_1? Will the airplane fly? Take an accident at Kennedy. An L1011 had just left the ground when the stick-shaker was felt: stall† warning! The pilot knew it might have been a false signal – but what if it wasn't? No time to contemplate, invaluable seconds had already been lost. He had to make a spot decision. His choice was to

*Op. cit.
†Stall results when an aircraft is trying to climb too steeply: the airflow is disrupted over the wing and can no longer produce lift.

abandon take-off, try to land and stop on the remaining runway. Others would have done the same. Yet the investigation blamed him for the accident because, in fact, there had been no stalling. The FAA aircraft certification allows less time for decision-making than it takes in reality. For even if a problem is recognized *below* V_1, the aircraft will have accelerated to *above* V_1 by the time a decision is made to abort take-off.'

Sometimes the dilemma is of the opposite kind: wait, think, do nothing but evaluate the clues. And that is no less unnerving.

It was not the Malay satay being served to the passengers that filled the cockpit of a BA Jumbo with acrid smoke in 1982. The windscreen looked as if the Kuala Lumpur to Perth flight had strayed into a *Star Wars* movie. Smoke and soot oozed out of the air vents. Then an engine stopped. Another faltered. Then the third and the fourth. A quadruple engine failure? It seemed an impossibility. *Where did I go wrong?* was Captain Moody's first thought. He shut down the engines, and decided to sit on his hands – do nothing rather than anything hasty. He sent a mayday call to Jakarta, set the autopilot on a slow descent from 37,000 feet, and reviewed his options. What would it be like to ditch a fully laden Jumbo into the sea? He ran through his checklist, and treated his passengers to a classic British understatement:

> Good evening, ladies and gentlemen. This is your captain speaking. We have a small problem. All four engines have stopped. We are doing our damnest to get them going again. I trust you are not in too much distress.

The cabin pressure dropped at 26,000 feet. Moody and the engineer donned oxygen masks, but the co-pilot got into difficulties with his. The slow descent would expose him to the crippling pain of anoxia, but Moody refused to do anything panicky. Hoping to gain time to restart the engines, he sat, 'winding his watch, as the Americans put it'. The terrifying display outside looked like St Elmo's fire (an electrical brush discharge with a mysterious glow around the mastheads witnessed occasionally by sailors), but that seemed yet another impossibility so high up in clear skies. At 13,000 feet, running out of theories and ideas for a solution, Moody had a moment to feel scared. But then, he managed to restart number 4 which had been the first to fail. Then the other engines could be brought back to life. With cool expertise, the pilots nursed the aircraft upwards, only to be hit by more St Elmo's fire. Although their windscreen had gone completely opaque, and the Jakarta landing aids were inoperative, they landed safely.

Only after the forty-minute nightmare would it transpire what had happened: a vast eruption of the notorious Mount Galunggung volcano had destroyed twenty-two villages, killed dozens of people, and filled the air with volcanic ash even 37,000 feet up. Apart from the great feat of the fine airmanship, Moody's actions – or rather, inaction – saved the aircraft and 247 lives. Because he had shut down all his failing engines without any delay, and refrained from taking split-second decisions, the aircraft had suffered no further damage and could be flown, once again, when reaching cleaner air.

NO HEROES, PLEASE

'The selection of applicants is an arduous process, but because of the glamour and good pay of the job, airlines can usually take the pick of the bunch,' says a training captain.

'We watch out for hazards in the personality profiles,' Dr Ruedi Knüsel, a SWISSAIR psychologist once told me. 'We look out for the characteristics of inner stability, flexibility, stress resistance' in the selection and throughout training. 'Does he panic? Does he seek excuses for mistakes? Can he work in teams? Can he bear the loneliness of a captain's leadership?' Gone are the days of the heroic macho image making an ideal pilot. 'It creates a tunnel vision, an urge to be right at all times.' They select people who can make decisions, face up to errors, and listen to critical advice. A very high degree of physical fitness is of course also a pre-requisite.

The basic training is expensive. Some people spend up to £50,000 of their own money to qualify. British Airways (when recruiting) sponsors successful applicants for fourteen months in a flying school. Others train their own or retrain military pilots. Most American carriers will not even interview anyone with less than a thousand flying hours in multi-engined aircraft, and only up to 15 per cent of the applicants are accepted. The training, with six-monthly refresher courses and check-flights to test proficiency, never stops even for senior captains. Flight simulators, now with a leading role in training and conversion to new types, have helped almost to eliminate training accidents. More is the pity that not all airlines can afford to buy and run the expensive installation. (Simulators are so effective that pilots can now convert on the ground to flying a new type of plane with zero flight time before actually starting to fly under supervision – a practice not recommended to any but the top carriers. The realistic feel of simulators is such that to crash into a computer-generated image of terrain is a terrifying, unforgettable experience.)

Unfortunately, the international level of training is very uneven, and the standard of licensing a pilot ranges from the excellent to the barely acceptable. The Swiss require a special 'mountain rating', Germany has an extra exam for long-haul routes. However in some Third World countries, the right connections can secure a left-hand (captain's) seat in the cockpit. In Sweden, despite strict controls, a flight engineer got away with flying DC10s for five years without a valid licence or medical certificate. This was discovered only when he was found to be suffering from a mental illness. (SAS claimed that licences were a matter between pilots and the Aviation Authority.) It was known to Japanese pilots that a captain, who eventually crashed into Tokyo Bay, was mentally ill, but nobody, not even his co-pilot, would criticize (let alone report to the authorities) a man of seniority.

Why are there so few women among airline pilots? No one disputes their potential flying skills, proven by the few women in service, but most carriers I questioned came up with rather coy answers. All of them were anxious to claim that there was no sex discrimination. Some of them mentioned concern about pre-menstrual tension, the risk of undue pre-occupation with family problems, difficulty with fitting into a 'male environment', and 'potential emotional situations in the cockpit'. Only Lufthansa trotted out once with an admission of commendable frankness that 'economic considerations' were the main obstacle: it costs 200,000 Deutschmarks (some £80,000) to train a cadet; add to that another DM400,000 for follow-up refresher courses, and no wonder that they want long service, preferably to retirement, in return; that continuity of service would be threatened, the airline feared, by marriage and pricey retraining after each pregnancy.

THE THREE HOBGOBLINS IN THE COCKPIT

are stress, fatigue and boredom. They seem to be set against each other – how can one be bored *and* stressed? – but they work in tandem as a tripartite menace, taking turns, one opening the door to another.

The periods of stress – dealing with the vagaries of bad weather, heavy air traffic near airports, and an assortment of infrequent but demanding problem situations – increase the fatigue generated by the long hours of either the frequent flights (up to four take-offs and landings a day on short-haul) or the wear and tear of dusk to dawn wakefulness and time-zone crossings on long-haul duty. Though on very long flights, a spare crew and bunks for a few hours' sleep may be carried, and although the daily, monthly, even annual duty time of pilots is strictly controlled in most countries, further studies of human fatigue and an update of regulations are still on the NTSB's 'Most Wanted' hit list of desirable safety improvements. After a twelve-hour non-stop flight the pilots may relax for twenty-four hours at some tropical pool-side, but there is no guarantee that they get a proper night's sleep to recuperate. Yet again, standards vary. 'Whereas pilots working for some airlines may remain on duty for no longer than fourteen hours, some of their colleagues remain in the cockpit for "as long as they can endure".'*

Duty hours start with clocking in at an airport, following, probably, a long, wearying drive or a night in a noisy hotel, early rising and a taxi ride. The availability of crew bunks on aircraft, such as the B747-400,

*System Errors In Aviation, op. cit.

MD11 or Airbus 340, may extend the duty time by 50 per cent in lieu of the hours spent horizontally. IFALPA suspects the demands to simplify the complex regulations will mean an extension of duty time.

The discretionary element in the interpretation of the rules creates a trap. A two-hour extension of duty for operational reasons is now a routine. If there is a delayed take-off because of traffic congestion or bad weather (and that happens frequently on short-haul in peak holiday periods) it is expected that the crew will exercise its discretionary power to exceed the limits. In Britain, a three-hour extension must be reported to the CAA – a longer one is seen as a *force majeure*. In some countries, and particularly when working for poorer carriers and small charter companies, pilots may be scheduled right up to the limit, so nobody can say that the law was *meant* to be broken, but then they are *expected* to act in favour of the airline as if the discretionary power was a business asset rather than the captain's sole preserve. (For example, a London to Los Angeles flight is delayed for four hours – the crew will be on duty for sixteen hours. Or, say, some maintenance hitch holds up a flight at a small Greek airport. Tedious waiting for a take-off slot comes next. There is no spare crew available. The captain must reckon not only with 300 sleepless, irritable passengers who are anxious to get home, but also his bosses who expect loyalty to the company that may be on the breadline – i.e. pressures to avoid the extra cost of hotels and the upset of flying schedules. Nobody will spell it out, but his job may be under threat, especially now that there is a pilot surplus.)

Every young cadet dreams about getting his own command and the absolute authority of captain, but the monotony of flying with universally marvelled devices of automation that have rendered engineers and radio officers superfluous, may come as a shock. Take-off, navigation to destination, and soon even the orders for an automated blind landing in any weather conditions, may simply be tapped into the control computers, but the job will entail duties for which humans are the least suitable – the incessant and exceedingly monotonous monitoring of instruments.

Airbus Industrie – a French, German, British and Spanish consortium – pioneered new technology, introducing the fly-by-wire concept. That means that computers play key roles in flying the aircraft. Instead of using a traditional yoke – the control column – pilots programme the flight and fly by manipulating small hand grips, not unlike those for TV games. Instead of rods, cables and pulleys, only wiring connects the 'joystick' to the moving parts of the wings and the tail, and the control surfaces respond to electronic signals.

Automation has vast advantages. It enhances safety by reducing the room for human error, 'ensuring more precise flight manoeuvres, providing display facility, and optimizing cockpit space,' says Agnes

Huff, USAir human factors specialist.* On the other hand, it may lead to the 'erosion of skills, perceived loss of control, and increased monitoring responsibilities'. Strict adherence to separate printed checklists for every single procedure in the cockpit was the fist to eliminate human memory lapses, and to augment skills with rules. Because of those rules, and now the high degree of automation – techniques the middle-aged captain finds harder to learn – RAF aviation psychologist Dr Roger Green sees a danger to pilots in becoming unable 'to handle any situation which requires knowledge- or skill-based behaviour'.

Early pilots flew by the seat of their pants. Sights, noises, vibrations used to give them vital clues. Electronic and digital display designs intruded between the machine and their senses. In their glass cockpits they call up speed, altitude, track, attitude, engine performance and other data in words, figures, dials, diagrams and coded messages on TV-type screens. Instead of using a mouse, like personal computers, the flat panel and CRT (cathode ray tube) displays are manipulated by touch-controlled cursors. Watching them for hours on end can be soporific. No wonder that the confidential British and American reporting systems are peppered with pilots' admissions: 'I fell asleep in the cockpit.' Fatigue and boredom work hand in hand. Salvation is sought with even more technology. Pilots may have to wear helmets with electrodes to monitor brain patterns, and alert them if they nod off or fail to respond to signals. Or the instruments themselves could demand attention: if a pilot does not acknowledge certain displays on the screen at given intervals, a 'rise-and-shine' buzzer will be sounded. Meanwhile, cabin attendants must visit the cockpit every twenty minutes to supply the pilots with liquids – and ensure they are awake.

Yet the pilots' 'safety first' attitude is borne out by the fact that there is no other professional who would be willing to work in the constant knowledge that . . .

. . . BIG BROTHER IS WATCHING

Every one of the pilots' actions – or failure to take timely action – is immortalized by flight recorders, every word they utter remains on a Cockpit Voice Recorder (see Chapter 25) that is strictly confidential, but certainly helps to stamp out the tabloids' favourite 'hanky-panky on the flight deck' rumours. The stress it imposes on pilots is obvious: 'All details of their work are recorded and can be scrutinized at any time later,' says Captain A. Holmes of BALPA. 'Intense commercial pressure can be and is applied . . . If something goes wrong . . . the crew's comments can be eagerly snapped up by the world's press and they can be found guilty by editorials, with no effective right of reply.' The

*42nd Safety Seminar of the Flight Safety Foundation, Athens, 1989.

benefits are, however, overwhelming, and examples of that are innumerable. After an accident, investigators can often pinpoint what went wrong, what information was available to the pilots (was there an audible warning signal?), and how they dealt with it.

SWISSAIR, for instance, scrutinizes the 'black box' after each flight. Did the pilots exceed speed limits? How precise was their ILS approach? For the sake of confidentiality, only three people in the company have access to the details. If those three recognize some potentially hazardous trends, they give anonymous reports to the management. In 1991, it was noted that significantly frequent approaches were made 'below the ILS path'. (Flying MD80-s, 6 per cent of the landings were faulty.) So was there something wrong in the training and the manuals? The handbooks were altered, refresher training began to lay emphasis on the risk – and the problem disappeared. In extreme cases, the pilot is called in for a discussion with the three men in the know, who are housed well away from the airport and the airline headquarters, so that nobody will see the pilots entering. The procedure is never disciplinary: the aim is to let the pilot learn from his mistakes or even volunteer for some additional corrective training. The analysis is also useful for introducing all-weather automatic landings: only if the data proves that in some 300 cases, at least 98 per cent of the selected flights have managed successful automated landings within the 'window' (the prescribed area) will the authorities accede to the general utilization of the technique.

The 'black box' can often exonerate the pilot. A red-faced BA captain once reported truthfully a 'very hard' landing – i.e. he had slammed the wheels on the concrete. His aircraft was immediately removed from service, but before the lengthy maintenance checks began, the Flight Data Recording group discovered not only that the landing had been well within the acceptable limits, but a comparison with other records also revealed that the landing, perceived by the pilot as 'very hard', was not without precedent at that particular airport: the runway there had a hump, and an excellent landing at that precise point could produce a disconcerting acceleration. The captain was reassured, and all his colleagues were warned to be prepared, but unfortunately no demands were made on the airport to deal with the problem.

Cockpit resource management, a relatively new science, is another potential beneficiary of the recordings. Communication and workload distribution between the pilots are an essential part of flying. Any breakdown in that respect can have disastrous consequences. National character may play an important part in that. While Australian co-pilots are only too willing to point out anybody's errors, their Arab and Japanese colleagues have an excessive respect for seniority, and an Iranian stewardess would have to find some tactful way to disturb her captain's peaceful snoozing.

The captain's resource management requires tact. Richard Offord, a senior BA Captain and BALPA official, says that 'Hardly ever will a captain feel that he must take over from a first officer who is flying the aircraft. Usually, a carefully phrased but authoritative suggestion will get the job done to his own standards. I had to give a firm direction, a direct order, that is, only once. It's always a hard decision, for at the same time we expect expert views and co-operation from people under our command. A captain may have to take control for safety, but it can cause hard feelings, a breakdown in communications, and may turn the flight into a virtual one-man operation. So it must be used as a last resort.'

A captain who expects to be treated as a demi-god may fare no better than the Swiss one who, flying to Paris, admonished his crew to keep their opinions to themselves unless he asked for their views. In the ensuing silence, the radio officer, still present in those days, tapped out his messages in Morse, and nobody warned the captain that he had made a mistake, landing at Orly instead of Le Bourget, the intended destination. When, with an obvious loss of face, he gave the order to notify Zurich that they would be a little late at Le Bourget, the radio operator informed him that he had already sent that message 'While we were on the finals . . . sir.'

There was no room for gentle irony when in 1978 Flight 173, a United Airlines DC8, approached Portland, Oregon. At 17.06, the flaps and the landing gear were lowered. Everybody on board heard a bang and felt a severe jolt. The aircraft began to yaw. The wheels position indicator gave some confusing information. So what was faulty? The instrument or the gear itself? There was plenty of time to investigate: the aircraft carried the regulatory surplus fuel for another sixty-five minutes' flying to cater for any necessary diversion.

The captain decided to circle at 5000 feet. The diagnostic checks were inconclusive. At 17.44, he radioed his base for a confirmation that no other check procedure was available. He then chose to burn up fuel to reduce the risk of fire in case the wheels collapsed on landing, and ordered cabin staff to prepare for an emergency evacuation. But the status of the gear remained his main concern. The CVR recorded some cautious hints from the crew regarding the level of fuel in the tanks, but there was no positive response.

'Less than three weeks, three weeks to retirement . . . you better get me outta here,' said a crew member at 17.48.

'Thing to remember is don't worry,' answered the captain.

At 18.06, they were seventeen miles out, flying away from the airport. Then two engines flamed out in quick succession because of fuel starvation. Nineteen miles out, the captain decided to go 'straight in'. The remaining two engines were crossfed from other tanks, but by 18.13 no more fuel was coming through. They tried to make it to a small airfield near Portland or an interstate highway to land on. They failed.

At 18.15, sixty-nine minutes after the first sighting of Portland, the DC8 cut a mile-long swath in a forest in a populated area. Mercifully 'only' ten people were killed, 179 others suffered mostly minor injuries. The investigation discovered that the landing gear fail-safe design had overcome some excessive corrosion, and it would not have collapsed on landing. The crash was caused by the captain's preoccupation with the wheels, the lack of clear assignment of responsibilities, and the crew's failure to communicate assertively their anxiety about the state of fuel.

That case helped the industry to recognize the importance of training pilots for cockpit resource management – yet its value took a decade to be acknowledged universally! Some situations are, however, almost impossible to cater for. When a young, probationary first officer was flying with his company president (known as a 'grumpy old captain') in a Twin Otter of an American commuter airline, he slowly came to acquiesce to his master's habit of not responding with anything beyond a grunt to his standard challenge-check calls. When the captain was about to land, coming in too steeply, the young man kept his head down, thought about his future with the company, did not query why his call-outs were not receiving even a grunt of acknowledgement, and let his boss get on with it – all the way into the ground. He survived, but the older man was dead. The autopsy discovered that the captain had been killed by a heart attack in the air – which explained his final taciturnity.

Despite occasional rumour-mongering, pilots rarely suffer from sudden incapacitation in the cockpit. For Big Brother is also watching them by medical means, and even if some unforeseeable illness strikes, the other pilot can almost always avert disaster. (In a seven-year period, ICAO recorded only seventeen deaths in the cockpits of mostly smaller aircraft, and only five of those had catastrophic consequences, killing 148 people in all.) Pilots are subjected to regular, exhaustive health checks. They are required to report even the mildest medication they take. In America, pilots over the age of sixty are not allowed to fly commercial aircraft with more than thirty passengers. This, in effect, limits the number of passengers the incapacitation of a sixty-one-year-old may kill. The US authorities are under pressure to extend commercial pilots' working life beyond sixty. In 1993, the result of a two-year study was published. Based on twelve years' accident data, it proved that pilots, approaching the age of sixty, had the same safety record as their younger colleagues. It did not examine, however, how much the *likelihood* of sudden incapacitation – due to strokes and heart attacks – might increase with age.

Medical certification is not foolproof. Some heart conditions may remain dormant for years, and cannot be identified by 'resting ECG' which is all that is required by ICAO. (Radioactive isotope inspection is not carried out routinely anywhere.) Minor symptoms, such as 'a bit of breathlessness when walking uphill' or 'an occasional pang of a chest pain, caused only by some indigestion' may be shrugged off, and go unreported by pilots. Bodies like the FAA and the CAA vet the pilots' medical checks – and not without good reason. 'Unfortunately, corruption in the medical fraternity is not without precedent,' Dr Frank Preston, a leading aviation consultant told me. 'There were such cases in the Third World, and some ten years ago the FAA noticed that a medical examiner in the Mid-West had a huge international clientèle. Some 3000 pilots came to him from all over the world because he was known as an easy touch for some consideration, I suppose. His records were checked, he was fined, and controls were tightened. These days all US medical certification papers must go to Oklahoma where even the slightest omissions are spotted.'

There are also occasional sensationalist reports about pilots who drink or take drugs. Though both hazards are on the NTSB's 'Most Wanted' hit list, relatively few real cases come to light. Only a Japanese freighter aircraft came to grief due to drunkenness some two decades ago in Alaska. The cheapness of alcohol and rest periods shared by pilots and cabin crews a long way from home give rise to many rumours about wild parties, but these are less frequent than popularly believed. Captains who are known to be 'nipping back to the loo to have a few snorts from a hip flask before beginning a descent' are now reported by colleagues to their airlines in most countries. In the former Soviet Union, where alcoholism is widespread, pilots have to report for duty, and stay dry, for twenty-four hours in advance. In Hungary, where the alcohol limit is nil even for car drivers, pilots are breathalysed before every flight. In Britain, no more than ten to fifteen pilots and cabin crew are under voluntary treatment and regular follow-up observation at any one time.

'Pilots have always maintained that they were a special breed who could control themselves,' says Rick van Woerkom of the NTSB, 'and everybody agrees that most of them are extremely responsible and safety-conscious. The NTSB has long been pushing, however, for stricter controls because different they may be, but not *that* different, and there's no reason to believe that the spread of dangerous social habits will not affect at least some of them. In ground transportation we saw alcohol, marijuana, and hard drug problems – driving along a railroad is an incredibly boring job – and then we had a commuter aircraft accident at Newark, New Jersey, in 1984, in which drugs played a part. Finally, there was Colorado . . . a major milestone in legislation.'

On the 19 January 1988, at about 19.20, Continental Express flight 2286, a Metro Fairchild aircraft, crashed into trees at Bayfield, on the approach to Durango, Colorado. Of the seventeen people on board, two crew members and seven passengers were killed. The one passenger who walked away uninjured alerted the rescue services who knew nothing about the accident. Survivors revealed that a few minutes before the accident, an abrupt pitch had been followed by a surge in engine

118

The Past and the Future

The Wright brothers' first ever man-carrying powered flight, airbourne for twelve seconds in 1903.

This Superjumbo for eight hundred passengers on three floors – complete with offices, a viewing gallery and surgery – is on the drawing boards for the next century.

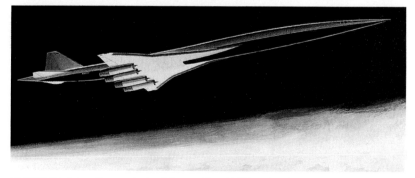

An artist's impression of hypersonic aircraft that may fly at 10,000 m.p.h. – fast enough to go into low Earth orbit.

'Glass cockpit' of an Airbus. (Later versions have joysticks, like video games for children, in lieu of the 'yoke'.)

Each dot is an aircraft. One of the dozens of screens in the London (West Drayton) Air Traffic Control Operations Room.

How the other half flies – *Air Force 1*, one of the two special Jumbos for US presidents.

A lounge for presidential aides and conferences.

Next to the airbourne Oval Office, is the lounge area for the President and First Lady.

From the armoury of crash investigators

Below, Giant jigsaw: meticulous reassembly of wreckage from the rear of the fuselage – something must have happened up front before the metal back there crumpled.

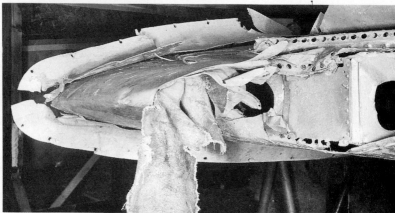

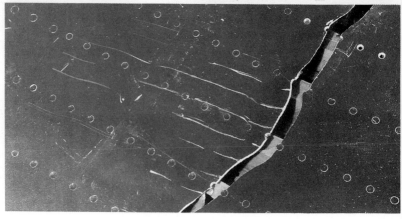

Scratches on two reassembled pieces stop at the fracture – the metal must have broken in two before one was scratched, so the marks are irrelevant to the search for the cause.

Resurrection of the past: computer screen reconstruction of an aircraft and its behaviour based on evidence from flight data and voice recorders.

An air-gun to test the strength of a flight recorder that must withstand impact, fire burning at 1100°C and ocean pressure at 20,000 feet.

Inset: A flight recorder 'black box' – that is orange-coloured.

'If you took a scheduled flight every day, it would take 4000 years before you were likely to be in some, probably minor, accident – and still have a fifty-fifty chance of survival'.
Carl Vogt, *Chairman of the US National Transportation Safety Board*

Hong Kong 18/11/93 – a China Airlines Boeing 747 skidded off the runway and into the harbour. There were no fatalites.

Hawaii 29/4/88 – the roof rips off an Aloha Airlines plane while in mid-air. There was only one fatality.

Some weapons of the battle against drug smugglers

One of the specially trained dogs sniffs out drugs in personal luggage and cargo.

Just a matter of patience: drugs hidden in the smuggler's body will sooner or later reappear in the glass toilet and the adjoining receptacle.

The electronic urine-testing machine detects minute quantities of drugs (cannabis, cocaine, amphetamines, barbiturates and opiates, including heroin and opium). Even if the smuggler has swallowed it in sealed condoms, leakages or traces on the package will show up.

Modern times: rows of airline food are assembled on one of the production lines of the SWISSAIR kitchens.

Aircraft cemetery: protected against rust in the arid Arizona Desert, miles of grounded machines await second-hand buyers and resurrection.

power, and the aircraft had rolled several times. The investigation soon established that the too-fast, too-steep approach had been unstabilized, and that the captain had conducted all the radio communications as customary whenever the aircraft was flown by the first officer.

It was the autopsy on the crew that produced the shock waves. Benzoylecgonine, the principal metabolite of cocaine, was found in the captain's blood and urine. His former girlfriend revealed that in 1987 'he wasn't himself any more', seemed nervous, scared and overweight. She thought it was a drug problem but did not inform anyone at the time. The woman he last lived with told a pilot (who at once contacted the NTSB) that she was 'Sure glad that we were able to bury him right after the accident, because the night before we had done a bag of cocaine . . . ' She had the 'burned out look' of an addict, and she confessed that her dead lover had been a periodic user of cocaine.

The examination of personnel records revealed further character flaws. The captain, rated by colleagues as a 'highly skilled pilot', had a tendency 'to rush things'. He failed to inform his company or the medical examiners that his driving licence had been suspended for various – some serious – traffic violations. All that added up to a 'cavalier attitude to the need for rigorous adherence to rules and procedures'. The first officer, a fully reformed alcoholic, had shown 'deficiencies in performing instrument procedures' during training. The investigation revealed that the airline had a bad maintenance record. (It was irrelevant as a causal factor, but the unpaid heavy fines hastened the company's bankruptcy soon after the accident.) Delving into the effects of cocaine, it was found that the drug had been taken the night before the crash, and that such a stimulant, causing insomnia followed by fatigue, must have impaired the captain's ability to fly or monitor the first officer's flying, as required.

While in most countries the current level of drug usage is not seen as a significant threat to aviation, the Colorado accident has led to new American regulations: the non-disclosure of alcohol- or drug-related car driving records will entail flying licence withdrawal, and the FAA can test American pilots at random, primarily for hard drugs – a rule that may eventually be applied to foreigners flying into the US.

TO ERR IS HUMAN – TO PREVENT, A MUST

If in doubt, blame the pilot – that used to be the simple answer to puzzling mysteries of the air. Baffled aircrash investigators resorted to it, licensing authorities, manufacturers and others potentially involved in disasters hid behind it. Unfortunately, and all too frequently, it is also the correct answer. A Boeing study of twenty international airlines with better than average safety standards found that 70 per cent of the major accidents were caused by pilots who erred in most disturbing ways, such as deviating from basic operational procedures or the co-pilot failing his elementary duty of adequately cross-checking every action.

That simplistic early answer was unhelpful: it only disguised the circumstances that had ensnared the pilot. For a better understanding of *errors*, the term 'human factor' was coined. It saw the pilot as a part of a system that allowed, facilitated, even invited errors, and encompassed errorprone human elements in aircraft design, air traffic control, airport management, airline procedures, training, etc. Genuine pilot error can be blamed only if it is proven beyond doubt that in the given circumstances, other, similarly trained and prepared colleagues would have been expected to act differently. Over-simplification precludes the discovery of the true causes of an accident and, above all, misses the opportunity to identify risks and so prevent disastrous repetitions.

A whole series of accidents right up to the 1970s could serve as classic examples. In each of these cases pilot error was blamed for crashing into mountains or even runways, until it was recognized that the various altimeters, then in worldwide use, could easily be misread by as much as a 1000 or even 10,000 feet. A wealth of other examples can be found. The pilot who, with plenty of fuel in reserve and no engine problem, missed two approaches in adverse weather, yet kept trying to land and eventually crashed, may have been guilty of bad judgement or a victim of let's-get-homeitus; a Russian captain might well have been responsible for the crash that killed eighty-two people at Ivanono, in August 1992, because he had continued descending in thick fog despite the traffic controller's order to 'ascend immediately and circle'. But it was a grave mistake to blame 'the sting in tail' and 'the bloody fools who came down at a too-steep angle' for several accidents in the 1960s, soon after the B727 had entered service, because it would transpire that though the aircraft only did what it was designed to do, the pilots had not been trained properly to take advantage of its 'high sink rate' that would get them into smaller airports with short runways.

The answers to the investigators' complex questions are, however, not always so clear and unequivocal.

On 8 January 1989, the British Midland London to Belfast shuttle was flying at 29,000 feet when dinner in the cabin was interrupted by loud bangs, rattling and vibration. Smoke entered the cockpit. It smelt like burning metal. The instruments did not indicate engine fire, but what else could have caused it? And which engine was responsible? The captain took command, and began to investigate by trial and error. He first tried to shut down the starboard engine. It seemed to be the right choice: the buffeting stopped, the vibration and smoke began to subside. The aircraft, an almost brand new B737-400, could fly on one engine, but for safety the captain decided to divert to Castle Donington airport. The port engine was throttled back for the descent, causing even less vibration. In 127 seconds, the emergency seemed to be over. Descending through 2000 feet, the landing gear and flaps were lowered. Engine power was increased to attain the proper attitude along the glide path to the runway. Then suddenly, and without any warning, the port engine they had been flying on died. Fire alarm and violent vibration. In the remaining fifty-five seconds, all attempts to restart the starboard engine failed. A glancing impact with an open field, then a crash into the wooded motorway embankment near Kegworth, Leicestershire. Thirty-nine people were killed, eight more were dying, almost everybody else on board was seriously injured.

What happened? The investigation (and, later, a Parliamentary inquiry) produced numerous cautionary discoveries to some of which we shall refer in later chapters. As for the causes of the catastrophe? It was found that the port, not the starboard engine, had suffered fan blade failure and fire. (It was a new powerful type of high bypass turbofan engine. Previous, similar incidents with the type in flight had been investigated but no improvement had as yet been deemed necessary. Was that decision a mistake?) Had there been no engine failure, there would have been no emergency situation. Be that as it may, it appeared that the pilots had shut down the healthy power plant, and tried to fly on the faulty one. An error of judgement? Even this simplified summary cannot give a clear-cut yes or no answer.

The pilots' first choice experiment *seemed* to have located the fault, leaving them with some twenty minutes to the haven of Castle Donington. Staying at a high altitude for safety, could they have sat on their hands and contemplated their options a little longer? Possibly. But they saw no reason to. Busy with flying the aircraft, they could not actually *look* at their engines. (Prior to that accident, the installation of rearward facing external TV cameras had been recommended repeatedly but in vain.) And all the while, unknown to the pilots, certain design features were compensating for the fault, reinforcing their belief that theirs had been the correct decision.

Among the numerous instruments in the sophisticated cockpit were two tiny engine vibration dials. Whatever operation manuals and training instructors might have taught them, pilots traditionally mistrusted those gauges which had a long history of giving misleading signals. On new types of aircraft, vibration dials are a prominent part of the alerting system, but on that B737-400 they were tucked away on a secondary panel, with no warning lights, as if relegated to a nice-to-have monitoring status. Among the many recommendations, the AAIB demanded a review of pilots' attitudes to those engine vibration indicators because, as Eddie Trimble, the investigator in charge, told me: 'Sadly, one look at those gauges could have prevented the pilots' mistaken judgement.' A year later, when an identical engine fault developed on a DanAir flight above the Channel, and again, two days after that, when yet another fan blade failed on another new British Midland B737-400, the pilots knew right away – because they had been instructed – where to look for the answer, and landed safely. Preventive measures, albeit belatedly, thus began to bear fruit.

Automation and more automation will make flying easier, but it will not eliminate human errors from the safety equation. Just as a new stretch of dual carriageway may only push that notorious traffic-jam black-spot further down the road, computers can create opportunities for human error outside the cockpit – or present the pilot with unforeseen problems. The screens of the glass cockpit aboard a brand new B757 recently suffered a complete blackout when the computers overheated and failed. The British pilots landed safely, and then the cause of the emergency was found: fluff from the new carpets and upholstery had clogged the filters of the computer cooling fans.

As automation and computerization are here to stay, the solution of the pilot error problem will demand a more pragmatic approach. The British CAA is the first authority about to take a new, most commendable initiative. It plans to train pilots to recognize situations in which human errors *may* be made. An examination in the subject will prepare them for their true role, neither demi-god nor sky cabbie, in this futuristic golden age of aviation. The ideas will be welcomed, one hopes, by all. For pilots are not suicidal maniacs. Only if they are clearly negligent should they be made to bear the burden of blame.

13

Guardian Angels with the Frozen Smile

You are about to board in New York. An attractive woman in a pretty uniform catches your eye. You disembark in New Orleans, and there she is again. And again and again, in Paris, Tokyo and Melbourne as well as in the romantic and efficiency-oozing advertisements on your television screen. But wait a minute: it might have been only the standardized frozen smile – *We're here to serve YOU* – and, more than that, the smart uniform that stood out in the crowd and grabbed your attention. If so, the dress designer has performed successfully the essential duty of creating a focal point for air travellers in moments of need: Can I have another coffee? – I feel sick – I'm worried – My child needs a change of nappy – Am I at the right airport? and, above all, though only once in a million life-times, How do I get out of here?

Most airlines are shameless in the exploitation of glamorously clad males and females to entice customers, and project a marketable corporate image. They play down, at least in public, the real objective for cabin attendants: to perform duties and handle emergencies for the safety of passengers. The size of the cabin crew must always be proportionate to the number of people in their care.

Some of the reasons for the 'winged waitress' misconception can be found in the origins of service in the sky. In 1930, Steve Simpson, a United Airlines area manager, had the brilliant idea of employing crews to assist passengers who usually suffered air sickness. As cabin ceilings were low, with space in the aisles at a premium, he thought small and slender Filipino males would be suitable, but then refined his proposal for 'young stewardesses or couriers or whatever you want to call them', preferably nurses, whose presence would be a 'psychological punch' and great for publicity. When the innovation was accepted, the job specification included nursing experience, and set the limits at the age of twenty-five, 115 pounds in weight, and 5 feet 4 inches height. The girls would have to carry baggages for passengers, serve food, and screw down seats that were then unfastened! Sex appeal, an unwritten but clearly understood requirement, provoked a wave of protests from pilots' wives (some made a habit of collecting their homecoming husbands straight from the cockpit), dented the machismo of airsick male passengers, but served as a distraction to fears, added a glamorous gloss to flying, and proved to be such a success that all the competing airlines had to follow suit.

Whatever the attractions and perks of the job, hard labour with Job's patience is the winged hosts' and hostesses' lot. Apart from all the preparations and briefing for a flight (Will there be babies, people with special needs?), it is a mad rush on a short hop, say, from London to Zurich, to greet passengers, seat them, check safety belts and the storage of luggage, give the safety briefing, change uniform, serve food, deal with requests, sell duty-frees, change again, and supervise disembarkation, only to get ready for the return leg with a repeat performance of chores that are overlooked by many applicants, thousands of whom approach airlines year in, year out, knowing full well that the competition is fierce.

Take Britannia Airways. Last year it sent out its application forms (deliberately complicated to weed out starry-eyed glamour-seekers) to 13,500 people who had answered advertisements. Only a third of them returned the forms. After the assessment of answers, education, health and general background, 1000 were called for tests and interviews – for 250 jobs. (Those with nursing experience, a proof of stamina and knowledge of first aid, enjoy some preference.) The selection process continued throughout the five-week intensive training course, when the lucky ones were subjected to daily test papers and three major examinations under the watchful eyes of the company and the CAA. Many trainees failed for a variety of reasons, such as the inaptitude for team work.

Airlines are less than candid about it, but beyond basic mental and physical attributes, looks do matter in the selection. 'Intelligent women tend not to be good looking – according to the head of the Thai national airline,' reported the *IAPA World* in its 1991 winter issue. 'Replying to complaints that Thai air hostesses are not pretty enough,' he revealed that candidates 'were vetted in the same way as beauty pageant judges select contestants'. The alluring invitation from 'Singapore Girl', advertised *ad nauseam* on television, is not only Oriental – but also openly sex-oriented, and may fail to comply with the trade description law if in reality she was substituted by girls from a neighbouring country. (In 1993, £40 million was budgeted for further Singapore Girl advertising, but according to *Travel Weekly*, 10.10.1992, fewer true Singaporean girls were available to the airline for selection because of the government campaign against large families.)

All airlines have a height-to-weight policy – nobody could serve as cabin crew if bulk caused difficulties in squeezing through emergency exits – and the crew's general appearance is under strict regulations.*

African and Oriental ethnic uniforms, kimonos, pencil skirts, and cheong-sams with revealing slits – though perhaps a welcome sight for the weary businessman – can be a serious safety problem. Stewardesses of Emirates Airlines sport purple djellabahs that could be, like beautiful saris, a serious hindrance to saving lives in water after a ditching. (The ability to do so is a universal requirement.)

Sadly, glamour and cheerfulness (on VARIG, stewardesses may put on an impromptu song-and-dance routine before landing in Rio) are often misinterpreted, particularly by drunken passengers, as an invitation to sexual harassment. 'There have been a large number of mostly drug- or alcohol-related assaults on stewardesses,' says Chris Witkowski of the American Association of Flight Attendants. 'One of our members is now suing a hockey team who kept fondling her claiming that "she only laughed and had fun" with them. What rubbish! Aggressive or amorous misbehaviour is often a cover for tension and the fear of flying, but fortunately other passengers tend to help the crew.' An executive of Britain's *Cabin Crew 89* shares his faith in passengers: 'Apart from the drunken holiday-maker, it is often the first-class passenger who takes out stress and irritation with things like security on the crew – particularly on us women. Experience teaches us how to help them relax, how to handle people, chat to strangers, ignore nuisance passengers or tell them off if necessary, but if someone makes a polite pass, most of us just take it as a compliment.'

If diplomacy fails, the captain has absolute authority on board. Passengers can be told that the police would wait for them on arrival, and a compartment in the cockpit usually houses a pair of handcuffs. 'I'm glad to say that I've only had to use them once,' says a British captain. 'A passenger, halfway across the Atlantic, put on his hat, moved to disembark, and told one of the girls to put his coat into the car! He went crazy when she wouldn't let him out, and had to be physically restrained. A more difficult case of disorderly conduct occurred when the cabin crew noticed that two young and pretty women kept going to the toilet even when we were having a bumpy ride and the seatbelts were on. Oddly enough, there were also men coming out of the same toilets. When the

*For example, MALÉV, that lists A-levels, preferably a degree, English and at least one other foreign language among its requirements for applicants, goes to great lengths in its rules for appearance. Manicured hands, minimal make-up, the length of hair (no unnatural colour), the size and style of jewellery (no multiple earrings or ankle chains), the size and style of watches, and even the colour of watch-straps (must be in harmony with the uniform) is prescribed. For stewards, earrings are out, beards and moustaches of a certain size and shape may be grown only during long absences. Men's hair must never touch the collar of the shirt, and the 'wet look' with the use of gels is disallowed for it may appear greasy. If they travel as passengers, they must not wrap themselves in blankets.

women were ordered to stay put, they started counting cash. As soon as the seatbelt sign was off, they were at it again. And I do mean *it*. They were earning back the cost of their holidays. What were we to do? Their behaviour did not endanger the aircraft, there was no pimp involved, so they were not running a disorderly house – we could only let them know we knew what was going on, and that they must cool it.'

A psychologist advocates more research into the cabin crew selection techniques. 'Scheduled airlines tend to go for slick, sophisticated types to attract business customers. Holiday charter operators prefer the mumsie type, a friend who can be trusted with kids. Both types might find it difficult to switch character and display serious authority. It's easier for older people, but would we want to rely on the physical rescue efforts of sexagenarians? Yet if some unions win equal retirement age for all, we may come to that.' (There is no US Federal age limit, and some attendants are in their sixties.)

Authoritativeness is an essential attribute that must be attained by cabin crew. And it is not only for the restraint of any misbehaviour. In an emergency, they must be heard and obeyed. Though they have loud-hailers, when SWISSAIR trainees shout 'This way!' or 'Follow me!' the volume must be sufficient to register on an audiometer in a full-size cabin mock-up. In some Oriental and Muslim countries, it is very difficult to train women to break social taboos, overcome traditional subservience, and shout at men. The first test of authority comes with hand luggage: where size restrictions are not fully enforced at the gates, people board with incredible pieces. The likes of tractor tyres, flat-pack kitchen units (even a sink), a fig tree, a slot machine, a 25-gallon aquarium, and a few lavatory pans have been noted on various flights. People insist on (and cabin crew often turn a blind eye to) placing bottles and other hard, heavy objects, i.e. potential deadly missiles, into the overhead bins. I once saw a pair of metal crutches in there, and the stewardess refused to do anything about it. (Companies can wrongly pressurize their crews to please customers.) Cabin crews and air safety experts have long been fighting for duty-free sales at destination only, losing out to the lure of profits, but the introduction of plastic bottles has at least alleviated the problem.

The worst situation I ever saw arose on a Biman Bangladesh flight. A vast amount of massive items, including large TV sets, were carried into the cabin without objection from anyone. None of them would fit into the bins above, let alone under the seats. So they were piled high in the aisles, atop oxygen bottles and fire extinguishers, blocking the exits. When the sari-clad crew tried to serve dinner, their trolleys had to be lifted repeatedly over the 'hand-luggage'. I shudder to think what chaos would have resulted if an emergency evacuation had become necessary. On the same flight, there was a serious fist fight involving several passengers, a steward and a pilot. People were flung against the wall, but a stewardess remained unperturbed: 'It happens on every flight. People are coming out of a dry country, demand alcohol, but can't handle it. What can you do?'

Refuse to serve them like European crews do when confronted with heavy boozers?

'What would that achieve? We'd lose customers to competitors.'

Service has always been an essential role of cabin crew. But as Sue Knight of the CAA says,* the promotion of the corporate image and emphasis on the commercial product and customer service have now created a new trend: some airlines 'restructure their management in such a way that Cabin Safety Departments report to Marketing Departments rather than the Operations Departments'. And if this is the case in Britain, no wonder that there is much unevenness in the international standard of . . .

. . . SAFETY TRAINING

All airlines must comply with the safety rules of their national authorities, e.g. the CAA and the FAA, but the level of training requirements varies alarmingly. Leaving aside the countries where being a minister's mistress may be a vocational qualification, safety aspects form a small part of the cabin training curriculum – most of it is taken up with service, self-care, food presentation, the answers to passengers' questions – and much is left to the airlines' discretion. Safety refresher courses are, however, compulsory, particularly when the crew is transferred to a new type of aircraft with different exits and location of equipment, or when somebody returns to service after a long absence, due to pregnancy and lay-offs, or to resume seasonal, part-time employment.

British cabin crews may be qualified to work on two aircraft types – possibly three with CAA approval, if the location and operation of exits and safety equipment are similar, but that may still involve thirty-seven different positions with specific duties. They may be assigned to any of these at short notice with hardly any time for familiarization. If they are transferred to a new type, they must be trained for it. An NTSB investigation into US flight attendant training and performance in emergencies found scores of shortcomings that had failed to prevent, or had actually caused, injuries. Here is one of those cases.

In 1990, when a B727 and a DC9 collided on the ground at Detroit airport, the structural damage was substantial, but nobody was injured aboard the Boeing. On the DC9, there were serious difficulties with the evacuation and eight people died in the subsequent fire. It emerged that the lead flight attendant, qualified for *seven* types (most US carriers do not impose any limitation), had not been in her jump-seat during the collision, could neither properly secure an escape slide nor fully open a

*Operational Considerations for UK Cabin Attendants, Presentation at the 10th International Aircraft Cabin Safety Symposium, California, 1993.

door, and, with three others, failed to inflate another slide 'thereby slowing the evacuation and increasing the number of evacuation-caused injuries'. Another attendant of twenty-two years' experience could not open the tail-cone exit because of inadequate training for its operation. The report criticized the FAA for allowing group demonstration for crews instead of 'hands on' training.

In other cases, crews discovered only too late that the real emergency exits were harder to operate than the training doors; that they were unprepared for the frightening darkness, noise and smoke of a survivable crash; that smoke hoods for the cabin crew could be in different locations on variants of B737s used by the same airline; that some of them had never actually been asked to remove a fire extinguisher from its brackets; and that the drill for coordination and communication among them had been insufficient. A lead flight attendant had difficulties with an evacuation slide because he had no 'hands on' experience, and had seen only *pictures* of the quick release handle. The twelve airlines in the sample used very different levels of training for the opening of emergency exits, the instructor/student ratio for drills ranged from 1:1 to 1:9, one airline spent thirty minutes on dealing with decompression, another allocated ten minutes to the subject, and there were serious variations in the recurrent training that should 'address degradation of human performance that can be expected during stressful' and 'especially life-threatening situations'.

The numerous recommendations in the report (issued in 1992) were taken to heart by the FAA and the US carriers, but the rest of the world would be well advised to follow suit. Studies by the Cranfield Aeronautical Institute proved that evacuation is up to 50 per cent faster with crew direction than without expert guidance. Aviation records are brimming with examples of cabin attendants' heroic self-sacrifice for their passengers, such as in the case of the Manchester disaster,* but stricter worldwide laws for training – along the lines suggested by the European Joint Aviation Authority, and with realistic emergency simulators that are used by Delta, BA, Air Canada, etc. – could help eliminate that wasteful call for any heroism. (Ditching training, for instance, is compulsory everywhere. But I have not yet come across any airline that conducts life-saving exercises with fully clothed rather than swim-suited crews in a pool, though swimming in uniforms could pose unexpected difficulties.)

The *duty time* of cabin crews also varies from country to country. Dr Hans Krakauer of IAPA has raised the question repeatedly: could the crew's ability to perform emergency duties be impaired at the end of a long flight? 'In no accident has cabin crew fatigue been indicated as a detrimental factor,' says Tony Broderick of the FAA. 'We know that in

*More about the survivability of accidents in Chapter 26.

some cases they work very long hours that might have a cumulative effect, but we've studied the problem, and never found quantifiable safety benefits from limitations. If you cannot identify a problem, you shouldn't try to solve it.'

Chris Witkowski disagrees: 'Some of our members may work twenty hours a day. They're told that in an emergency, the adrenalin starts flowing, so everything will be OK. But when they're crossing time zones, when the rest they get is of questionable quality, and the sufficiency of their four-hour anchor sleep is suspect, they may behave as if they had a 0.1 blood alcohol level. We want a fourteen-hour maximum duty time. Congress was for it, but President Bush vetoed it. He said it would impose a financial burden on the operators, and give an unfair advantage to their foreign competitors. We have managed to negotiate contracts with the big lines, but regional carriers claim that such limits would kill them off. If it was a law, duty time would cease to be seen as a mere bargaining chip.'

The FAA now proposes to impose a minimum rest period and maximum hours of flying in order to eliminate the obvious abuses that, though quite rare, did sometimes occur. 'The approach we came up with', says Tony Broderick, 'is of modest cost to the airlines and, we hope, will eliminate the few rare but nevertheless existing occasions when cabin crew schedules were outrageously long. Of course, the rule will also now restrict flight attendants in some cases from rearranging their work schedules to suit their own preference in cases where those rearranged schedules would exceed the rule limits.'

In Britain cabin crews enjoy virtually the same limits as pilots, and must get a full day's break after a sixteen-and-a-half-hour-day (including waiting for, say, repairs), but in 1991 BA cabin staff went on strike, causing twenty-nine cancellations, because a new rostering technique could stretch their duty time to nineteen hours. 'The legal maximum must never be allowed to become the standard minimum in practice,' says Gordon Bennett of *Cabin Crew 89*. 'Third World countries are just beginning to recognize the problem and seek advice.'

Improved international standards are overdue. So what if cabin attendants were to be licensed, like pilots, by government agencies? France, Hungary and a few other countries have long subscribed to that idea. Elsewhere, proposals are still debated. New European thinking advocates National Vocational Qualifications (computer records of personal standards in expertise and proficiency) which could amount to just another name for licensing. In Britain, the CAA monitors the training, and the argument is that licences would only generate more bureaucracy, and fuel higher pay demands on the basis of a greater cudos the job might attain.

The US Association of Flight Attendants believes that licensing would improve cabin training, and lead to strict testing of efficiency. But an

American lawyer, devotee of the 'if in doubt, sue' school, believes that cabin attendants would lose out on licences: 'It would turn their occupation into a profession, and as professionals they could be sued more easily, like doctors, if there was the slightest hint of alleged negligence.' An ICAO technical commission, representing 153 members and more than forty observers, 'concluded that there would be no safety benefit from cabin crew licensing,' says Tony Broderick. 'If Third World and various vanity airlines fail to adopt American and British training standards, what guarantee could we get against some incompetent governments issuing yet another piece of paper?'

Once again, ICAO and other international bodies cannot enforce worldwide standards. Much is left to us, the passengers, in choosing whom we trust to fly us. And it is for us to complain vociferously if we see anything in the cabin that seems inadequate, unacceptable or outright dodgy.

14

Do-s and Don't-s

Before reading on, you may like to answer a quiz. It is based on the questionnaire with which the American AFA tested 800 people in flight. The average participant got only half of the answers right. Hopefully, the previous chapters have already given you a distinct advantage, at least in some respects.

True or false
1. If you carry a portable typewriter or lap-top computer, it will be best protected in the overhead storage bin.
2. If you are a nervous passenger, ask for a seat near an exit, and carry a torch-light.
3. When cabin attendants are busy, e.g. serving dinner, be considerate, and do not bother them with your questions or observations.
4. If there is decompression, and the oxygen mask comes out, just lean forward until your face reaches it.
5. Try to find a snug fit for the mask over your mouth.
6. In decompression, every second counts, so if you are travelling with a child, you must ensure that the child can breathe safely before attending to your own mask.
7. After the initial ascent, the seatbelts sign is switched off, but experienced fliers keep their seatbelts fastened.
8. Seats at the rear of the cabin are the safest.
9. It is permissible to smoke in toilets but only if they are fitted with smoke extractors.
10. Cabin crews have extinguishers to fight in-flight fires.
11. Not every aircraft carries life-jackets under the seats.
12. If the aircraft is on the ground, and there is an order for emergency evacuation, head for the nearest exit without waiting for detailed instructions.
13. Before you leave your seat to evacuate, collect your valuables, including identification papers, and some cash.

14. During an emergency evacuation, you should preferably exit through the door you used for entry.

15. If there is no cabin attendant available at a door, check that there is no fire outside, then try to open it yourself.

16. Although aircraft doors vary in size, their operation is basically identical.

17. If smoke fills the cabin, you must escape on all fours.

18. If you have to use an escape slide, the best way is to jump into it, without first sitting down, however frightening that may seem.

19. After an evacuation you must always stay close to the aircraft to be counted, and to avoid getting lost or hit by emergency vehicles.

The answers will be found at the end of this chapter.

To break a wage strike by pilots, Indian Airlines wet-leased (aircraft and crew) seven TU154s from Uzbekistan Airlines. On 6 January 1993, one of those aircraft took a wrong turning, and tried to land at an air force base instead of Madras airport. A military training flight was about to take off, but fortunately air traffic controllers managed to intervene and prevent a collision. Three days later, 167 people aboard another of those TU154s had an even luckier escape. Their flight from Hyderabad was told by air traffic control to avoid New Delhi because the airport was fog-bound. Nevertheless, it tried to land. Apparently, the Russian and Uzbek pilots' English was not good enough to comprehend fully the expressions of standard international communications.

The aircraft missed the runway, and slewed from side to side for thousands of feet, smashing its landing gear, losing both wings, turning on its back, and breaking into sections. Smoke filled the cabin. People were hanging by their seatbelts upside down, and had to lower themselves on to the ceiling. Miraculously, there were no fatalities. Apart from a few broken bones and minor burns, there were no serious injuries. If passengers needed even more luck, that was the day for it. The first fire engine arrived *twenty minutes* after the crash. After evacuation, the dazed passengers just stood by the wreckage, waiting for help. Almost an hour later, a bus came out of the misty Indian dawn. The driver picked them up, took them on an aimless tour around the airport, and finally parked the bus some 50 feet away from the wreck which then exploded and burst into flames. Yet nobody was hurt from the blast or the heat. One of the passengers, an oral surgeon from London, told *The Times* that he had tried to help the injured, but in the first-aid room only cotton wool and headache pills could be found, and there was no medical staff on hand.

One wonders how many passengers were told – or if any of them tried to query – what kind of aircraft and whose crew would actually fly them. And was there nobody concerned when, having been told to read the emergency cards, the few available copies were only in Russian or Uzbek? They ought to have asked questions and demanded answers.

A CAA-sponsored study by the Applied Psychology Unit at the Cranfield Institute of Technology revealed that passengers tend to underestimate their chances of survival in aircraft accidents. They believe, wrongly, that there is no need to assume any responsibility for their own safety and escape. The airlines themselves could do more against people's complacency. Not all that long ago they used to cover emergency exits with pretty little curtains, and banned newspapers from distribution on board if there was an air accident headline, to spare passengers from any unnecessary fright. Now they are compelled to give safety instructions, but could impress us more seriously with the importance of those briefings. A captain told me that some cabin crews crack jokes to make people listen, and 'threaten' to conduct mock exams, offering prizes for a pass. Funny? Not at all. If nothing else works, a joke or the lure of a free brandy might grab passengers' attention.

Do-s

Do listen to safety briefings when flight attendants point out where the exits are, how safety belts and life-vests work, where emergency cards will be found, etc. Understandably, it often transpires how bored the crew become with their endlessly repeated lines. Recorded briefings on television screens may be more effective than live presentations: video culture has turned most people into watchers, not listeners, but the 'show' often appears to be less gravely serious than a few well-chosen words from the crew. (A screened shoot-out may be exciting, but deep down we know that it is not for real!) Many people, especially men, fail to listen, hoping to appear as cool, frequent travellers. Truly experienced fliers may indeed know more about the safety features, but without reminders they may forget them in an emergency.

Do ask questions if you do not understand something.

Do complain if you cannot see the screen or hear the words (e.g. at the rear of the cabin), and also if you feel that the briefing was not given properly. It is also helpful to complain about that after your flight to the airline or the authorities.

Do try to operate your seatbelt repeatedly. (Only in the 1970s, some carriers recommended their use 'for your comfort'. If that was true, fireside armchairs would have been manufactured with seatbelts. This euphemism was later revised to 'for comfort and safety', until finally 'comfort' was dropped altogether.) When an aircraft is hit by rough air, those who do not wear seatbelts may suffer injuries. You must obey the 'fasten seatbelts' sign every time, but when the sign is off and you are seated, it is best to keep the loosened belt buckled. Many injuries to cabin staff on the move, caused by unexpected turbulence, prove this point.

Do feel the location of your life-vest under the seat, and try to think through how you would use it. Tests have shown that most people understand how and when to inflate a vest, but do not know how to don one.

Do look at every detail on your emergency card: those little drawings may well be inadequate or even somewhat confusing and misleading but they will give you some idea of what to do in an emergency; for example, how to open exits.

Do learn how to adopt the brace position recommended by your airline. In America, three basically similar positions have FAA approval. In the rest of the world, there is a bewildering variety of recommendations. After lengthy research, the CAA wants a standard position to be introduced by all British carriers from April 1994. (For a detailed description, and a fuller discussion of the problem, see pages 228–9.) The main objective is to protect the head – a cushion or blanket atop may also help. In a survivable SAS crash-landing at Copenhagen, heavy objects falling from burst storage bins could have caused injuries if heads were above seatback height. Feet must rest on the floor. If you raise your knees to protect against forward motion, they may transmit the impact, fracturing your hips.

Do plan your escape. Don't just watch the cabin attendant's fingers pointing vaguely towards exits: look at those doors, and count the number of headrests between your seat and the *two* nearest exits. In thick smoke, you may not be able to see, but will be able to count your way out. The operation mechanism may differ from door to door so, following the emergency card, try to figure out how you would open them.

Do be prepared for unexpected difficulties with opening an overwing emergency hatch. Though many emergency cards show a woman lifting out that 'plug' with the greatest of ease, those doors are heavy, and must be thrown out, through the opening, and *not* deposited on a seat, usually occupied in any case, or dropped between seats where they would obstruct other people's egress.

Do pay attention to what is said about the use of oxygen masks: on some jets it is not enough to pull them to your face because they may need a gentle tug on a plastic tube to start the oxygen flow.

Do raise hell if you see that passengers are allowed to place large pieces of luggage in the aisles where they may create an obstacle course for an evacuation.

Do object if passengers are allowed to store bottles and other hard, heavy objects overhead. (Those storage bins are designed to hold soft items, such as coats, and they are liable to burst open, particularly in emergencies. That has caused numerous avoidable head injuries. (In 1991, the FAA admitted that such bins on some 1400 B737s and B757s, for instance, failed to meet the requirements. Boeing and other manufacturers are now designing stronger ones with better locks, but to improve existing bins to comparable standards may take 'many years', for refitting would require taking each aircraft out of service for some 200 hours.)

Do tell the crew if you see something unusual, or anything you may find worrying. Nobody else might have noticed it. Accident investigator Eddie Trimble says: 'Don't assume that the crew knew about it. Warn them, call the purser if necessary or even insist on telling the pilot. Don't be afraid of making a mistake – rather you than the pilot. In the Kegworth accident, several passengers and even cabin staff noticed that the smoke was coming from the allegedly healthy engine, yet everybody assumed that the pilot would know!'

Do try to stay calm in emergency situations, but do not be ashamed to run for dear life. Crews and aircraft are tested and certified for ninety-second evacuation, and that helps to make an amazing number of crashes survivable, but safe escape is often a matter of knowledge, and willingness to follow the crew's instructions. You are never further than 60 feet away from the nearest exit. Feeling panicky is not surprising, though survivors often claim that 'there was no panic', e.g. allegedly in the New Delhi crash. Those who do not scream or run may have frozen stiff from negative panic. (There were cases when people in such a condition refused to move and get through the open door, and the crew had to fight or push them. In Athens, a bunch of doctors stayed so calm and cool after a crash that they waited until everybody else was out and the aisle was completely clear, but before they could start to *walk,* fire broke out, preventing them from escaping.) A degree of controlled panic can, in fact, be beneficial; in tests, a cash bonus for the first passengers through the doors worked as a panic substitute to speed up evacuation.

Do lower your head as much as possible if there is smoke in the cabin, because smoke rises fast. Near ground level the air is cleaner, and you get a better view of the emergency lights along the floor. It is dangerous, however, to try crawling along the floor, because in a stampede you may not be able to get up.

Do leave the vicinity of the aircraft after an evacuation, for there is always the risk of delayed fire and explosion, but watch out for emergency traffic.

Do report if you discover on arrival that your luggage might have been pilfered, even if nothing or nothing of any value has been taken: in baggage areas, where thieves are free to operate, saboteurs may also have an opportunity to plant a bomb, and security should be told about it.

Don't-s

Don't pack valuables and dangerous goods (see Chapter 3) in your luggage.

Don't take knives, weapons (even toy guns), fireworks and other dangerous items on board.

Don't carry packages for other people or check in someone else's bags. (Best to leave your own gifts unwrapped, and your camera unloaded, for that makes it easier for security to check.)

Don't drink excessively or use drugs in flight. The effect can be unexpectedly strong. (If you get drunk before the flight you may not be allowed to board. If you are on a package tour, you could lose the entire cost of the holiday.) During a flight, drunkenness is illegal – in America, drunken and disorderly conduct may attract a $2000 fine and/or a prison sentence. Passengers often overload when going into or coming out of a dry country. They may be met by police on arrival. If the crew refuse to serve you with any more drinks, do not turn to your duty-frees.

Don't get into fights in flight. Most disorderly conduct cases are due to alcohol. (Three recent examples: a man flying from Aberdeen to Newcastle was arrested and charged with endangering the safety of the aircraft by brawling; after a drinking bout, two Canadian rugby teams played havoc on a flight to London – the women the worst offenders, with a mass scrummage and tackles in the aisles, mooning and clambering over seats, until the captain threatened to land and offload them at Newfoundland, and finally radioed ahead to Gatwick for a police escort for the pack; a Lufthansa jet had to make an emergency landing at Salonika after a drunken passenger fought the crew who tried to prevent him from opening a door in flight at 10,000 feet.

Don't panic if during a cabin decompression no oxygen mask appears: some aircraft of the former Soviet Union do not carry masks, only oxygen bottles. Even worse, aircraft flown by Azerbaijan Airlines may have 'seatbelts on/off' signs – but no seatbelts!

Don't smoke anywhere, particularly not in toilets, except when you are seated in a designated smoking area. (Many in-flight fires, including fatal ones, have started in toilets where addicts have sometimes covered the now compulsory smoke alarms with condoms.)

Don't use mobile phones and electronic equipment, including certain toys, without clearing them first with the crew. (At Geneva, in 1991, when a jet was only 50 feet from the ground during an automatic approach, the computerized controls initiated sudden banking. Due to that, the right-hand landing gear touched down first and dangerously hard on the runway. The malfunction had been caused by interference from a mobile phone a passenger had used despite a flight attendant's warnings. On a flight to Brussels, a child's radio-controlled toy interfered with the navigation computer, and the aircraft suffered a course deviation of ten degrees that could have taken it into the path of other air traffic.)

Don't jump out of your seat as soon as the flight has touched down. Many passengers refuse to believe that there is no time to gain: they would have to wait for their luggage in any case. On the other hand, unbuckling their seatbelts and standing up whilst the aircraft is still moving, to be first to gather up their belongings, might earn them quite serious injuries. Aircraft may sometimes have to make sharp turns or sudden stops when taxiing to the terminals. ('It might, in fact, help to reduce that lemming-style rush if airlines conducted disembarkation the way they board passengers – rows 1 to 30, etc. – in an orderly fashion,' suggests Roy Humphreyson, the editor of *Focus*, the magazine of Britain's Flight Safety Committee. 'Clear directions would also help the elderly and people with babies who may now have to wait to be the last out.'

Airlines and aviation authorities recognize that people need better, more attention-grabbing safety briefings, and greater awareness of how much they could do for themselves. When the American NTSB conducted a special study of Airline Passenger Safety Education, it discovered many mistakes and inconsistencies in the presentation of the legally required instructions – including faulty public address systems, and two airlines that told passengers 'Please refer to your safety cards' instead of giving verbal briefing. Most of its recommendations were followed, video presentation, where available, brought some standardization of quality, but the last thing airline managers want to do is call attention to danger in the product (implied by the word safety), and nobody has yet found a technique that would substantially improve the passengers' motivation to listen and pay attention.

In the early 1950s, it was still easy to give a meaningful briefing. There might have been no more than two dozen passengers on a flight, cabin staff would gather them in a small room before boarding, and tell them all they needed to know, mostly about the use of life-jackets because engines were less reliable and ditchings at sea could be expected. Besides, passengers could easily walk up to the cockpit where they would find four or five officers to talk to.

That kind of personal contact would, of course, be impossible on a Jumbo, but several safety specialists would like to see door mock-ups and life-vests made available in terminal areas, so that passengers could try them out before boarding. Some airline executives oppose the idea, saying that 'hands on experience would make it easier for madmen to try opening doors in flight.' A less nonsensical argument is that there are so many door variations that it would be impossible to crowd waiting rooms with all that paraphernalia. Aircraft manufacturers admit that, with mutual agreement, it would be possible to standardize the operation of exits. That would only apply to new designs, but perhaps it is time to start planning this at least for future aircraft. And there could be a useful temporary measure: these days check-in clerks and cabin crew ensure that seats adjoining overwing exits are allocated to able-bodied passengers – why not let them alone try out opening the cumbersome hatch, and appreciate its considerable weight?

One of the NTSB recommendations (advocated repeatedly by many people, including this author) never came to fruition. It suggested 'pre-landing safety announcements to re-inforce the pre-take-off briefings on the release of seatbelts, the location of exits, the location and operation of life preservers* (in the case of overwater landings)' and that passengers should be urged to study safety cards once again, prior to landing. 'Unfortunately, the FAA refused to make pre-landing safety announcements a legal requirement,' says Matt McCormick, Chief of the NTSB Survival Factors Division, and Gordon Bennett of *Cabin Crew 89* comments: 'This good idea will never be introduced without a regulation because the airlines will claim they would accept it only if all their competitors did the same simultaneously.' The airlines also argue that a repeat performance would be superfluous because if people paid attention in the first place, they would remember anyway. A few experiments gave some substance to that argument, but the observations concerned only the use of life-vests, and the memory span in the tests was limited to four hours. It appears to be extremely doubtful that at the end of a long flight – after eating, reading, watching films and sleeping intermittently – people would remember readily what they heard twelve or fourteen hours earlier . . . let alone the number of head-rests between their own seats and the nearest two exits.†

*The NTSB also recommended that cabin crew should demonstrate how to open the sealed protective pouch that contains the life-jacket.

†At the risk of appearing repetitious, some of these points are also reviewed, and expanded upon, in Chapter 26, which deals with some crucial aspects of survival in an accident.

ANSWERS TO THE QUIZ

1. *False*. Heavy objects may fly and cause injuries if the bin bursts open or if someone tries to take something out of it.

2. *True*. The nearness of an exit may soothe your nerves, but usability of a particular exit is never guaranteed. A torch may be useful if all lights fail in an emergency, and also after a night evacuation.

3. *False*. If you have any questions regarding safety or any observations (e.g. smoke inside or around the engines), *do* take a chance on making a fool of yourself or appearing to be a busybody, for if you are right, you may save the aircraft and the lives of all on board.

4. *False*. Do not get up, do not release your seatbelt, just pull the mask to your face – the pull will start the oxygen flow on most aircraft.

5. *False*. The mask must cover tightly your face *and* nose.

6. *False*. Your own mask has priority. If you lose consciousness, you cannot help the child.

7. *True*. The aircraft may be hit by unexpected turbulence, and seat-belts are a protection from potentially serious injuries.

8. *False*. In accidents/incidents, the movement of and damage to air-craft are unpredictable, because there are too many variables. (Some statistics that indicated added safety at the rear were based on a sample of older cases, too small in number to be significant.)

9. *False*. It is not permitted to smoke in toilets – indeed, anywhere except when seated in the 'smoking' section – under any circumstances.

10. *True*. If you suspect that there may be a fire, call a flight attendant right away. (Do not be afraid of erring on the side of caution!)

11. *True*. Overland flights may not carry life-vests or flotation cushions. (In America, the law does not require them if the aircraft is not meant to be more than fifty miles off shore.) The safety briefing will clarify that.

12. *True*. Flight attendants may be incapacitated, struggling to open doors, too busy to direct evacuation or their instructions may be lost in the noise. Stay as calm as possible, and try to make your own way out.

13. *False*. Do not waste time gathering any of your belongings. (People seem to be most reluctant to part with their duty-free bottles.) Carrying anything may impede your own and others' escape.

14. *False*. Leave through the nearest and most accessible safe exit.

15. *True*. Hopefully, you will have studied the instructions on the emergency card before take-off.

16. *False*. Some doors are operated automatically or manually; others, such as overwing exits, can be opened only manually. Even the direction in which a handle must be pulled or turned varies. The markings on the door could be a better guidance than the emergency cards which are often confusing. Nevertheless, studying the cards may save you valuable time.

17. *False.* Smoke rises fast, so it is best to keep your head as low as possible, and cover your nose and mouth, preferably with a wet cloth. In a hotel fire, escaping on all fours can be a good safety measure, but in a crowded aircraft anybody on the floor could be trampled on.

18. *True.* Any hesitation, trying to sit down on the edge of the door, wastes precious time. Slides can withstand the jump that will ensure fast, unimpeded descent. (High-heel shoes must be removed because they may damage the slide, but on the ground, if there is ice or fire, shoes will protect your feet.)

19. *False.* As post-crash fires and explosions are always a possibility, you should move away from the aircraft quickly, but try to stay in groups, and watch out for traffic.

15

Food for Thought

It will surprise no one, not even the airlines whose wrath I tempt, if I claim that eating in the air is more in the hope of passing the time than stumbling on culinary delights. Many of the passengers are not even hungry when it is feeding time in flight, particularly on a short-haul, yet when the trolleys begin to clatter, a hush of expectation spreads along the cabin. Toys and papers are cleared away, books are shut (even if the cliff begins to crumble in the hero's grasp), tables are folded down, and hostile glances greet the stewardess who pushes her starboard trolley faster than ours on portside – the dish in the *other aisle* always looks more appetizing. And let's not forget the gasps of disappointment when the jug of coffee or tea runs dry just at the row in front of us where the bastards are already on their dessert anyway!

Although people expect to be served plastic food, and claim that it tastes plastic (even when it does not), they consume with gusto whatever is put in front of them (it is free, after all), and eat with a concentration you hardly ever see in a restaurant for gourmets. If the quality is disappointing, the marketing and PR whizzkids of airline promotion have a lot to answer for: proposed dishes must pass muster by juries that taste the food but regard it as a top priority that the presentation *looks* appetizing and be photogenic enough for the brochures and advertisements. Once a dish in a given form is accepted, it must never vary one iota as long as it stays on the menu – imagine the murderous glances of envy if the guy in the next seat received an extra blade of haricot bean! (Nobody would, of course, bring up *that* fact: the bean in the bonnet of the injured party would translate into general complaints about 'bad service'.)

Unduly enhanced expectations apart, airline chefs must live with special problems beyond the usual limitations imposed by tight budgets and mass catering. When Bernard Gaume, the executive chef of the London Hyatt Carlton Tower, was asked to create menus for the United Arab Emirates Airline, he had to keep in mind that food in flight may not taste the same as in the kitchen. The difference 'is not only the effects

141

of altitude and the pressurized cabin,' he told *The Times* in February 1993. 'The food must be prepared in advance, then transported, then reheated or finished in flight. We try to find dishes whose flavour will improve with keeping.' Even though Emirates is not a dry carrier, and its wines are chosen with as much care as those served by its competitors, Gaume could not use any alcohol in his cooking, and had to substitute a lot of orange blossom water for Grand Marnier to avoid offending strictly religious Muslims. For the same reason, pork could not appear on the menu, and the use of beef was banned on flights to the home base.

Pâtés are out as they are liable to go off; green salads lose their crispy appearance in the pressurized cabin; lamb is fine for African and the Middle Eastern passengers, not for the Japanese; poultry is usually the safest bet.

'With the limited elbow-room in mind, the food we serve on aircraft must be easy to eat,' said József Csányi, catering director of Pannonia, the hotel chain that supplies MALÉV as well as other airlines on their return journeys from Budapest. 'Bones, not to mention potentially dangerous fish bones, must therefore be avoided. The serving dish determines the quantity, but it must be packed to show generosity. In my opinion, people in flight eat too much anyway, only to complain afterwards of flatulence. Traditional Hungarian dishes may be too heavy. Paprika sauces could be too spicy for the international palate, and might stain clothes if spilt.'

'It's hard to be creative without extra cost, keeping in mind that most of the air food is prepared thirty-four or forty-eight hours in advance,' said Hansueli Meili, General Manager of SWISSAIR's Inflight Product Planning, with a sigh. 'Then there are other considerations. Everybody wants to offer something unique and characteristically national, but *Rösti*, a Swiss speciality of boiled, peeled, grated and baked potato with pork, used to be too greasy. Now we serve it with minimal oil, in small quantities, with veal Zurich-style.

'In our country we used to have mostly vegetables, a lot of cabbage, with hardly any meat, and so there's no great Swiss kitchen. Our airline cooking had to be internationalized, mostly the French way, with Swiss chocolates and pâtisserie thrown in.' (Walking through the SWISSAIR 'candy-factory' the sweet air first induces an excruciating desire for chocolates, then baffles the visitors how those who work there could ever eat a bite of their product.) 'I mentioned vegetables. Even those can be a problem for aviation catering. Brussels sprouts, cauliflowers and pepperoni are not easily digestible, so we keep away from them as much as possible. For the same reason, I suggest that passengers should avoid eating a lot of onions or garlic before a long flight.'

Apart from national specialities, international airlines try to offer some dishes that are familiar to the natives in taste and presentation, for example Japanese ones on flights to and from Tokyo. They also cater for those who require special diets. Baby food, as well as vegetarian, properly stamped and sealed kosher, Muslim, Hindu, salt-free, low-fat, low-cholesterol, diabetic dishes, food only with milk products or strictly non-cow milk products, even ulcer-friendly meals, are served if ordered in advance, preferably at the time of booking a seat. Depending on the destination or origin of the flight, some of the more frequent of the unusual demands are readily complied with even at the last minute. But if you need something truly extraordinary, it is best to make advance enquiries – and you may get unexpected surprises, such as kosher meals served without any fuss by some Arab airlines.

In the early days of flying, an airship was four times the size of a Jumbo, and tried to imitate the grand style of ocean liners with wicker chairs, mahogany walls with mother-of-pearl inlay, and cabins with a sofa for afternoon naps. The chef on the *Hindenburg* had five cooks to prepare gourmet meals for the fifty-foot dining room. Aboard the flying boats nobody would have dreamt of serving food that had been heated up, and there was even a promenade deck from where the scenery could be enjoyed through binoculars.

When commercial air traffic began to grow, airlines served rolls, fried chicken and coffee from steam chests, and food in the air had the personal touch. 'Serving a meal was an art,' said Ivan March, a former Chief Steward. 'My training began in the BOAC directors' club. Only if they were satisfied with the service could I graduate to flying. Mind you, it was mostly first-class travel, with several overnight stops on long-haul. I'd take my passengers to their hotels, check out that their accommodation was comfortable, often spend the evening with them, taking them around, and collect them in the morning in time for the onward flight. I would plan their menu myself, order supplies, and ensure that we had sufficient quantities of fine glass, napkins, cutlery – silver service, that is – for two sittings. Frozen food was a novelty, with fruit salad being a favourite, and I would have to prepare and cook the food on board for my passengers.'

Such luxury, including March's noticeably frequent reference to '*my* passengers', would of course be unimaginable in these days of mass travel. Porcelain tableware and silver cutlery are retained, and the culinary finishing touches may still be added for those flying first class, but mass catering must be concentrated in the vast kitchens that match the planning and logistics of a Normandy invasion to ensure that every flight gets the right kind and quantity of food, everything from champagne to toothpicks, on time. The figures are quite staggering.

The new British Airways Catering Centre at Heathrow occupies a site that equals four soccer pitches. It can produce 29,000 meals a day. Its bakery can churn out 6,000 rolls an hour, the ice-making machines can satisfy the need for 15,000 pounds of ice a day, the cutlery sorting and wrapping machines can process 6,000 pieces an hour and wrap forty-two sets a minute. Just to take a few examples of the quantities involved: 7 million rolls, 130,000 kilograms of salmon, 500,000 kilograms of strawberries, 1.4 million litres of wine, and 28 million pieces of cutlery passed through the centre in 1992. United Airlines serves some 30 million meals a year. First-class passengers flying on various airlines out of Zurich alone swallowed 8500 kilograms of caviar in 1992.

Hygiene is of even higher priority in such kitchens than in those catering for the earth-bound – stomach complaints in the air could be more frightening – and SWISSAIR's five dishwashers, for instance, can handle 1.5 million items an hour. (The machines work round the clock, and gargle every day with 100,000 litres of demineralized water that leaves no stains and thus needs no drying.)

A Jumbo, with 380 passengers (a quarter of them in first and business class), would have ninety container trolleys, twenty hot-air ovens, ten coffee machines, 1000 headsets, 2000 plastic cups, and 200 sachets of artificial sweeteners, to mention but a few items on board. The bar would contain an infinite range of wines, beers, whisky, brandy, about a thousand miniature bottles of liqueur, a hundred litres of Coca-Cola, twice as much mineral water, and gallons of fruit juices. There are always a few meals to spare, in case some passengers ask for a second portion or there are late boarders. The pilots get the first-class menu, but must not eat identical meals in flight or within six hours beforehand, for there is always a faint risk of food poisoning. (For the same reason, no shellfish is served for them.)

The heating and service of meals is yet another operation planned and executed with military precision. On short-haul, the slightest hold-up could throw it into disarray, preventing the leisurely sale of duty-frees from which the crew get a commission.

Much of the food on board is thrown away, costly packaging and all, so Crossair, a Swiss regional carrier, now wants to capitalize on that wastage: because on short flights many passengers do not want a meal, those who are hungry will have a choice of dishes, decent plates and cutlery. It wants to be the first to offer everything fresh, even in economy – fresh orange juice, a variety of fresh bread, champagne truffles and pastries from a famous pâtisserie. As the head chef says: 'We intend to make the airline meal an attraction rather than an aggravation.'

And talking about aggravation, food on the ground must not be left unmentioned. Passengers often believe that everything is duty-free, hence cheap, at airports. Not so. Apart from expensive restaurants, one often finds only the quick-food variety at its worst, and in some countries you may have to pay a king's ransom for the privilege of passing the time while waiting for your flight. The prices can be particularly annoying when, after check-in for a return flight, and running already short in local currency, you are charged almost twice as much for an elderly sandwich at Malaga airport, for instance, as for a truly fresh *boccadillo* in

144

town. In Britain, the *Egon Ronay Ratings* for airport catering quality and service act as a public guardian. The guide's comments can be devastating, and usually lead to urgent improvements. In 1993 it gave the top Heathrow rating to The Granary in Terminal 3. Regarding some other establishments, it did not refrain from comments such as 'the cappuccino contravened the Trade Description Act: it was a sludge-like liquid resembling the Thames estuary' or demanding that a 'leaden quiche with grotesquely thick pastry' should be removed from sale.

Overall airlines do their best, within the constraints of eternal cost-cutting, to feed us well at 30,000 feet, and if the braised escalope of beef with peas tastes a little like the veal in some non-descript sauce with a fanciful name (and more peas) on a previous flight, blame the blandness of it all on the demands of the international palate rather than the lack of trying.

16

How the Other Half Flies

In the early days of mobile communications, Lou Grade, the not-yet-knighted television mogul, was reputedly among the first to install a telephone in his car. Sydney Bernstein, also a commoner at the time, was quick to follow suit, and under the pretext of having something urgent to say, dialled his great rival, Rolls-Royce to Rolls-Royce, just to let him know that he was not the only one who could talk on the move. But Grade was still a step ahead: it was his chauffeur who answered the call, asking Bernstein to hold because the boss was *on the other line*.

True or false, the anecdote comes from the lower echelons of keeping up with the Joneses. Had the two illustrious gentlemen been flying, neither would have qualified for genuinely exclusive treatment: the sky is not the limit of upmanship – that is where it truly begins.

Many people see themselves as *very important persons*, and expect VIP status that spares them from queuing with the hoi-polloi at the check-in desk, opens the door to VIP lounges that proliferate at airports everywhere, allows them to board at their leisure, stretch out in armchair seats with free drinks in hand before gourmet meals, and then work or fall asleep in comfort. They are regarded, however, by those in the know as mere CIPs, *commercially important persons*, to be humoured and resisted discreetly if they try to sweep through customs and immigration without stopping. Pop stars may enjoy an airline's private lounges and special facilities, but they tend to feel offended when the difference between a VIP and a CIP is explained to them. When, prior to achieving a certain notoriety, the Duchess of York arrived at London aboard an ordinary Jumbo, some fellow first-class passengers failed to recognize her and understand why she could walk straight into a waiting limousine, without going through the normal channels.

You and your entourage may fly into Heathrow, for instance, with your private, custom-built jet, yet you will not even set sight on the three real VIP suites that are tucked away in unmarked buildings on airside. Not that there is anything special about these lounges. They are more spacious but no more comfortable than the increasingly plush ones provided, with full communication facilities, by airlines for CIPs. Their blue-grey armchairs and sofas, with plenty of stylish scatter cushions, coffee tables and a sprinkling of palms, spread out under modern, rather non-descript paintings, might have come from any hotel room of a reasonable standard. But being used briefly by no more than 3000 people a year, they offer the *penultimate* status symbol: it is the treatment you get there that makes you special. To qualify, you must be on the list compiled by the Foreign Office. On arrival, as you descend from your aircraft, a limousine is waiting at the foot of the stairs to run you to a VIP suite, often no more than a hundred yards away. Your passport is then collected by an official who takes it for immigration clearance, while you read the papers and have some coffee and biscuits – no free drinks as in the airlines' CIP lounges. Meanwhile, a Skycap identifies and collects your luggage in the baggage hall, and puts it in your car. Occasionally, customs officers may visit you in the VIP suite. It is a case of the mountains coming to Mohammed. If the government in its wisdom deems it is necessary to get a bottle of champagne opened for you, it must pay for the extra cost.

The *ultimate* status symbol is the use of the Queen's own royal suite, reserved for royalty and visiting heads of state. A grey, bullet- and bomb-proof bungalow, with a small pyramid adorning its roof, it is situated in a secure area of the airport. The jets can drive right up to about 30 feet from the door. Embedded in the tarmac, leading from the parking spot to the entrance, there are small metal hooks: they hold the red carpet in place when it is laid out. With its modern furnishing, the suite is more a press facility than a show-piece to be opened to the public.

At the Northolt Royal Air Force base, used by British ministers, and occasionally the royal family, the 'VIP lounge' is a glorified Nissen hut. Tight security and complete privacy compensate for the lack of refinements.

In terms of private-transport creature-comfort, the Queen travels mostly in the relative modesty of converted RAF aircraft. Her own quarters, with two dressing rooms, occupy about a third of the cabin. (Her massive, leather-clad steel wardrobes and chests of drawers can be wheeled on and off the plane. She is usually surrounded by familiar items that reduce the stress on long trips – crates of Malvern water to eliminate the risk of tummy upset abroad, favourites like pork sausages from Harrods and Oxford marmalade, Earl Grey teabags, a hot water bottle, cutlery and decanters with the royal cipher, and, allegedly, a white kid-leather lavatory seat cover that must be the most-travelled personal belonging in the world.) The red-carpeted lounge and dining room areas – originally the first-class section – is where the Queen receives her briefings, the correct, knowledgeable questions to ask, and the introduction to photographs of people she will have to 'recognize and remember readily' from previous meetings. Ladies-in-waiting, equerries, secretaries, cooks, maids and the rest of the entourage travel at the back of the aircraft.

US Presidents come, US Presidents go, but the two aircraft used by them are always known as *Air Force 1* and *Air Force 2*. After thirty years of service, the two B707-320s have now been replaced by specially modified B747-200s. The 4000 square feet of floor space of each Flying Oval Office contains living quarters for the President and the First Lady, conference and dining room, offices and sitting areas for the staff, full medical emergency facilities (an office can be converted into an operating theatre), two galleys that can feed a hundred people, interior stairways into the hull below that stores mission-related paraphernalia and food for 2000 meals, and a vast amount of normal and secure communications equipment (238 miles of wiring, more than twice the length of that in an ordinary Jumbo, eighty-five telephones and multi-frequency radios for air-to-air and air-to-ground satellite transmissions). With their own power supply, Air Force 1 and 2 can be self-sufficient anywhere in the world, and the aerial refuelling facility gives them a virtually unlimited range. (At the height of the cold war, they were designed to stay aloft, serving as a command centre, for the duration of a nuclear war.) They are always fuelled by JP1, which is safer and less flammable than JP4, with which commercial fleets fill their tanks. Airlines ignore the advantage of JP1, using 'cost and availability' as their excuse.

Arab rulers, and numerous oil-sheikhs, specify throne rooms, and plenty of gold fittings, when ordering their private jets. One of them, whose identity is withheld by the manufacturer, has a mini-mosque with a revolving prayer platform that is governed by a compass to face Mecca at all times, whatever the direction of the flight. King Khaled of Saudi Arabia used to have a direct line from his Jumbo's medical section to a specialist hospital in Cleveland, Ohio.

President Clinton's $200 haircut, that was reported to have held up Los Angeles air traffic for hours, was a rather pedestrian show of privilege compared to that of Carlos Menem, the Argentine President, an eager patron of Ferrari salesmen and cosmetic surgeons, who used a special credit from the World Bank for his B757 – to be known henceforth as *Tango 1*. He might have been tempted to call the aircraft *Hair Force 1* because the $66 million cost included the installation of working and living quarters as well as a hairdressing salon where his two barbers, each on a monthly retainer of $4000, can attend daily to his 48,000-piece hair transplant (*The Sunday Times*, 6.12.1992).

Michael Jackson's jet has everything from state rooms to showers, but anybody would find it hard to match *Playboy* emperor Hugh Hefner's flying mansion of the 1970s. His black *Big Bunny*, a stretched DC9, had handcrafted rosewood panelling, a disco and a dance floor in 'caves'. His huge elliptical bed, complete with bedbelts for turbulent weather, had master controls for all entertainment facilities, which included a Cinemascope screen. The seven stewardesses were, of course, Jet Bunnies in black uniforms of skin-tight, shiny nylon, white scarves and thigh-length boots.

Descending further down in status, appropriately converted though elderly B707s are advertised as 'executive, head-of-state aircraft' for lease or sale. (Leasing, presumably, would suit rulers who enjoy limited prospects, and could be more economical than frequent hiring of luxury planes. Big spender Jacques Attali forked out £22,000 from the funds of the European Bank for Reconstruction and Development for his flights – £600,000 on private air transport in a single year.)

Some 16,000 airborne boardrooms, turbine-powered aircraft, including 200 big jets from Airbuses to a DC10, fly corporate flags all over the world. Their prices range from tens of thousands for a second-hand few-seater to millions of dollars. A second-hand BAe125-800 – like the one Gerald Ronson, the tycoon now reviving his fortunes after a stretch in jail, is trying to sell – may fetch £5 million.

THE COMPETITION TO ATTRACT CIPS

is unremitting because their seats are the most profitable part, in fact the *lifeline*, of air carriers. Cabin crew get an extra week's training before they are allowed near first class, yet many of them claim that 'our most beloved and most pampered passengers have more money than sense, and even what they spend isn't theirs, because you hardly ever meet one who pays for the privilege with his own money. No wonder they want Johnny Walker *blue label* at eighty quid a bottle.'

In 1992, £8.8 billion was spent on air tickets – more than a billion less than three years earlier, due to recession, better communications, less travelling, and fare cuts. In the same year, the upper crust spent some 20 per cent less because many companies switched from first to business or from business to economy seats for their staff. A first-class ticket may cost anything from three to ten times more than economy. (The cost difference is the same whatever gimmicks and euphemisms the airlines dream up to entice customers and avoid offending those who cannot afford anything but the lowest fare.) British companies spend some £18 billion a year on business travel and related expenses such as hotels, meals, entertainment and car-hire. While more than a third of British directors are entitled to first-class tickets, only a fifth of their French colleagues enjoy that privilege. The Brits also outnumber the Germans three to two in executive-class entitlement.

Despite staggering losses by the airlines, there is plenty of room for fare-slashing because of the numerous discrepancies in the cost of business travel. Some tickets are offered at give-away rates to undercut competitors, others may be a brazen rip-off: why does a London–Oslo cost half as much as Paris–Oslo? Or why do they charge the London businessman as much for flying to Brussels as to Dusseldorf, which is further away?

Silver, gold, diamond or royal club memberships and various 'frequent flier' bonus schemes, offering free tickets and upgrade vouchers for proven loyalty or a complimentary seat for the companion of a first-class passenger, are a thinly veiled form of cut-throat competitiveness. Inspiring loyalty is said to be the key to airline profitability because the cost of grabbing a customer from another airline may be as high as 90 per cent of the profit on an existing one. Yet the schemes can be almost suicidal. They were blamed partly for the collapse of PanAm. In the United States, where the idea of bonuses was hatched, half the passengers pay nothing on many flights. American Airlines have 20 million AAdvantage members. If you fly with United from London to San Francisco, you may get a free European flight with British Midland to a city as far as Paris or Amsterdam. When BA introduced Air Miles in 1988, 391 collectors took advantage of it during the first year. By 1992–1993 some 6000 people travelled free with Air Miles each week. In addition to free flights, Virgin throws in prizes – hot air balloon trips or free golf tuition. The schemes not only separate chairmen of multinationals from 'granny visiting the family once in a blue moon', but also induce high-fliers to demand that their companies book seats, irrespective of cost, on the airlines whose points they collect for private use.

The industry was howling with judicious uproar when in 1993 British Midland cut its business-class fares quite radically – offering its newly invented Diamond Euro-Class, better seats in a segregated area for the price of economy tickets – yet within days, others copied the idea. The thought behind British Midland's move was ingenious for it recognized the greatest lure to the most lucrative passenger: extra *status* (no airline would risk upgrading a passenger of uncouth appearance) and *comfort*.

Top status comes with flying on Concorde. Supersonic crossing of the Atlantic costs £4220, whereas the cheapest APEX ticket is about £240, the standard scheduled fare about £400, business class more than five times that, and first class £3800. What extra spending buys in comfort, i.e. arrival in better shape, is considerable. (Seats on Concorde are more cramped than in first class, but if you leave London at 10 a.m., you arrive in New York at 9 a.m.) On long-haul, in first class, you get up to 62 inches of legroom, with seats that are 20 or 22 inches wide (28 on All Nippon), and recline up to 60 degrees. BA has now introduced heavily advertised sleeper seats – while you sip your hot chocolate, and change into freebie cotton pyjamas in the lavatory, the crew convert your seat into a bed with crisp cotton sheets, proper pillows, a duvet, earplugs and a sleep mask.

As only a limited number of people travel first class, 'service with a smile is no longer enough: knowledge of the individuals and their characteristics is essential,' Martin Tyler Bennett, general manager of the International Customer Loyalty Programmes, told *The Times* in April 1993. *Good morning, Mr Smith* and *How are you today, Herr Schmidt* feed the egos more than the choice of delicacies and free drinks, that are, of course, just basic frills that come with pricey seats, but it is a sign of the times that more and more airlines have calorie-coded meals and health diets on the menu.

Wooing with competitive perks begins and ends on the ground. Free car parking, chauffeur-driven limousine service, free or cut-price hotel accommodation, accelerated check-in facilities, express retrieval and free delivery of baggage to your hotel, luxury lounges with the use of showers, computers, fax and Telex communications, the loan of portable telephones or free phone cards, even priority service in duty-free shops, are just a few of the temptations. (Fast Track check-in at Gatwick ran into trouble: airlines are reluctant to foot the bill for an extra 50 pence per classy passenger – £250,000 a year – for they are afraid that in peak seasons ordinary holiday-makers will swamp the route of the privileged.)

In the air, individual TV sets with multi-channel videos and mementos are now standard. Apart from the neat bags of comfort goodies (anything from cosmetics, toiletries, shoe-horns and slippers to BA's new aromatheraphy products against dry, itchy skin) the value of gifts is no longer limited by international agreements. In search of something unique – what rich executive would want another watch or gold pen? – SWISSAIR, for instance, gives away otherwise unobtainable CDs for which they commission special performances. Some perks on offer are not very imaginative or clever. SkyClub, the business class of MALÉV, flaunts a not exactly unique service of 'refreshing, warm napkins before meals'. Emirates Airline advertises that 'every passenger gets the best seat in the house' – just imagine the ensuing battle for it if there was 'a best seat' aboard. (Or do they mean the best *remaining* seat?)

What a pity that airlines cannot go the whole hog and follow the example of the Spanish hotelier who, so the story goes, found the ultimate answer to it all. He added showers to every room. When his neighbour, his greatest competitor, not only did the same but also built a new bar, he copied the idea *and* put TV sets in the rooms. Moves and countermoves followed until his competitor built a swimming pool – something for which the hotelier had no room in his garden. So he began to advertise his hotel as being complete with showers, bars, TV sets, sea-views, balconies, travel bureau . . . and a swimming pool next door.

Worldwide communication facilities are both a threat and a bonus to business travel. While fax and the availability of conference calls substitute some face-to-face meetings, save costs, time and fatigue, thus reducing the need to fly, the possibility of staying in touch at all times in flight removes the strain of not knowing for several hours what goes on in the markets, the boardroom and the world in general. Electronic companies now fight for a share in the approaching in-flight-communications bonanza, worth about £2 billion.

The first telephone call by a passenger from an airliner was made in 1984. The system spread fast, first of all in America. Currently, a million such calls are made every month using a network of ground stations. In 1991, Singapore Airlines was the first to introduce a satellite-based telephone service. With the help of satellites, passengers on most international airlines will be able not only to make but also receive calls from the ground and other aircraft by 1994. First-class seats will, of course, have individual phones built in. (The cost is not thought to be prohibitive: a two-dollar connection fee and two dollars per minute are charged if the call is made from a flight over the continental United States. A call via satellite costs about five times more.) Data services, now available to airlines, will also be extended to passenger use. The flying office is going to be offered as the ultimate perk, but many executives are not entirely pleased with the idea: it is good if everybody believes that the boss never stops working on his laptop, but even better if, discreetly, he can rest and enjoy the isolation from the ringing of telephones and the buzz of fax machines.

The use of laptop computers, one of the great status symbols in flight, has now been banned by many airlines during take-off and landing, because they may interfere with the controls and navigation of the aircraft. Although there is no hard evidence for the risk, the use of high-energy devices, including personal stereos, CD players and personal organizers, may be banned at all times except during the cruise phase.

However ingenious the perks may be, what flying executives continue to value most is *punctuality*. In this respect, SWISSAIR, British Airways, SAS, Singapore Airlines and Lufthansa were voted the best, in that order, by readers of the *Business Traveller* magazine in 1992. (Alitalia, Iberia, TWA, Air India and Garuda were found to be the worst.) BA came first for 'best airline overall', Virgin for 'best business class' and American Airlines for 'best airline in North America'.

The passenger–crew ratio is also important to those who demand good service, but few if any could hope to get the amount of attention Joan Crawford received from Chief Steward Ivan March some forty years ago. The film star, then married to the chief of Pepsi Cola, had two seats reserved on a Bermuda to New York flight: 'The second seat was for her Pepsi ice-box. Thinking that she liked Pepsi, I offered her one from the trolley, but she just opened her own box that contained four bottles of gin, a bottle of dry Vermouth, loads of ice, a silver goblet for mixing, and her own glass. "Now, my dear boy, have you any fresh lemons? Good. Choose a big one. Peel the zest, and that's all I want from you. I'll then show you, step by step, how to mix my dry Martini with the merest hint of Vermouth, how to stir it, gently, gently, and how to pour it lovingly. Every time you come by, you just mix me one exactly like that." I must add, she never got through her supplies, and although I passed by frequently, the drinks had no visible effect on her.'

17

What If . . . ?

It helps to be prepared for the unexpected – eventualities that may be anything from the bizarre and outright ridiculous, to the dangerous, such as being involved in a skyjacking.

What if your bulk hardly fits into a seat, and the seatbelt cannot embrace your girth? It may happen even if you are not a sumo wrestler, so airlines are prepared for it, and can provide an extension belt. (If it is a struggle to leave your seat, beware when using a toilet. A huge West African woman once got stuck in the lavatory, pressed the emergency button for help, but could not reach far enough to unlock the door, which then had to be unhinged and removed from the outside. She was still so firmly wedged in her seat that attendants had to extract her like a cork from a bottle.)

What if there is a sudden loss of pressure? In a severe case, there may be loud, startling noises as air leaves the cabin with the speed of sound; dense fogging may occur due to moisture condensation that would be cleared by an onrush of wind that makes loose articles fly; there will be an extreme drop in temperature; a feeling of chest expansion will be followed by forced exhalation; pain may be experienced in the ears and the abdomen, accompanied by a release of abdominal wind. Despite such worrying events, there is no need to panic, but as mentioned earlier you must act instantly. In a sudden decompression, never try to hold your breath: this could damage your lungs. Put on your oxygen mask without any delay, because you will soon be unable to do so unless help is available. Prolonged hypoxia can cause brain damage. (If you relish tit-bits of not-many-people-know-that information, you may like to note that full pressurization may add a ton to the weight of a Jumbo.)

What if you fly into a thunderstorm? You will end up with an exciting tale to dine out on. With the help of weather watchers and radar, pilots these days circumnavigate or fly above storms that can give a very uncomfortable ride. (It is not true that jets always fly above the weather – storms can be encountered even up to a height of 45,000 feet.) The bumps, the noise and blinding lights can be frightening, but the seatbelts and the strength of the structure will protect you. If lightning strikes, a flash may seem to run through the cabin, but the electrically bonded surfaces of the aircraft, and the wicks on the wings and the tail, will dissipate the electrical charge. The experience will be safe rather than enjoyable.

What if you have a bout of motion sickness? Best known as air sickness, it is related to an over-stimulation of the sensory perceptors, worsened by the fear of feeling sick. However this is becoming so unusual in modern passenger transport that, as I mentioned earlier, airlines rarely need to replace sick-bags – except when they have been used for rubbish disposal. The condition could be caused by a combination of turbulence, travel excitement and anxiety. The most likely sufferers are those who also tend to feel sick in cars. Fatty foods, too much alcohol and smoking could trigger an attack, and a bumpy ride may upset the balancing mechanism of the inner ear. The symptoms begin with feeling unwell, nauseous, and hot even though the skin remains cool and moist, and culminate in rather painful vomiting. The best thing to do is loosen your clothes, recline your seat, keep your head still, apply a cool cloth to your forehead, seek some reassurance against your worries, and *do not resist vomiting* which will usually bring some relief. If much of the flight is still ahead of you, let the cabin attendants give you a seat where the movement of the aircraft is less noticeable. Air sickness drugs have side-effects, so ask your doctor before flying – particularly if you are pregnant. If you are given such a pill during the flight, and it fails to produce the expected result, *do not demand a second dose.*

What if you (or somebody near you) suffer moderate to severe chest pain radiating, possibly, down your left arm and fingers? Yes, it could be a heart attack. Call an attendant immediately. You will be given oxygen, helped to loosen your clothes (particularly at the waist and the neck), and placed in a relaxed, reclining position. The assistance of a doctor will be sought if there is one on board. If the attack seems serious and it is possible, the pilot will divert the flight to the nearest airport, and radio for an ambulance to wait for you.

What if you suffer hyperventilation (emotional overbreathing)? In most cases, it will be due to fears and anxiety, rather than a lack of oxygen. Reassurance, and breathing in and out of a paper bag or an empty oxygen mask (it restores the carbon monoxide content in the blood to normal level), will help to stop the symptoms.

What if you find yourself grounded at an airport you never intended to visit? The airline will sort out the problem that may be technical or due to pilot error (landing at the wrong spot) or brought about by news of a sudden outbreak of hostilities in the airspace ahead. If necessary, the airline will try to find another flight for you with minimum delay, because otherwise it must pay for your food and accommodation. If the reason for the unwanted stop-over is something quite outlandish, passengers may be able to help themselves: in April 1990, a Paraguayan Airlines flight to Brussels was scheduled to refuel at Dakar; the pilot mistook Conakry for Dakar, landing in Guinea instead of Senegal, where suspicious airport officials refused to accept the airline's credit card for buying fuel. The passengers were about to pass around the hat, when one of them produced $7000 in cash as a loan to the pilot.

What if you have a sudden urge to make love at 30,000 feet and qualify for membership of the notional Five-Mile-High Club? It may well sound crazy, but there are plenty of precedents. On the old Strato-cruisers, where bunks could be rented, the crew could judge what was going on from the number of early cups of tea ordered for a bunk. In the 1960s, no jet-setter worth the name would fail to lay claim to five-mile-high sex. Air crews reputedly enjoy the experience, but several of them told me that usually they are too tired to indulge in it. If you find the temptation irresistible, long flights with half-empty cabins are the ideal setting, especially when the lights are dimmed to let people sleep or when everybody is busy watching the movie, and most of the cabin crew take a rest. But beware: if caught, the captain has the right to report you to the police and charge you with indecent behaviour likely to cause a public outrage – though it is debatable what will or will not outrage your public. (In 1992, a young couple experienced eighty-mile-fast sex on a train from Margate to London. The girl went to the toilet, and returned carrying her jeans and wearing only her knickers. She sat on the man's lap, and they had intercourse in full view of the crowded compartment. Nobody raised any objections to the spectacle. Not until they lit a post-coital cigarette. Then hell broke loose because it was a non-smoking carriage. A guard, summoned by the indignant passengers, radioed Victoria station where police arrested the couple. They pleaded guilty to committing an indecent act, and the Horseferry Road magistrate imposed a fine of £50 each plus £25 costs – their admitted smoking in a non-smoking compart-ment weighing heavily against them.)

What if you notice a fellow passenger's rather abnormal behaviour? The person may be quietly nutty, cause commotion, upset others, initiate violence or act peculiarly, embracing hand-luggage at all times. In case the crew have failed to spot it, it is best to call it to their attention.

Odd behaviour may be due to drink or nervousness or some unstable personality trait aggravated by fear of flying and claustrophobia. The crew may try to pacify the wrong-doer, and the captain has the right to discipline, even restrain, anyone who jeopardizes good order in the cabin, but as a handbook for pilots says, 'Bear in mind that a person behaving abnormally could be an intended hijacker or an intended suicide carrying explosives in his luggage.'*

SKYJACKING

Like the fashionable length of skirts, the fads of terrorism come in waves. Pictures of a big jet standing, exploding, burning in the desert, are etched indelibly in everybody's memory. In a single year to the summer of 1978, more than 2000 people suffered, if not died, at the hands of murderous skyjackers. That particular wave produced so many examples that certain peculiar trends became discernible – in Europe, the United States and South America, Friday was the most popular day for air piracy, in Africa and Australasia, Wednesdays were the most dangerous, and people travelling on those days were advised to go to the lavatory before or just after starting a long flight, because the terrorists, who were likely to strike within the first hour, might not allow anyone to move about in the cabin for a long time.

Do not be misled by the fact that these days skyjacking figures in the headlines only infrequently. The threat is alive and thriving wherever there is political conflict, oppression, and real or imaginary hope for extracting cash or concessions by this variety of blackmail. In the investigation of such cases, aircrash detectives could turn to Rudyard Kipling for guidance:

> I keep six honest serving-men
> (They taught me all I knew);
> Their names are What and Why and When
> and How and Where and Who
>
> *(Just So Stories – The Elephant's Child)*

Looking at the threat of air piracy, the *What* is the crime itself, *When?* Mostly in quick succession of each other by way of copy-catting. *Who?* It could be a single terrorist, a political ring, a madman or a criminal chasing a dream of untold riches through extortion. And let us not leave out the person trying to escape political persecution in this way – hoping to win sympathy and deserving of compassion, but endangering, nevertheless, the lives of a planeload of passengers. The fact that the bomb with which they make the threat is sometimes non-existent does not

---

Fit To Fly, A Medical Handbook for Pilots, compiled by the BALPA Medical Study Group, and published by BSP Professional Books.

reduce either the gravity of the crime nor the risk it creates. Here are some recent examples.

Flights from China were hit by a classic series of copy-cat skyjacking by would-be refugees of allegedly political motivation. In 1988, two men with pistols and a fake grenade diverted a B737, and gave themselves up in Taiwan, where they received a mere three years' jail sentence. In 1989, after a pro-democracy demonstration, a man pretended to have a bomb, and forced a New York-bound Jumbo to land in Japan. He was extradited and sentenced to eight years' imprisonment. In 1990, a Chinese regional flight of Xiamen Airways was ordered to divert from its destination in Canton, to Taiwan. Pilots are under orders to comply with the gunmen's instructions for the sake of their passengers' safety, but the Chinese captain tried to play a trick: hoping that people would not recognize airports from the air, he was about to land at Guangzhou, as originally intended, when the skyjacker realized what had happened, and detonated a bomb or a grenade. The B737 crashed on to a B757 which was on 'hold' near the runway, and large parts of the wreckage also hit an empty B707 in a parking area – 127 people were killed outright, sixty were seriously injured.

In 1991–1992, Ethiopian Airlines suffered an outbreak of skyjackings, mostly by former members of the deposed president's security forces. In one such case, they allowed most of their hostages to go free at a refuelling stop, but created havoc in air traffic over three Middle Eastern countries until they surrendered, with their weapons, in Rome, asking for political asylum. In the same year, after the breakdown of the Middle East peace talks because of the mass-expulsion of Palestinians by Israel, the world braced itself for yet another spate of skyjackings. Due to tight security – and, presumably, some sensible recognition that terrorism is ineffectual – it did not materialize, but the risk of a recurrence of the 1970s is still on the cards.

Skyjacking from Cuba is a fairly regular event for political reasons, and the United States refrains from harsh sentencing – also for political reasons. In 1992, one of the pilots himself, supported by his family, most of the cabin crew and all the passengers (48 out of the 53 people on board), overpowered and tied up the co-pilot, knocked out the armed security agent with a rug soaked in ether, and landed in Miami, where émigrés celebrated their arrival. Two months later – in the wake of President Clinton's call to halt the exodus of refugees from Haiti, and threats to renege on his campaign pledge of easing restrictions on political asylum – a Haitian soldier with a gun took a woman hostage on the ground, marched her on to a DC3, fired a shot that holed the roof to demonstrate that he meant business, and forced the pilot to fly the damaged aircraft to Miami.

Barely three months earlier, long after the end of the Vietnam war, Ly Tong, a former South Vietnamese fighter pilot, vented the fifteen-year grudge he bore against the new regime. He had once been shot down by a Soviet missile and tortured for five years in 're-education' camps from where he made a daring escape. Having walked, swum, cycled through the jungles of three countries, he eventually reached America. President Reagan congratulated him, and granted him US citizenship. He studied for an MA in New Orleans, but nurtured his thoughts of revenge. In 1992, he boarded a Vietnam Airlines Airbus in Bangkok and by grabbing a stewardess hijacked it with its 152 passengers. He wrapped some wire round her neck, and threatened her with a steel knife from his in-flight meal tray. (Airlines do not regard cutlery as a potential weapon.) Forcing his victim on to the flight deck, he ordered the pilot to make five dangerously low passes over Ho Chi Minh City (formerly Saigon). Passengers were on their knees, praying, when the captain just managed to pull the aircraft out of a stall. Ly Tong sprinkled the city with political leaflets, then opened a window in the cockpit, and jumped out with a cheap parachute he had bought in Bangkok. Five hours later he was captured. Disaster had been averted only by superb airmanship. Bangkok security, that claims 100 per cent efficiency, failed to spot the suspicious item in his hand luggage, but admittedly almost anything can be a weapon – the means of *How* – in the hands of the determined skyjacker, because once the threat is made, nobody would risk taking a closer look.

Apart from real guns and explosives, swords, an axe, toy weapons, razor blades, large nails, a bottle of hairspray containing (allegedly) nitric acid, scissors, a scout knife, a can opener, and petrol in babies' feeding bottles have been used for air piracy. When two Burmese captured a Thai Airways A300 on a flight from Bangkok to Rangoon, and forced it to land in Calcutta, the 'weapon' was a ceramic doll with a switch dangling from a wire – the effective threat was that any resistance by the captain would be countered by pressing the switch of the 'bomb'.

It is, perhaps, understandable that a doll could pass through X-ray machines, but how do Frankfurt security men explain an Ethiopian student smuggling a starter pistol with blanks, hidden in a cowboy hat, aboard a Lufthansa Airbus? He ordered the pilots to fly him to New York instead of Addis Ababa, asked for political asylum for himself and his family who were still in Africa, and demanded that America should intervene in the conflict in – Bosnia! At Kennedy airport, he gave up his gun without a struggle, but several passengers suffered lasting emotional trauma from their ordeal.

Special army and police anti-terrorist units everywhere are trained to negotiate the release of hostages and, as a last resort, storm a hijacked aircraft, but foolishly hasty acts can have disastrous consequences. In 1986, when Pakistani negotiators failed to achieve quick results with those who were holding a PanAm Jumbo to ransom in Karachi, a sharp-shooter tried to kill the leader of the hijackers while he was in the cockpit. Obviously, the trigger-happy man or his superiors knew nothing about the necessary velocity of the bullet to penetrate an aircraft windscreen which was only 'starred' – and the terrorists responded with the massacre of twenty-two passengers on board.

Whatever the motivation of skyjackers, precautions alone cannot stop air piracy (and sabotage) – not without putting an end to the kind of treatment the Korean government dished out to the glamorous mass murderer mentioned in the earlier chapter on security. So . . .

What if you find yourself a hostage of air piracy? Apart from trusting the sensibility of the well-prepared pilot, the negotiators and anti-terrorist squads, what can you do for yourself? The answer must be: very little. In fact, the less you try to do the better. Obey orders, never try any heroics, keep a low profile, avoid eye contact with your captors. If for any reason you are picked on, try to stay cool without being provocative, do not argue, but do not cringe: any survivor of the Soviet Gulags will tell you that the one who trembles most will get beaten first and most regularly. Co-operate, expect some physical deprivation – such as cramp, hunger, heat, the discomfort of not being allowed to go to the toilet – try to occupy your mind with something else, and never make sudden arm movements if you try to do some invisible exercise. Do not make demands – even polite requests for food or fresh air in a hot cabin can be a hazard: skyjackers watch out for potential leaders in the crowd, and if they want to set an example, it is the too loud, too meek, and the menacing-looking body-builder they tend to go for. If the aircraft is stormed with tear-gas, stun grenades or gun fire, throw yourself on the floor and lie low. Be ready for the trauma that may follow, and seek counselling.

What if you find unattended luggage on board? This question arose when a man joined a Jakarta–London flight in Bangkok, placed his bag on the floor, and disappeared. A reader of *Flight International* in the adjoining seat, as well as some others, grew uneasy when twenty minutes later the doors closed, with the owner of the bag still missing. A stewardess was warned, but her English was 'insufficient to appreciate our concern' (letter in the magazine, 1.12.1993). A more senior member of the crew remained similarly unimpressed, though by then the engines were started up. Should passengers create a scene, demand to see the captain, and cause a long delay – perhaps unnecessarily? They chose not to, but searched the bag, trusting their inexperienced eyes to spot whatever might be suspicious. Fortunately, they saw no bomb, the flight was uneventful – and the missing passenger was found later, fast asleep in another seat. No question about it: they were right to make a fuss, and should have insisted on informing the captain.

18

Your Health in the Air

Is it a boy or a girl? Do you need to notify my mother? Is it healthy? Red hair — what will my husband say? Obstetricians have heard it all. But few of them could match the American flight attendant's astonishment at the young mother's first question: 'Will it be entitled to American citizenship?'

The passengers' wild applause shook the US registered aircraft when the captain announced the successful delivery of a baby some 30,000 feet above the Bay of Bengal, but the Indian mother's anxious enquiry revealed that the 'sudden early birth' might not have been entirely unforeseen. Sadly, that was one question the purser could not answer. As it would eventually transpire, the law was even more disappointing: irrespective of the nationality of the aircraft, citizenship could be claimed only if the baby was born in American airspace over the territory of the United States.

Cabin crews are capable of handling such emergencies, but most airlines do not accept passengers beyond the thirty-sixth week of pregnancy (thirty-fourth week on long-haul flights) unless a doctor's certificate is presented, and even then the airline has the right to refuse carriage. If a pregnant woman is allowed to embark, a warning is issued to the crew because it is not always obvious to the check-in clerks just how advanced a pregnancy may be, and a transoceanic flight may not be able to divert and make an unscheduled landing in time. Laboratory experiments have succeeded in inducing premature labour at high altitude and reduced oxygen pressure – but only in goats. Such tests offer scant reassurance to experienced flight attendants, like those of British Airways, who know of cases when cabin pressurization, reinforced by the heightened natural tension of the rush to the airport, the check-in procedures and flight, brought about not only real but also phantom symptoms of premature labour.

Pilots and cabin crew are trained in first aid techniques. Though one of them may well be a nurse or paramedic, their first resort is usually to find a doctor among the passengers, because they are discouraged from administering any medication that may have side-effects with which they cannot cope. (It is only a doctor who can give injections, morphine or any of the five prescribed substances carried in the standard drug kit.) There are also legal considerations. As *Fit to Fly*, the BALPA medical handbook for pilots, points out, the geographical location of the aircraft may create a dilemma: while in most European countries (and their airspace), 'It is a criminal offence *not* to render assistance to those in need,' in the United States, for instance, the law 'denies any obligation to give aid to a stranger,' and a first-aider may be held responsible for resultant death or injuries.

Hyperventilation (mentioned in the previous chapter) is one of the conditions cabin attendants may have to deal with. In fact, it would help the crew if they were forewarned by the nervous passenger. The same could be said about various medical conditions that in themselves are perfectly safe to fly with. 'It is up to the passenger to call attention to potential problems,' says Dr Frank Preston, a consultant in aviation medicine and former head of BA medical services. 'If in doubt, ask your doctor or the airline. Unfortunately, many people fail to do so.' A BA purser has the same experience: 'I don't know why that is. Shame, shyness, ignorance? Instead of being prepared for it, often the first we know about a potential problem is when passengers demand diabetic meals that could have been pre-ordered or ask us to store their insulin in the fridge. It is always more difficult to deal with the unexpected, such as a request for a seat near the toilet that may alert the crew – the passenger might have failed to notify the airline about carrying a catheter or a colostomy bag.'

Fortunately, there are relatively few airborne medical emergencies, but their likelihood increases with the capacity of the aircraft as well as the range of non-stop flights, and some incidents may be difficult.

So why are the airlines so reluctant to urge passengers to disclose their medical condition, seek professional advice, and, in certain cases, not fly at all? The usual answer is that it would be wrong to frighten passengers unnecessarily. Also they would alert them only if all their competitors were compelled to do so as well. They may argue that the small-print on the ticket is already overcrowded by items of liabilities, baggage and dangerous articles, but health warnings could be issued on a separate sheet at the time of booking just as some airlines attach security advice to each boarding card. The standard IATA 'Conditions of Carriage' – the document for which only one in a million will ever think of asking – refers to health rather coyly and unhelpfully. Under Article 8 it declares that the airline can refuse carriage if someone's age or mental or physical state 'is such as to . . . cause discomfort or make himself or herself objectionable to other passengers; or involve any hazard or risk to himself or herself or to other persons or to property . . . ' Though the range of such conditions is well-known to doctors and the industry, not all of them may be obvious to all passengers or easily recognized by the carrier.

YOUR CHECKLIST

The following are contra-indications to air travel – medical conditions you should *definitely not* fly with – from the lists compiled by Dr Preston and the US Aviation Consumer Action Project:

- *Severe anaemia* (less than 6 gram per cent of haemoglobin)
- *Severe sinusitis* and *severe otitis media* (infection of the middle ear)
- *Acute contagious or communicable disease*
- *Recent coronary* (within previous thirty days. If it occurred two or three years earlier, it is advisable to tell the crew)
- *Uncontrolled cardiac failure* (serious heart condition)
- *Recent cerebral infarction* (stroke)
- *Peptic ulceration, duodenal or gastric ulcer with recent haemorrhage* (within the previous three weeks)
- *Post-operative cases* (within ten days of simple abdominal, or within fourteen days of major chest surgery)
- *Skin disease that is infective or repulsive in appearance* (Dr Preston: 'This is a controversial issue. Some airlines are rather uppity about it because of the fear of upsetting other passengers, though it could often be covered by gloves or a scarf. Check-in clerks are trained to notice it and may be inclined to turn people away. Yet somebody may be covered with a rash from a bad sunburn just as well as chicken pox or scarlet fever. Headmasters and parents can get rather furious at the end or beginning of a school term when the little darlings are returned to them from the airport.')
- *Fracture of the lower jaw with fixed wiring* (even worse than starvation, choking can result from air sickness – unless the patient carries his own wire-cutters to open his mouth)
- *Mental illness* (may cause additional problems in an enclosed environment unless the patient is suitably sedated and escorted)
- *Advanced pregnancy* (36 weeks, or 34 weeks for a long-haul flight)
- *Introduction of air to body cavities for diagnostic purposes* (air may be injected into the chest or brain cavities – do not fly within seven days)
- *Severe lung disease* (removal of lobe or lung creates a risk when flying)

The American Medical Association also mentions *epilepsy* (unless well controlled medically and at cabin altitudes below 8000 feet), *recent eye surgery*, certain *intestinal virus infections*, a *recent skull fracture*, and *haemophilia with active bleeding*.

Not many people will accept the warning not to fly with a very heavy cold. In the case of flu or a cold, the sinuses or the Eustachian tube to the middle ear can get blocked, and pressure changes in the cabin may cause pain, inflammation of the ear drum or damage to the middle ear. If you must fly with flu, it is suggested that an oral decongestant is taken 'an hour before descent and/or a decongestant nose spray or drops before and during descent'.

Though an unexpected tooth-ache may become excruciating in flight, there is no need to panic: the probable cause is an air pocket trapped in the tooth root – as air expands at altitude, it presses on the nerve. You only find out about it by default, and even though the pain will be gone by the time of landing, it is well worth seeing a dentist. (The occurrence is more common to pilots and scuba divers than others, who may only need a filling.)

People at risk from thrombosis are warned to get medical advice, especially for long flights. (Exercise, drinking plenty of water, resting the feet on hand-luggage, and the avoidance of tight trousers/underwear may reduce the hazard.)

HAVE A COMFORTABLE FLIGHT

Air pressure On most modern aircraft, few people are susceptible to serious pain from pressure changes, but even mild flu can exacerbate the condition, mostly during descent. If your ears begin to pop, take a deep breath, pinch your nostrils – blowing out at the back of the throat against the closed nose and mouth will usually help. In December 1992, the technique received some free earthbound advertising: according to *The Times*, a man was shot in the temple by another quarrelsome motorist. While waiting for emergency treatment, he blew his nose – and ejected the bullet through the hole it had made; apparently it had been lodged in his sinuses. (Fighter pilots, wearing an oxygen mask, and so unable to pinch their noses, do a modified Valsalva manoeuvre: they drop the jaw as if yawning, push it forward and swallow, while exercising the jaw muscles. It works, but needs practice.)

Sucking boiled sweets or chewing gum is also a good idea. The distribution of free sweets went out of fashion when airline accountants demonstrated how many thousands this wasted: 'Will anyone refuse flying with us only because we stop the practice?' they argued. It is only now that airlines are beginning to realize once again that chewing, like listening to piped music, gives people confidence and helps them to relax, as well as reducing ear pressure.

Shoes There is a lot to be said for old pairs retrieved from the black bag destined for Oxfam. Familiarity breeds comfort. Thick woollen socks, boots and trainers may generate too much heat on a long flight. Kick off or not to kick off? Some travellers swear by slippers (several airlines include them in their freebie packs) but at the end of a long flight, your shoes may have to become hand-luggage. Lace-up shoes may be a better solution. The BA purser is convinced that exercise is the answer: 'Just moving your feet frequently, without even getting up, helps to prevent swollen ankles. My feet get more tired flying as a passenger than working in the air, when I may have to walk twelve miles between London and New York. Admittedly, it also helps to keep my weight down!'

Clothes Many people dress to kill, and there is nothing wrong with that as long as they are not killing themselves with some tight-fitting garment, particularly around the waist. The looser, roomier it is the better. Wearing layers of clothing allows you to adjust to changing temperatures. (On some Russian-built aircraft, the air conditioning may be a match for a Siberian welcome, and the window seats can be draughty.)

There have been some reports that on long-haul flights, pilots raise the *cabin temperature* to an unacceptable level after the main meal to induce sleep, make heavy drinkers and unruly passengers drowsy – and give a well-earned rest to the crew. Passengers may welcome this help to doze off, but ICAO is investigating the practice because the high temperature may not be healthy and will cause extra dehydration.

Skin dehydration This is a constant feature of air travel. No make-up will survive it. Frequent application of moisturizing creams (free on many flights) is recommended.

Liquids and alcohol Dehydration is an even greater menace to the body than to the make-up. Eyes can feel sore and contact lenses dry. Many people counter it with alcohol. It may indeed help them to relax, but those who light-heartedly advocate getting drunk are quite wrong. Alcohol accelerates the dehydration, and altitude heightens its effect. (If you get on to your bottle of duty-free, beware: its alcohol content may be higher than you are used to.) The British Airline Pilots' Association urges its members to keep their bodies well topped up with fluids but *mix* their drinks: too much coffee and tea may cause indigestion, 'carbonated drinks can cause discomfort due to the low cabin pressure, encouraging the release of CO_2 in the alimentary canal', many soft drinks contain too much sugar, and aircraft water may taste foul – plenty of non-fizzy, bottled water at hourly intervals may be boring, but that is the answer.

Food Particularly on long-haul, multi-sector flights, meals seem to arrive ceaselessly. At last you feel drowsy, hoping to sleep across another time zone, but here it comes, you are woken up to take yet another breakfast. Most people complain about the dullness and plastic quality of airline food, yet they gobble up everything in sight – and manage to get painfully bloated. Stewards and stewardesses are often amazed at how much people can put away if it is free, munching and complaining about growing discomfort all the way.

Exercise This may bring some relief from discomfort. Wiggling toes, circling movements with feet and neck, clenching and de-clenching fists, gripping armrests and lifting the body, as well as walks down the aisle (when the seatbelt sign is off!) are the usual recommendations.

Jetlag The most common cyclic activity of the body is governed by the twenty-four-hour circadian rhythm. It is synchronized by external cues – light, darkness, the clock, and even social factors. When it is disrupted (your body-clock tells you to sleep but your watch commands a visit to the beach or an important meeting), you may feel like a zombie, and nod off in mid-sentence, spending the nights twisting and turning sleeplessly. Non-stop east–west or west–east crossing of up to a dozen time zones can leave you tired, listless, disorientated, and even constipated. Numerous miracle cures are bandied about. Build up your sleep 'credit' in advance, trying to establish sleep patterns similar to those at your destination – your odd behaviour of snoozing at your desk may be explained away, but it is no guarantee of sleep at the right time after the flight. Take a walk and a hot bath before your new bed-time. Reset your biological clock by timely exposure to very strong lights (in the air or on arrival in moonlit Singapore?), and wear dark goggles at other times to trick and stir melatonin, a light-related chemical, into action.* Melatonin pills may soon be available. Apparently, they help blind people who tend to develop a form of permanent jetlag with a free-running rhythm that may be up to 30 hours or longer. The same happens to people going to the Arctic or the Antarctic winter where there is perpetual darkness for months at a time. (Melatonin was also found to be effective when taken by people with perfect eyesight if the medication coincided with light requirements – exposure to natural or powerful artificial light at the start or end of the day according to the direction of travel.)

Captain Steve Last, a senior BA pilot, relies on his own remedy: 'Most people tend to feel sleepy soon after a meal. So I try to synchronize my dinner with my plan for sleep. If I arrive home from a trip in the early hours of the morning, I sleep an hour or so, then adjust to the local pattern. Jetlag is dangerous: it can build up long-term fatigue.' Some pilots go even further with their planning: because they drink a lot of water against dehydration in the air, they may go to bed full of liquids, only to be awakened by their bladder some fifty minutes later, with not a chance of going back to sleep. Therefore they try to pee, have that big meal with hardly any liquid, and pee again before retiring in hope.

The Buley formula is a scientific equation of various co-efficients to calculate the necessary rest time. For example, many big corporations will not allow their executives to take major decisions for twenty-four hours after a five-hour flight. The American Argonne medical research

*Melatonin is a naturally occurring neuro-hormone secreted by the pineal gland, a small pea-like organ at the base of the brain. Its rate of secretion is increased by darkness, causing the individual to feel sleepy. The reverse is the case in daytime: as the melatonin secretion lessens, so the individual tends to wake up.

laboratory devised a most elaborate ninety-six-hour diet with alternating feast and fast days. You determine your destination's breakfast time, and begin with a high-protein breakfast and lunch, followed by a high-carbohydrate dinner, to prepare for the salads, fruit and juice of the following day. If nothing else, it may work wonders on your figure.

This author believes in a simple technique: set your watch to your destination time on embarkation, try to eat and sleep according to the new time pattern, keep awake on arrival until local nightfall, and then take a sleeping pill (which tends to be more effective the less you are used to it).

'I've spent twenty-five years working on jetlag, without finding a satisfactory answer,' says Dr Preston. 'I've tried all the diets, even an aromatherapy. A firm once sent me a whole course – morning bath with one tablet in it, evening bath with another tablet – and tried it out in New Zealand. The fragrance I carried all day improved the air quality of offices and hotel corridors, but I felt no better for it.' (An in-flight comfort kit from chemists offers rehydration gel, exercise rub, mouth rinse and eye compress, but according to Trevor Webster of the *Evening Standard* (14.12.1992) the real winners are those long-haul travellers and members of the Royal Family who use two fragrant magic potions called *Awake* and *Asleep*. They are given to first-class passengers of Air New Zealand, with the suggestion to develop and nurture 'relaxing thoughts' at nighttime.)

Dr Preston subscribes to the idea of adjusting meal times and a little of the sleep pattern according to destination in advance: 'That calls for a very determined, precise traveller. Sleeping pills are also useful now that we have short-acting, so-called hypnotic drugs. They work for two or three hours, and are available on prescription, except in Singapore and Bombay. You may take one en route, flying westwards, and something stronger in the evening of arrival. Valium is bad, especially for pilots, because it has a long 'half-life', and may still have an effect thirty-six hours later. Your doctor will know what is best for you. Some people claim that jetlag is more likely to occur when flying eastwards. We studied flight crew reaction, but found no scientific evidence for that. If you want insurance against jetlag – fly north to south.'

Air sickness   See Chapter 17.

Radiation and ozone concentration   Affecting passengers on supersonic flights, these have caused some concern ever since Concorde went into service. The risk to flight crews was thought to be the greatest, but no serious scientific evidence was discovered, and it was not thought necessary to protect the aircraft nose with an anti-radiation shield. However, it is sometimes suggested that women in the first three months of pregnancy should avoid going supersonic. (Check with your doctor or the airline.)

Fresh air at 30,000 feet Ever tried sharing a small room with eleven strangers? Aboard aircraft, fresh air supply is well below the minima acceptable in other enclosed areas, such as offices, where, admittedly, people are more active and require more oxygen. On a long-haul flight, that may result in drowsiness, fatigue, nausea, headaches and respiratory problems. Seat density (the greater it is the cheaper you fly) may have an additional detrimental effect.

Aircraft cabins used to be fed only fresh air, until the beginning of the 1980s when oil crises and the dramatic increase in fuel costs lent fresh muscle to the accountants. As the ventilation system is bled from the engines, it was found that a DC10 could save more than 60,000 gallons of fuel if *recirculated* air rather than fresh air was pumped into the cabin. So pilots came under pressure to save fuel by shutting down 'air packs' and reducing the flow of air into the cabin. Some airlines go as far as offering a bonus to the thrifty pilot. In modern aircraft we breathe a mixture, but more than half the air is filtered and recirculated at seven-minute intervals. (SWISSAIR is experimenting with chemical absorption and ionization to clean the air and eliminate odours.) While passengers continue not to complain about the stale air, not much will be done about the increased CO_2 levels which, in turn, may induce more intensive jetlag, occasional migraines and nausea.

It has also been suggested that viruses, as opposed to bacteria, thrive on dry, recycled air, and a bad cold could be transmitted easily to other passengers. People who have tuberculosis are a special hazard. A sudden increase of TB cases has been recorded in many parts of the world, even in Britain where it had been virtually extinct, and in the recycled air of an aircraft infection can occur. (An American stewardess recently passed the illness on to another two crew members.) The airlines deny that fuel-efficiency measures create a risk, but the International Airline Passengers' Association has now sounded the alarm bells (*IAPA World*, Winter 1991): it warned that shutting down air conditioning packs may reduce costs, help to extend the range of an aircraft, and protect the engines from long-term wear and tear, but the practice may create a health hazard to passengers, and requires guarantees that an adequate minimum rate of fresh air-flow will always be maintained.

Hay fever This seems an unlikely risk in the sky, but if you suddenly suffer symptoms aboard a B747-400, it may be due to a powder that is used for cleaning the plane's air conditioning system!

19

Flying with Special Needs

Patronizing, politically correct euphemisms have mushroomed, particularly in the United States. Many are verging on the ridiculous. Someone who is bald is 'follicularly challenged', the deaf are 'aurally inconvenienced', the blind are 'optically challenged', the dead are 'terminally inconvenienced', a healthy person is 'temporarily able', and it is easier to admit to a 'nondiscretionary fragrance' than to foul body odour. Call it what you choose, one must discuss the problems of travelling with a physical impairment or disability.

Moving through busy, noisy, overcrowded airports, boarding and disembarkation procedures need no more fill the 'differently abled' with dark forebodings. All it requires is not to be too 'motivationally different' (lazy) to make some advance enquiries and requests. The majority of airlines are well prepared and airport information services, such as those at Heathrow, are most obliging. The provision of wheelchairs and electric buggies is a standard facility. Devices for the hard of hearing, marked with an 'ear' symbol, offer induction loops, and minicom phones are becoming widespread.

The more demanding somebody's needs, the more important it is to obtain some specialist publication such as *The World Wheelchair Traveller*, or booklets available from airports, airlines, disabled living foundations, fliers' organizations or ministries of health and transportation. The *Your Patients and Air Travel* and similar guides are available to doctors.

A few hints are, however, well worth remembering. Allow for transport delays to and at the airport during peak periods. Enquire about parking facilities, and ascertain which terminal you need. If possible, inform your airline about your special needs well in advance. In some cases, British travellers and their doctors must complete an INCAD (Incapacitated Passenger Handling) form. There should by now be no shortage of wheelchairs, yet dozens of justifiable complaints arise every year against airlines that fail to arrange for them to be available. Some ramps are quite steep at certain airports (e.g. between Heathrow

Terminals 1 and 2), where controlling or pushing a wheelchair may be an effort, requiring extra muscle.

Britain's Air Transport Users Committee (AUC) gives this warning in its *Care In The Air* booklet: 'If a charge for special ground services is requested, resist it strongly, and if you are compelled to pay at the time, obtain a receipt and endeavour to obtain a repayment.'

Be sure to have a sufficient quantity of medicines for the flight, and carry a copy of the prescription not only for the replenishment of reserves, but also to prove that your medical needs are genuine, and avoid difficulties when entering a country where the importation of certain substances may be prohibited or restricted.

The American regulations for handicapped travel are exemplary, and eliminate the old and discriminatory requirements. Carriers may not refuse transportation on the basis of disability, must not limit the number of handicapped people on any particular flight, and have to accept individuals whose appearance or involuntary behaviour may offend, annoy or inconvenience other passengers. American airlines may demand advance notice about handicaps only in certain conditions. (For instance, if an electric wheelchair is to be carried in an aircraft with fewer than sixty seats, if medical oxygen or a respirator hook-up is to be provided or if a stretcher needs to be accommodated. New aircraft with more than a hundred seats must offer priority space for storing a passenger's folding wheelchair in the cabin. Battery-powered wheelchairs have priority over other luggage in the hold, and must be transported, with batteries packaged as hazardous goods, free of charge.) New widebody (twin-aisle) aircraft must have accessible lavatories.

Respirators and kidney machines can usually be carried, but cabin power varies from airline to airline. Stretcher cases are charged at four times the normal fare, plus one extra seat for the mandatory escort.

Only in certain circumstances of severe impairment may an airline require a handicapped person to travel with an attendant. If there is disagreement about the need for an attendant, the airline may assign someone, even a volunteering passenger, to act as one.

People with a disability must submit to the same security screening as anybody else, but problems may arise with heart pacemakers that could be affected by the types of electronic screening equipment used by several (not British) airports. (It is essential to obtain advice in advance, and if still in doubt, to explain the problem to the security staff who should be able to provide some alternative means of screening.)

Cabin staff are trained to help disabled people, but they are not required to hand-carry or feed any passenger, perform medical services and, being 'food handlers', they must not give any assistance in the toilet.

It is essential that disabled passengers should receive the standard safety briefing before take-off. The new video presentations, if large enough to be visible to all, carry captions and a 'window' on the screen for a sign language interpreter. A discreet individual briefing can be given to a handicapped passenger who chooses to board before others.

Some American organizations have campaigned to give blind people the right to occupy seats adjoining the doors or overwing exits. While their concern is understandable, and such an arrangement would be a considerable advantage in ordinary circumstances, the FAA has rightly ruled that those places must be secured for only those passengers who are capable of opening the exits in an emergency. Blind people, travelling for non-pleasure purposes (business, medical, etc.) can get special concessions: on British domestic flights their escorts go free.

Though water will always be provided, airports lack special facilities for guide dogs that may travel within national boundaries in the cabin with their charges but they must not obstruct the aisles or access to emergency exits. If international borders are crossed, the laws of the receiving country apply. It is essential not to rely solely on information obtained on the telephone. (For example, a British Airways reservation clerk admitted he had never handled a query regarding guide dogs. He then, commendably, made some enquiries, and suggesting that precise details should still be obtained at the time of actual booking, came up with the answers that a free seat would be reserved for the dog if the passenger's needs were properly documented, and if tranquillizers were carried in case the dog became too agitated in flight. The dog would have to be muzzled – but only if it had been trained outside the United Kingdom.)

20

Flying with Children

Hopping on an aircraft may seem a doddle to you, but are you fit to fly with a baby, a toddler or a young child?

Having negotiated the traumas of packing (no, you did not forget the extra nappies, no you have not left behind the seven essential dolls and 15 kilograms of selected specimens of the highly educational crystal rock collection) you may think the worst is over – at least until you reach the long check-in queue in the hot and overcrowded terminal. Sometimes, particularly if you ask for it with a baby on your back, queue-jumping will be allowed. If so, just ignore the comments and dirty looks that mark your progress.

If possible, reserve your seats and ask for any special meals in advance. ('Special' may mean the dizzying heights of cordon bleu cooking, such as bangers or hamburgers, if you know from bitter experience that the 'finely cut veal in creamed mango sauce' would be rejected with a yuck and snarl.) Failing that, be at the airport early, and point out at the check-in desk that you want to sit with your child. Airlines will do their best to accommodate you. For once you are aboard the flight, you are at the mercy of fellow passengers, and that mercy is not always evident. You did not listen to their comments in the queue, now it is their turn not to hear the attendants' pleas for a change of seats.

While you are bustling with checking in, shifting bags and fishing out documents, with one eye on the luggage to see if it is labelled properly, it may be easy for an adventurous inquisitive toddler to get momentarily lost in the commotion. It is therefore a good idea to let them wear a badge of pride – with easily legible name, address, destination, passport number and, above all, flight number so that airport staff can easily reunite the family.

Be prepared for delays. Strong nerves, with the determination to relax no matter what (it is the beginning of a lovely trip or holiday, after all), are just as important as toys and games for the waiting around (for hours if you are unlucky). Most airports have nurseries with toys and facilities for babies. Some of them are staffed by trained nurses, but beware: quite a few of the nurseries are closed at night when you may need them most! Others are tucked away, out of sight, without signs to direct you, so if you do not ask, you may never find them. Also, a few airports may discriminate against men: the nappy-changing facilities being housed in the women's toilets. Virtually all airport restaurants can provide high-chairs, and offer special cheaper menus for children. Junk food with chips can extend children's patience – and soothe your nerves.

In the air, babies under three months of age seem to be unaffected by jetlag or any interruption of the circadian rhythm. The disadvantage of this is that their eating and sleeping cycles do not alter – to the chagrin of parents who may try to sleep and adjust to the changes of time zones on a long flight, the children may want to sleep and be fed at the wrong time. Babies and small children are more vulnerable than adults to dehydration, and should therefore drink plenty of fluids. Dehydration could be a cause of seemingly inexplicable excessive crying. During the descent of the aircraft, sucking dummies could minimize babies' discomfort; feeding could achieve the same. If all that fails to pacify them, do not get angry, do not persist with sweet-talking them – *let them cry*. Sooner or later it will force them to swallow, and the pressure will be reduced. It is sound advice that in the first ten to twelve days of life, newborn infants should not fly, for tiny air pockets, not yet expanded in their lungs, might cause distress in the pressurized cabin. Children with a bad cold, tooth or ear problems should be treated before flying.* Sucking sweets or chewing gums will do the same for them as for adults.

Most airlines provide sky-cots and carry-cots for babies, but it is best to make advance enquiries if they will let you take your own carry-cot or even a push-chair into the cabin. Usually the crew have powdered milk, baby food, lotions and spare disposable nappies available, and they can warm bottles and store your own baby food in the fridge. Aircraft toilets have pull-down desks for changing nappies, but be prepared: space will be at a premium, to say the least.

Travelling with babies or children imposes heavy demands on the capacity of your hand-luggage. A tip from a stewardess: you can take only one piece into the cabin, but the size of a woman's handbag is unlimited – so carry a large one.

THE END JUSTIFIES THE GAMES

Especially on long flights, it can be a mammoth task to keep children busy and happy. Toys, games, reading and drawing material are worth their weight in gold. Most carriers, particularly the charters for holiday-makers with children, provide these, as well as cartoon films and audio entertainment, but the above stewardess has another useful tip: have a

---

The Curse of Icarus by F.S. Kahn (Routledge, 1990).

secret weapon, a surprise toy your child has never seen, in that large handbag. With an eye on future customers, most airlines offer children special status: such as 'Skyfliers' on BA, 'Jet Cadets' on Britannia, and members of the 'Skyrider Club', a junior version of Emirates' 'frequent fliers', with a logbook, gifts and birthday cards each year.

Some toys and games are, however, dangerous. Electronic devices, particularly remote control toys, must not be used because they might interfere with the navigation of the aircraft. To avoid temptation it is best not to pack them in hand-luggage. If any such equipment is with you, clear its use first with a cabin attendant. One should also watch out for children's 'treasures' that might be considered to be weapons. A writer vented her fury in *The Times* (18 August 1992) because a daughter was upset when her teddy bear had to go unaccompanied through the X-ray machine, and the mother was interrogated about her son's Swiss army knife: 'There are probably terrorists sneaking through at this very moment while I'm springing him from a body search and wondering how a small boy is going to hijack a 747 with something that takes stones out of horses' hooves.' If she had stopped to think for a moment, she would have never written that piece. Teddy bears can, and did, hide explosives planted by a 'generous friend', and knives can be handed over to adults who travel with malicious intent. The security officers who spotted and checked those items deserve nothing but praise.

Occupying children during a flight helps to keep the family, as well as other passengers, happy. In March 1993, a reader wrote to a newspaper wondering if it were possible to segregate families from the rest, offering 'children' or 'non-children' options, just as the choice of 'smoking' or 'non-smoking' seats. Cruel as it may sound, the idea would be supported by many parents who battle to keep their offspring from annoying others by running up and down or pummelling the seatback in front. One problem is: where will the segregation stop? Some people want to be kept away from drunks and too high spirited travellers. In the United States, a clampdown on perfumes has begun, there are demands for aroma-free zones in offices, restaurants and churches, some cinemas have already stopped using air fresheners, objections have been raised to the smell of freshly cleaned shoes, and in a recent airline survey, respondents claimed they were more bothered by heavy scent than crying babies and rumbustious fellow passengers.

Unaccompanied children are well catered for by most airlines, but usually there is a minimum age limit for acceptance. Older children get assistance, younger ones are taken care of, but the guidelines issued by the US Department of Transportation are well worth remembering: unaccompanied children, carrying sufficient identification ('travel cards' with all the relevant details) must be handed over by an adult to an airline employee, must be taught never to leave the airport with a stranger, and must be delivered on arrival to a responsible adult whose name appears on the 'travel card', and who must sign a receipt.

Much of all this may appear, of course, nothing but trivia when it comes to the consideration of . . .

CHILD SAFETY IN FLIGHT

In most countries, children up to the age of two or three can travel free on the lap of an adult. Some special promotions by tour operators offer free seats even to teenagers who fly with two fare-paying passengers. Ordinary seatbelts, no problem to such youngsters, could create serious difficulties, or an outright hazard, to a three- or small four-year-old in a separate seat. And what about the baby on the mother's lap?

It is far from reassuring that the most advanced aviation countries – including America, Britain and France – allow contradictory principles to prevail concerning infant seats and seatbelts. Advice and regulations must not be based on guesswork, logic and opinions. Safety, just as flying itself, belongs to the realm of technology and science, and international research ought to be conducted in order to achieve a universal consensus among experts. Short of a single indisputable view, it is worth reviewing what some airlines and responsible exponents of the clashing arguments think.

For children occupying their own seats, the CAA has approved the Carechair, a new child seat designed specifically for British airlines, and now allows the use of purpose-built children's car-seats if they are in a good condition, with a proper restraint harness, and are capable of being secured, facing forward, in an aircraft seat. The use of such car-seats is subject to the age of the child, and to acceptance by the airline. (Depending on the age limit imposed by the carrier, if a child has his second birthday during a trip, he may sit on a parent's lap on the first journey but must have his own seat, paying some two-thirds of the fare, on the way home.) Airlines have been given guidance, with advice from the Cranfield Impact Centre, on the acceptability and fitting of privately owned infant seats at their own discretion. So BA, for instance, offers no special seats, but passengers can take their own car-seats if suitable. (Advance enquiries should be made.)

'To mandate airlines to provide child seats would impose a serious commercial problem, because they would have to hold stocks all over the world,' Michael Willett, the CAA Safety Regulations Director, told me. 'Some airlines would provide one if the passenger demanded it. So it's worth asking questions when booking. Sadly, the sort of person who doesn't bother to buy a car-seat would usually fail to do so. Our research has shown that it is extremely dangerous if two small children share a seat, so that's forbidden in the UK, but French airlines may allow it, for over there it's not illegal.

'On British airlines, unlike in America and most other countries, a mother who holds her baby on her lap gets an attachment that is looped through her own belt, so it takes only the child's weight. No, it's not the optimum means of retention. More accidents are these days survivable, but there are higher acceleration forces working on the body. Unfortunately, it's virtually impossible to protect a baby, whose head mass is disproportionately large to the body weight and weak muscles, and who is too fragile in a physiological – one could almost say engineering – sense to withstand forces of nine g-s.'

ACAP (American Aviation Consumer Action Project) warns in its *Facts and Advice for Airline Passengers* booklet that although many approved infant seats are available, some US airlines do not permit their use, and it is essential to find out about the rules of your carrier in advance.

'It is a Catch-22 problem,' says Tony Broderick, Associate Administrator of the FAA. 'When we improve, say, the wings, every passenger shares the cost. This wouldn't be the case with infant restraints. Car-seats for children up to two years of age are compulsory in the United States. It's been the rule for eight years that those seats must be suitable for aircraft use. We urge air passengers to book a seat for every child, and bring their own infant restraints. But if we mandate infant restraints and a separate seat for each passenger, only parents will have to bear the extra cost, many families will find flying too expensive, take to the highways, instead, and we'll end up with far more car casualties than we could save in aircraft accidents. The proportion would be some 50 to 1 plus serious injuries. Mandatory child restraints on US aircraft would cost some $250 million a year – and save, on average, only one infant's life every ten years.

'Extended seatbelts? I think it's a terrible idea. We don't allow them in the United States because our tests have proved that on impact, the parent would jack-knife, and virtually kill the child. So if you can't afford to buy an extra seat where your own infant restraint would fit, we advise that in the air, having a baby on your lap and in your arms is marginally safer than the use of an extension belt – and a lot safer than driving.'

Willett disagrees: 'It doesn't work. In a just about survivable accident, the parent will often let go of the child, because when there is severe deceleration, your limbs are flailing, trying instinctively to protect your head. I'm not happy with either method, but extension belts are still better than just trying to hold on to a baby.'

Tom O'Mara of ACAP is also critical of the FAA view: 'It is absurd for the FAA to require that baggage on the plane be restrained while infants and small children are not.' He fights for compulsory child restraints, and criticizes the FAA that lets 'lap children continue as a norm in commercial air travel'. He finds support in the attitude of the NTSB, the US Airline Pilots' Association, the US Association of Flight Attendants, the Air Transport Association, crash survivors and next-of-kin of crash victims, and quotes a case history:*

In 1989, a United Airlines DC10 crashed at Sioux City, Iowa – 112 people were killed (including O'Mara's daughter), 186 survived. 'One lap child perished. Two lap children lived. Two parents had to suffer the agony of seeing their child torn from their grasp . . . ' Some parents 'wrapped their infants in blankets and placed them on the floor between them a few minutes before the crash. Then they prayed for strength to hold on to their children during the emergency landing.' They could not. 'The infants were hurled through the air just like the luggage, coffee pots, trays and other debris . . . One infant was knocked unconscious when she hit the bulkhead, and died of asphyxiation' when black, toxic fumes filled the aircraft. Another child remained in the parents' grip. A third one flew forward, landed on some luggage, cried for help, and a brave passenger re-entered the burning cabin to save her. None of the parents had been warned against the dangers to their lap children in turbulence or emergency landings.

In February 1991, Matthew McCormick, chief of the NTSB Survival Factors Division, testified before a Congressional subcommittee: 'As we have seen during our accident investigations, it is impossible for an adult to hold on to an infant or a small child in a survivable crash. These children literally become projectiles and strike the inside of the cabin and other passengers.' The NTSB 'recommended that the FAA require infants and small children to occupy FAA-approved safety seats, and to conduct research on ways to restrain small children who have outgrown safety seats. While the FAA responded to our recommendations, they are currently classified as "Open-Unacceptable response". The FAA [then] proposed to prohibit air carriers from denying the use of' privately owned safety seats. As the proposal would still not make the acceptance of such seats mandatory, and infants would still be exposed to the same hazards, the NTSB continued to urge the FAA to introduce legislation. When I saw McCormick in Washington in November 1992, he still held the same view – by then with obvious frustration.

The FAA remains unconvinced by the validity of his argument and his evidence from crashes. The British CAA rules that infants under six months must be secured on an adult's lap by a supplementary loop belt. The Cranfield research found that the evidence available from accident data was insufficient. The impact tests with adult- and baby-sized dummies proved however (a) that the practice of carrying 'lap children' without some 'approved form of restraint [i.e. loop belt] is likely to promote fatalities or injuries . . . ' and (b) that a young child of any age, travelling on an adult's lap, will *not* enjoy as much protection from supplementary loop belts as adults get from their own ordinary seatbelts

*Article in *The Advocate*, Stamford, 16.9.1992.

when sitting in a forward facing seat. In other words, loopbelts may well be an imperfect solution, but remain the lesser of the two evils.

The child who has just turned two, and for whom a separate seat must be purchased, could be the most exposed to risk: the Cranfield test results, published in December 1992, did not mention that age group, and showed that 'the minimum age of a child who can be safely restrained by a lap belt' (the adult type) lies *somewhere* 'between the ages of three and six years'. In other words: entrusting a small child to the protection of an ordinary lap belt in a separate seat is not a solution.

With the prevalence of such uncertainties, child restraints (car-seats) ought to be made compulsory. Unfortunately, neither of the two leading authorities, the FAA or the CAA, has made a clear-cut decision for parents: they leave it to the lay individual and the cost-conscious airlines for whom it is not mandatory even to *accept* approved car-seats that parents may care to bring along for their children. Yet the Cranfield tests found that the protection provided by such 'child restraints was superior to that provided by other devices, e.g. supplementary belts and lap belts'. Aviation authorities in many other countries choose to pretend that the problem does not even exist.

The chance of extra hazard, to which air travel may expose small children, is minuscule. But who will explain that to the parent who may come to grief through lack of more thorough research, better guidance and appropriate legislation?

21

Flying in Odd Company

The Queen's and other diplomatic messengers do not qualify as 'odd company': passengers will be unaware of their presence because couriers are driven right out to the aircraft to board before anybody else so that they can store their precious pouches in special lockers, concealed by flower arrangements or magazine racks, in first class. Unaccompanied diplomatic mail bags (that may contain anything from secret documents to contraband whisky and drugs, weapons or luxury goodies for embassy staff in some outpost where such items may be in short supply) are sometimes in the charge of specially accredited pilots.

Similarly, passengers will never know that they may be sitting, literally, atop a gold mine or a huge heap of diamonds, valuables that zigzag the airways in vast quantities – to the delight of thriller writers searching for a plot.

Live animals are, however, another matter. The roar of a lion from below or the appearance of a snake in the aisle may shock passengers but will not entirely surprise the industry. The export and importation of animals is governed by strict regulations in every country to prevent the movement of prohibited species and the spread of diseases transmitted by non-human creatures. Consequently, the legality of their transportation is subject to global monitoring, and Quarantine Stations exist at all major airports. Illegal importation of any animal will attract massive penalties and imprisonment. Yet smugglers and eccentrics are forever trying to beat the system.

In America alone, more than 2 million live animals travel by air every year. The annual animal traffic through Heathrow is approaching the million and a half mark. Pets can be carried under certain conditions within national boundaries; some European countries will allow them to enter but only with sufficient veterinary certification. Usually, pets would have to fly in their own containers, stored in a pressurized hold. Airlines would require advance notification – detailing the size and gross weight of the cage – but will charge only 'excess luggage' rates that may amount to no more than £10 or £12.

American regulations for travelling pets are very detailed. US airlines may supply 'sky kennels', but accept cages only if they are standard for size, ventilation, strength and sanitation, and are designed for safe handling; dogs and cats must be at least eight weeks old, and must have been weaned for at least five days; specific water and food requirements exist for puppies, kittens and older animals. As a general guidance it is suggested that the animal should already be accustomed to its kennel, should be walked and not be given solid food or too much water for six hours before the flight, and should not be sedated without veterinary approval.

Some carriers allow a caged pet to fly as cabin luggage if it fits under the seat. (But if there is a pong in the cabin, do not always blame somebody's pet: it may be due to the spillage of some cargo on a previous flight. In 1992 on a BA Boeing 737, a plastic drum of a thousand litres of diluted garlic split accidentally while being unloaded. The pungent smell contaminated not only the aircraft, but also the hangar where it had been parked. A dozen different steam-cleaning treatments failed to eliminate the smell, keeping the aircraft grounded, until a small Sussex firm pumped its specially developed BVD, a non-toxic cleaning agent, through the air conditioning system. No other aircraft will ever be as clean as that B737.)

Animals are sometimes sent by air in quite appalling conditions. Several monkeys were crammed into small crates, leopards suffocated in 'safe' containers with no ventilation, starlings and parrots were caged as live meals with birds of prey, poisonous snakes were stuffed into a shoe-box-sized metal container (a favoured device to conceal a consignment of heroin). On cargo flights, overcrowding, heat exhaustion, distress-related heart failure or suffocation may kill calves and sheep. And these are only a few examples of careless yet perfectly legal shipments. The smugglers, who run an international multi-million dollar trade in rare and endangered species, take more precautions against discovery than slaughter. Vast differences in the price of tropical birds, gibbons, snakes or even striped squirrels, and the huge demand by collectors of rare species, make smuggling such a profitable business that animals which are dead on arrival represent only a small increase in overheads. Fortunately, with concealment (often in hidden compartments of hand-luggage or false-bottomed suitcases) being the prime consideration of the trade, passengers are unlikely to encounter odd company from that source.

Eccentrics represent, however, a different kettle of fish. Yes, *fish*. On a hot day at Perth airport, a Japanese passenger was noticed wearing a large overcoat with pockets that seemed to have a life of their own. It was found that he was carrying large, sealed plastic bags full of water – and fish. At Heathrow, humming birds, snakes, live lobsters, and once a dead pig, were discovered in hand-luggage. Next to a Jumbo on the tarmac, a legless live lobster was found – a passenger must have dropped it accidentally. Customs officers still dine out on the tale of two Shetland ponies that were caught trying to walk through the 'green' nothing to declare channel: nobody would hazard a guess as to how they got inside the airport. But the catch in Kenya probably beats them all: a nun from Greece tried to smuggle in several thousand bees with their hive under her habit. Under questioning she broke down and confessed that all she wanted was beeswax for candles in her Greek Orthodox missionary church.

Stowaways, which occasionally startle passengers, range from birds to snakes and mosquitos that may sneak into the cabin without waiting for the 'aircraft now boarding at gate seven' final call. The greatest threat comes from rats that may gnaw their way into every nook and cranny, chew up electrical and control cables, and compromise safety in the air. If it is suspected that a rat is on board, the flight must be postponed or substituted with another aircraft. Even a mouse can be a problem. In January 1993, American Airlines had already announced its departure from Manchester to Chicago, when a mouse was spotted in the business section. It caused a major delay: most of the 111 passengers had to wait twenty-four hours for the next flight.

In India, particularly in Bombay, where some Hindus, including airport workers, regard rodents as holy, rats escaping from flooded sewers during the monsoon are often caught in traps only to be released unharmed. As reported in *The Times* (14.8.1991) the Indian government instituted an extermination campaign because rats had delayed several international flights despite frequent fumigation and trapping. An Air India flight from the Middle East had to return when a rat was seen in the cabin soon after take-off. In Bombay, slums are only a few hundred yards away from the airport catering buildings, and rats can burrow through walls. Though food preparation is subjected to regulations of the utmost hygiene everywhere, international airlines take extra care with their catering in India, Pakistan and the Middle East.

22

Spaghetti Junctions in the Sky

CLOSED FOR LUNCH: PLEASE CALL LATER! The sign in the sky over Scotland was actually invisible, but the message could be heard on the airwaves – and it was no joke. Some 500 people on two cargo flights, a holiday charter from Florida and another from Palma were kept circling above Glasgow airport that closed for seventy-five minutes on 9 October 1991.

There is a worldwide shortage of air traffic controllers (who earn up to £35,000 a year), and Glasgow is no exception. On that October day, one of the three duty officers reported sick. The other two held the fort, but the law states that each controller *must* take regular breaks, for meals as well as a half an hour's rest after each ninety minutes on the busiest frequencies, to break the strain and monotony of the demanding job. They could have staggered their lunch hour – traffic was light enough for one controller to handle – but one of the two was not fully qualified to work without supervision. So to minimize the length of closure, they chose to eat together.

The passengers, stacked over Glasgow, might have seen nothing but unnecessary irritation in the delay (a diabetic, who had forgotten to take an insulin shot in Florida, suffered some discomfort), but for the rest of us, the episode is very reassuring: strict regulations and uncompromising individual responsibility worked in tandem for our safety.

AIR TRAFFIC CONTROL (ATC)

the traffic police of the skies, places notional road markings and traffic lights into the airspace. Its work is often described as a Gargantuan chess game in three dimensions, but in fact it is *four*-dimensional, with *time* being the fourth factor, because it is essential to know how long a particular aircraft will take to fly from point A to B, turning, ascending or descending. The primary function of ATC is to facilitate the flow of traffic with optimum safety, and prevent collisions. On a clear summer day, you scan the sea of blue over London – an airspace that is reputedly among the most crowded in the world – but may find no more than two grey dots traversing slowly and painting white (condensation) stripes across the sky. So it would be quite natural to ask: what's the problem?

The problem is manifold. Distance is always hard to judge. Those

DISTANCE BETWEEN TWO AIRCRAFT	960 mph	600 mph	360 mph
	COLLISION IN SECONDS		
10 m	37.5	60	100
6 m	22.5	36	60
5 m	18.75	30	50
4 m	15	24	40
3 m	11.25	18	30
2 m	7.5	12	20
1 m	3.75	6	10
0.5 m	1.8	3	5

RECOGNITION AND REACTION TIMES
in seconds

SEE OBJECT	0.1
RECOGNIZE AIRCRAFT	1.0
BECOME AWARE OF COLLISION COURSE	5.0
DECISION TO TURN LEFT OR RIGHT	4.0
MUSCULAR REACTION	0.4
AIRCRAFT LAGTIME	2.0
TOTAL	12.5

seemingly lazy speckles may be travelling at 500 or 600 knots (roughly so many miles per hour), and if they are converging at the same altitude, their closure speed will double. As the chart shows, the pilots could spot and perhaps recognize the other dot as being an aircraft when it is some four or five miles away. If the closure speed is 960 m.p.h., from three miles onwards they would not have enough time to become aware of the risk, make a decision, act and allow the aircraft to obey. Add to that the difficulty that over the UK virtually all flights are climbing or descending, criss-crossing each other's paths, albeit at lower speeds. So one cannot rely on the pilots' skill alone: they must be kept apart by other means. Separation of *all* the air traffic (corporate jets, leisure and military flights, even hot air balloons) is the complex art of ATC.

The process begins with the *ground-movement controller* who, using frequencies jam-packed with radio traffic, juggles with flying machines and a multitude of road vehicles at the airport (see Chapter 6). When an aircraft reaches the runway, it is handed over to the *departure controller* whose job it is to issue instructions and take-off clearance to the pilot, watch and maximize the use of available runways, and feed the voracious airways. When, in the Departures Lounge of a terminal, you see five identical times on the board, it is obvious that if there is only one runway those five flights cannot all depart at once: four will have to be delayed because many of the busiest airports – including the likes of Heathrow, but excepting the US ones – are short of concrete. Which one of the five will be the first at the starting line hinges on the controllers' information of a guaranteed route and arrival 'slot' for each, depending in turn on the hundreds of other aircraft intent on simultaneously using the same air-space, particularly the most congested European 'junctions'.

Once airborne, the aircraft is the *air traffic controllers'* responsibility. The London ATC Centre, for instance, is located a few miles from Heathrow – distance makes no difference for they work on radar screens, watching and governing the entire airspace up to the Scottish border, halfway across the Channel and the North Sea, Wales, and a long way out over the Irish Sea and the Atlantic, communicating with and handing traffic over to the adjoining control areas, such as France and Holland. Perhaps the most precarious and skilful task is to guide pilots in and out of their terminal area, dodging incoming flights and those leaving the holding stacks, give them the required rate of climb and acceleration to keep them well behind others ahead of them, and slot them into the airways higher up. As the green dots, representing aircraft, move through the intricate traffic patterns on the radar at peak times, it is not unlike trying to cross the Etoile in the Paris rush-hour – at high speed.

At the destination of the flight, the process is reversed. It is handed over to the controllers for *approach, arrival* (some eight miles out from touch-down), and finally, *ground-movement* for guidance to a gate. (At Heathrow, there are about 400,000 landings and take-offs to be taken care of every year, and each of these must be coordinated with the arrival and departure of private aircraft. It is estimated that commercial air traffic will grow by some 50 per cent by the middle of the next decade, and without major technical improvements, ATC would become unmanageable.)

The airspace is divided between controlled and uncontrolled areas. The *controlled airspace*, that must be used by all commercial traffic, is in three layers like a wedding cake. The terminal zones extend from ground level to 5000 or 7000 feet. Above that, to 24,500 feet, is a mesh of airways for commercial aircraft. From certain altitudes (24,500 feet in the UK, 18,000 feet in the USA) upwards, all traffic is under ATC control, and higher up, on the Atlantic routes, for instance, special rules apply. In *uncontrolled airspaces*, embracing the lower terminal zones, most non-commercial users inform ATC of their presence and intentions though they are not obliged to do so. Confusion over the mix can, and has, led to catastrophic air collisions.

Each of the airways forms a ten-mile wide corridor that can be used by several flights simultaneously – as long as they maintain the compulsory separation in distance and altitude. Long before departure, each pilot must file a flight plan. (The plans for regular services, stored in the computers, are just activated before each flight.) Accordingly, ATC allocates a notional, brick-shaped 'moving box' that gives the pilot five miles on either side, *at least* five minutes' flying time (that could be fifty miles!) in front and behind, and a minimum of 1000 feet above or below. On transoceanic routes, where pilots and autopilots are left to their own navigational devices, the separation is doubled, but when an aircraft flies under radar control, such as approaching a terminal area, the horizontal and time separation can be reduced. Over Britain, for instance, unlike in many other countries, virtually all the airspace is covered by radar surveillance.

MASTERS OF THE UNIVERSE

In the semi-darkness of the large halls of major centres, sound is hushed as if in a church. Green radar screens cover the walls, and although nobody is spared the incessant banter and leg-pulling that help to break the strain of concentration, a degree of tension is obvious. Controllers are drilled never to forget that each slow-moving dot on the screen may represent hundreds of lives. (A study by R. Roske-Hofstrad of NASA, the US space authority, found that the screen images are so powerful that they can become a more intense and convincing reality than the occurrences they denote. This is due to a weakness in the human psyche rather than any lack of responsibility. A controller told me how he solves the problem for himself: 'I think of the pilot alone. I talk to him, he is reality. What sits behind him might as well be cargo. It's easier to care for one real person than hundreds of phantoms.')

When an aircraft takes off, a new dot appears on the screen, and it is labelled with its airline code (for example, KL for KLM), its altitude (transmitted automatically from the altimeter of the aircraft), and its destination code (for example, CGK if it is Jakarta-bound). The computer can also project where the aircraft will be, at its given speed, in so many minutes, so that potential conflicts can be predicted and prevented. Information is also pouring in about flights that are to enter a controller's area in the near future. When that airspace is already full, the would-be newcomer is told to delay take-off (it is better for passengers, too, to wait in departure lounges than to sit cooped up in an aircraft) or to slow down (if it is already in the air) or, if it is about to arrive at a busy airport, to hold, circling at 1000-feet intervals atop each other in a stack, from where it will be peeled off in ascending order, usually on a first-in first-out basis.

The selection and training of controllers is an arduous process that takes at least three years to full qualification. Due to miscalculations of traffic growth, the intake was minimal in the late 1980s, then had to be trebled by 1991. 'As it's a well-paid job, huge numbers apply in Britain, but few satisfy the stringent requirements,' says Colin Chisholm, Deputy General Manager of the London En-Route Centre. 'Apart from intellectual qualities and good mathematics, we're looking for self-assurance, spatial capabilities to visualize events in four dimensions when you only see them in two with coded data on the screen. We want team-players who are quick-witted, willing to take decisions with confidence, who do not fluster easily under pressure, and usually turn out to be extroverts. We need people who can work shifts [called 'watches'] because we provide a service round the clock. The selection tests give a reasonable, though not foolproof, indication of the type of person who can quickly absorb and act upon a lot of information thrown at them, as well as recognize, admit and correct mistakes at speed. Those who can't cope with the stress are weeded out in the first two years of simulator and on-the-job training.'

'It is a requirement of the state licence that controllers should report if they are taking any medication,' says Dave Vaughan, a watch manager of the London En-Route Centre. 'If they have a personal problem, they are expected to report it and, despite their reluctance to put an extra load on colleagues, take a few days off rather than work with their minds on something else. Yet the solution varies. One of the chaps had a major family drama and preferred to be among his friends to "work off" the problem. We said OK, but you'll have to work a few days off radar, then on radar but under dual control, with another qualified controller at your elbow, until we're satisfied that you're comfortable once again to handle the job on your own. It worked out beautifully.'

Though an increasing number of women can be seen facing the radar screens ATC is still a male-dominated world, and many old hands (men, that is) claim, 'It's like on the road: some women are better drivers than any man, but most of them are worse, and too emotional for the job, complaining that the ghostly green hue lends them an unflattering complexion.'

The workload is tailored to fit human nature: if there is too much to do, stress could lead to rushed decisions; if there is too little to occupy the controller, inattention and dangerous complacency may result. Oddly enough, the serious risk of boredom, just as in the case of pilots handling automated flights, has been less researched than the effects of strain.

Stress becomes inevitable if there is an emergency in the air. 'In a difficult situation, you're the pilot's anchor,' says Paul Rundell, Vaughan's deputy. 'If a wing fell off, you'd be powerless beyond alerting the emergency services. Luckily, that doesn't happen. If there's a problem, even a major one out there, but the aircraft is still controllable, pilots tend to be reluctant to call mayday. Sometimes the information needs to be elucidated because pilots may not be very forthcoming. They think about their company's commercial interests, and are aware of others listening in. If there's a serious problem, the pilot will report it without any delay. We're his lifeline, but we need to know details, such as his position and the nature of his difficulties, before we can clear the airspace for him and offer him the option to turn or descend safely, and choose an alternate airport for an emergency landing. The flying fraternity is good in those situations: they shut up at once to clear the airwaves for a colleague in distress. We may give the captain gentle hints on what to do or we play devil's advocate if he opts for pressing on because his troubles *seem* to have gone away, but the final decision must always be his alone.

'There's no way to *train* and fully prepare us for special situations that may arise and grip you inevitably. You can't dream up and write a scenario for a terrified co-pilot reporting that his captain has been half sucked out of the cockpit, like in the case of BA's blown-out windscreen incident. There's no time to contemplate, finish your coffee, consult the charts. It's all experience, judgement, gut reaction. To retain our own cool, and help our charges to stave off panic, we must set the right tone. The busier we are, the greater the emergency we handle, the more slowly, deliberately we talk – excited transmissions may need to be repeated, and when every second counts, the message must get through right away, with no time to ask or be asked to say again.

'The language of the air is English, but in an emergency some pilots may revert to their native tongue. Even if they remember the standard phraseology, the mainstay of our radio communications, they may find it difficult to explain a problem in English. Yet language discipline is essential. Standard transmissions, however broken the English spoken, can be understood by all.'

The lack of such discipline can lead to misunderstandings, and has been a factor in several accidents, such as a Yugoslav DC9 crashing into a mountain and killing 180 people in 1981. French, Spanish, Russian and Chinese pilots and controllers seem to have a notorious reputation for using their native tongue whenever possible. It is permissible to use the national language if a flight does not leave the boundaries of its own country, but even that can impose extra difficulties on other pilots in a busy airspace where they want to listen in, just to be aware of what is going on around them – such as naughty favouritism by controllers who allow their own countrymen to jump the queue for landing. Pilots and controllers everywhere must acquire some basic English to pass their exams. Interpreters may be on hand in some towers, but the repeats can waste precious time. British controllers can cope with a bit of pidgin English, but their own heavy Irish, Scottish or Cockney accents could create difficulties.

In US airspace, the natives' frequent use of 'NewYorkSpeak', Chicago jargon and CB language, not to mention American slang, can be an enigma to everyone else. (What would you make of this? Fighter pilot to tower: 'This is chrome-plated stovepipe, triple nickel eight ball, angels eight, five in the slot, boots on and laced, I wanna bounce and blow.' As the reader would know, of course, to the old-timer in the control tower it meant that it was a jet, callsign 5558, flying at 8000 feet, five miles from the airport, with gears down and locked, requesting to do a 'touch-down and go' exercise.*

Callsign confusion has long been recognized as another potential hazard. Air India can be misheard as Air Indiana, SWISSAIR may sound like US-Air, and the pilot of one may not realize that a certain altitude was given to the other. Abbreviated callsigns have now been revised by ICAO, but the proliferation of airlines in deregulated America and Europe, in China and the former communist states, is bound to exacerbate the problem. (In 1992–1993, ninety-nine new airlines have been registered.) The ultimate solution will only come with automated direct data link between aircraft and ground radar to eliminate the fallible human element of speech and hearing.

Perhaps the greatest and most demanding emergency a controller may have to face is when it seems imminent that there could be . . .

A MID-AIR COLLISION

It must be said, however, that the risk and frequency of such occurrences are much smaller than we are often led to believe. It is a highly emotional subject, the ogre conjures up harrowing images in the mind, and the slightest hint of a possible case can trigger off press campaigns. (It is interesting to note that a banner headline is usually followed by a short period of hysteria.) Pilots must report an 'airmiss' if *in their opinion*, more often wrongly than rightly, two aircraft came too close together, that is, lost compulsory separation. In Britain, for instance, about twelve such incidents are reported by pilots and controllers every year: if it involves a public transport aircraft, it falls automatically into the most serious category, even if the two – say a jet and a leisure flight – were still half a mile apart. All reports, even the most insignificant ones, are thoroughly investigated – an independent commission can fully reconstruct the event from the continuous record of flight data, ATC instructions, and video tapes of the ever-changing picture on ground radar screens – and 80 per cent of them prove to be false alarms due to the difficulty of judging distance in the sky. Cases of some 'definite risk' to public transport aircraft occur about twice a year.

'Conflict alert' is initiated whenever two aircraft come into a configuration where they are liable to collide or the separation is likely to be lost. Air traffic controllers usually notice the chance for conflict even before modern computers could flash to alert them. A conflict may be due to misunderstandings, pilot errors ('altitude busting', i.e. flying at the level assigned to someone else, route deviation caused by punching incorrect

The Final Call, op. cit.

data into the autopilot, etc.) or mistakes by the controllers (giving wrong instructions, failing to spot a developing situation, miscalculations, forgetting during a busy period to turn an aircraft at the right time etc.). An incident in the London sector was a classic demonstration of unforeseen pitfall potentials: the terminal and en-route controllers used to work in the same room, and formed part of a single operation; when terminal controllers were transferred to the new operations room, coordination was degraded, and there was some confusion about deciding who was in charge; two aircraft came too close for comfort though too far from a serious risk of collision; nevertheless, the investigation led to some retraining for the controllers involved, and the introduction of joint briefings.

'Avoiding action' – an immediate turn to the right by each aircraft – in an emergency situation may be initiated by pilots if they see each other, or the controller when the pilots are not even aware of the other's proximity. If all else fails, this rule of the air can save lives. When two flights were converging in broad daylight, 18,000 feet above Lydd on the Kentish coast, 553 passengers and crew had no idea that they were minutes from disaster. ATC failed to spot the likely close encounter. Aboard the BA Tristar, a stewardess was serving yet another cup of coffee to the pilots. She looked up – and screamed. A Tupolev 154 seemed to be heading straight towards the windscreen. By then the captain had seen it too, and pulled instinctively up and to the right. Stunned passengers saw the Bulgarian aircraft flash by the windows. The crew thought the Tupolev (military codename 'Careless') was no more than five feet away. The investigative reconstruction found that the gap must have been 300 feet. Whoever was right, 'It was', as the captain put it, 'a very close shave'.

On July 10 1991, a Continental DC10 was flying north at 33,000 feet near Hawaii. In complete darkness, using the same airway, *Blue 474*, a Qantas B747, was southbound at 31,000 feet. The air traffic controller then made a mistake, authorizing the Jumbo to climb to 35,000 feet – and cross vertically right in front of the DC10. The Qantas pilot would never have known what hit him, but on that occasion the captain of the Continental was forewarned long before a hazardous situation could develop – his ACAS (Airborne Collision Avoidance System),* a relatively new instrument, was watching the black sky and everything that moved within a forty-mile radius. It alerted him that an intruder was starting to climb into his path. It also suggested what evasive action he should take, but there was still plenty of time. On a common radio frequency he contacted the Qantas pilot who agreed to stop climbing until the DC10 could pass safely overhead.

---

*Also known as TCAS (Traffic-alert and Collision Avoidance System).

'As there is constant pressure by airlines to cram more aircraft into the airspace, and by the general aviation lobby that wants freedom "to ride the range", we've long been fighting for the introduction of ACAS,' says Rick van Woerkom of the NTSB, 'and legislation is now in place at last.'

'Yes, the United States forced the pace, all US aircraft with more than thirty seats, and foreign fliers who visit US airspace, will have to be equipped with ACAS by 1994, but it's a major investment, and there're problems,' comments Air-Vice-Marshal Mike Gibson, head of the CAA air traffic control policy and planning. 'ACAS works very well but only if both aircraft are equipped with the latest, state-of-the-art transponders. Early models always assumed the worst scenario, and pilots might have been induced to chase phantoms. New types interrogate each other regarding speed, altitude, rate of climb or descent, information is bounced back and forth, and colours on a screen indicate the level of hazard: blue means "close but no threat", amber means "beware and look out for it" with an advisory for action, and if it turns red, it suggests a quick avoidance manoeuvre. In Europe, ACAS won't be required before 1998, maybe earlier for the upper airspace, and we must be certain that on the busy European routes, pilots won't be flying in a state of constant red alert. We try to reduce the risk, but some residual risk will always remain. Still, I find it more frightening to drive *in* than fly *to* Brussels.'

ACAS is an ingenious device, but in a way it only helps to patch up the gaps in precise navigation as well as air traffic control that is, in many areas of the world, some twenty years behind the development of aviation itself. New ATC facilities are often obsolete by the time they are installed. US modernization programmes have been delayed for years even though the money was available: from the taxes of air passengers and shippers, the Airports and Airways Tax Fund has accumulated a huge surplus, now expected to exceed $7 billion, but in blatant violation of its intended use, the government keeps raiding it to balance its budget. French, Spanish, Greek, Russian and other controllers often strike not only for better pay but also against their outdated hardware, and in some countries they are expected to work a terrifying sixty-hour week. It is only now that Greece plans to provide radar cover for non-military flights.

When radars were first introduced, they were expected to watch no more than a hundred aircraft at a time. Now they have to keep an eye on twice as many. It is expected that by 1995, London's three main airports will be handling 150 landings and take-offs an hour, in addition to another forty, mostly climbing or descending, overflights.

Right up to now, parallel to computers, London ATC has retained the old manual system (strips with flight data details are printed out, and passed in plastic holders from desk to desk where they are stacked in front of the radar screens). If there was a total power failure, as happened once some fifteen years ago when the lights went out and the telephones were dead, batteries would keep the radar system going for nine minutes, but it would be a traumatic experience. RT communication would work a little longer, and all pilots would have to be advised not to make any movement that might reduce their separation.

In Europe, the airways are choking. Many of the computers work to different specifications, and simply cannot talk to each other. Traffic flow management, keeping aircraft on the ground until the 'road is clear' or slowing them down en route until the destination airport can receive them, has helped to reduce wasteful 'holding'* but the procedure may still depend on steam-age practices. If a pilot wants to fly from London to Athens, ATC must try to slot him into the flow. It calls Paris ('Please, please, can we go through French airspace at that time?'), then puts the same question to Switzerland and Italy, and if they all give the green light, Greece may still say, 'Sorry, we're too busy.' Then it can start all over again a little later. Despite careful planning and scheduling, the system often seems to be taken by surprise because there are no allocated slots according to the timetables. It is only three hours before take-off that airspace can be booked (two hours until recently), and traffic must take experience into consideration – in the summer, the routes to Greece are for some reason very congested on Wednesdays. One gets the impression that it is sheer human dedication and ingenuity that make it possible for most aircraft to arrive on schedule.

The Continent is peppered with bottlenecks. Just as on major roads, when one is eliminated another is created a few miles further on. When long-delayed passengers vent their anger on 'bloody Heathrow' or 'bloody Rome/Malaga/Oslo/Prague' that, they have been told, 'can't receive us', they ought to blame some unheard-of junction, such as Nattenheim, where many north-south and east-west airways converge to form a blockage in the pipeline. (Clacton used to be Britain's bogeyman in the woodpile. Handling most of Europe's inbound traffic, it now provides a much improved service, but Germany and Belgium, for instance, having had to impose their own flow restrictions, still use the 'jam at Clacton' as an excuse for delays.)

US flow management is far ahead of Europe's, but the growing traffic density in airways and at 'hub' airports imposes plenty of frustration and resentment: when airlines are losing their shirts in cut-throat competition, it is hard to tell them, 'Don't leave the ground, slow down, waste fuel, be late, we've no room for you in the air or at your destination.'

---

*The last time detailed figures were gathered, it transpired that in 1991 Lufthansa passengers, for instance, spent 14,600 hours cooped up aboard aircraft on the ground, waiting for delayed take-off, and the airline wasted 50,000 tons of fuel when its flights had to 'hold' for a combined 13,700 hours. 'Holding' over London has now been halved.

On transoceanic routes, where there is no radar cover for the ever-increasing traffic, and where aircraft may stray sideways, up- or downwards (hence the double separation requirements), ATC must rely on pilots' transmissions for the estimated time of arrival. Over the Atlantic, wind conditions can change the duration of a flight by up to ninety minutes, and affect punctuality. (Until recently, nobody in Britain could be sure when the bulk of Atlantic traffic might arrive. It often coincided with the domestic peak, and those long flights could claim landing priority – to the chagrin of delayed commuters from Edinburgh, Glasgow and Belfast.)

Fortunately, major advances in technology and planning are now visible on the horizon. International co-operation is improving. The worst services will be brought up to scratch and, barring likely delays, flow management will be centralized in Brussels by 1995, so that the various nationalities will lose their excuses for blaming each other for hold-ups. (Computers will forecast where traffic jams may develop, and offer options to the carrier: delay taking off for ten, twenty, thirty minutes – or accept a longer route that may be costlier to fly but will help you maintain your schedule.)

The London Centre is soon to move home and work with far better facilities. Together with a new En-Route Centre, it is a part of a £750 million investment for the future that will weed out obsolete computers as well as twenty-year-old radar displays for which spare parts are hard to come by. Approach controllers for the three London airports will work together in a huge operations room by 1996. The new Centre will be able to handle more traffic than the airports can receive without building new runways and stands for aircraft. It is expected to satisfy the growing demands for the next forty years by introducing the safer and more efficient CCF (Central Control Function) concept that is already practised in some other places, such as the busy New York area. Replacing the interweaving 'plate of spaghetti' air corridors near airports, *tunnels* will be created in the sky. Fed by the airports at one end, and by the big international airways at the other, each tunnel will be distanced from the others by three miles horizontally and 1000 feet vertically, and will carry only one-way traffic. Each will be policed by a single controller, so that the need for time-consuming coordination could be reduced.

'Automation in the new centre poses some difficult questions,' says Dave Vaughan. 'If people are reduced to monitoring duties, as in a modern cockpit, their ability to quickly step in and take over if necessary may diminish. In the intermediate future, we'll have a computer-assisted but human-dominated system. Long term? Anybody's guess. One can foresee demands for leaving controllers completely out of the equation. But in my view, as opposed to what pilots claim, you could leave *them* on the ground before you'd take out the controllers. On the other hand, how many people would want to fly if nobody was minding the shop up front? Unfortunately, if controllers were eliminated, the passenger wouldn't even know.'

While various ATC modernization systems are running several years late, two American projects, costing an estimated $32 billion, will truly revolutionize transoceanic travel. To step into the control rooms of those projects in the FAA's Washington headquarters is like crossing the threshold of the twenty-first century. Pressing a button can conjure up a picture of all commercial aircraft in flight in American airspace, focus in on the traffic position over, say, the whole of California, or just Los Angeles, label each aircraft symbol with its estimated time of arrival, or survey the situation over the Atlantic (represented, for the time being, by electronically generated markers).

The Global Positioning System (GPS) will use satellites to give the exact location of every flight in real time, irrespective of what pilots report regarding their assumed location in the air. 'The inaccuracy of the current inertial navigation system and the fallibility of autopilot programming are the obstacles to packing the Atlantic routes, for instance, even more,' says Joe DelBalzo, a leading FAA executive in charge of Systems Operations. 'According to wind and weather conditions, there is only one optimum route between Europe and the United States, and it is, of course, impossible to allocate the same to all. That is not only frustrating but also costly to the airlines because the less than optimum routing means extra fuel, possibly even a need to refuel en route, and pilots are rightly concerned about any erosion of the separation standards. GPS could minimize those risks because human voice communication would be replaced by on-board computers talking via satellites to others in the air and on the ground, and because the pilots would also know precisely where they were at any time. The system is already operational with twenty-four satellites. We've offered it to ICAO, free of charge for a minimum of ten years, and promised not to raise any charges without a six-year notice. GPS will be much cheaper than installing, operating and maintaining the current worldwide radar and ILS systems, and satellite technology would be available to everybody. It could also help the poorest countries that now find the cost of ATC modernization prohibitively high.' (The system would not require expensive ground radar coverage, and would offer the Third World a short-cut to precision approach for which much more investment in technology and training would be necessary.)

'Currently, we have just one BA aircraft equipped for trials of what we call an Automatic Dependence Surveillance,' says Air-Vice-Marshal Gibson. 'Without any action by the crew, the instruments on board report to ground control via satellites in two-minute intervals, and if there's any straying because of, say, navigational errors, it will immediately be recognized and corrected. If the trials are successful, we could be equipped for the system and start using it by 1998 or 1999. In areas of high density, ever-climbing and descending traffic, such as Europe, we'll of course have to continue using ground-based, state-of-the-art radar surveillance and guidance.'

Meanwhile, DOTS (Dynamic Oceanic Track System), the other great American innovation, aims to manage transoceanic flights (in accordance with traffic demands, weather forecasts from Bracknell, and reports of wind conditions from pilots). It would offer alternative 'tracks' to flights to avoid congestion and bad weather, and could blend in the vast, now uncontrolled, airspaces with the flow management over continental United States. Once all aircraft are suitably equipped, it will be possible to fly safely with much less separation, and save time as well as fuel. The DOTS centre is already operational at Oakland, and using 'flexible tracks' through the South Pacific airspace, it controls some 200 departures a day. (When Qantas tested the system, the flight time of each aircraft was reduced by fifteen minutes, and the airline saved $15,000 on fuel in a single week.) It is estimated that DOTS could reduce delays by 50 to 90 per cent, and save some $19 million (including the cost of 1.4 million gallons of fuel) a year for the airlines flying the South Pacific alone – an area that represents only 4 per cent of the total Pacific traffic. Industry profitability would also increase because each flight could leave up to 4000 gallons of fuel on the ground, so that the lighter take-off weight would allow them to accept extra pay-load, passengers or cargo, on board.

As of now, if the whole of worldwide air traffic control were a centipede, it would seem to have ten feet in the next century – dragging the ninety others through the 1970s.

23

The Ogres We Live With

Among all the vagaries of the weather, it is probably the glorious summer day, rather than fog-bound airports, that is most likely to upset the average traveller's plans, for it is then that the whole world seems to be bent on taking to the clear skies – and the huge hold-ups develop. The 1992 Olympic Games almost led to a melt-down of the ATC systems over Europe. In one year delays and holding cost Air France, for instance, some Fr400 million (almost £50 million), and when, in the summer of 1991, a third of its flights could not take off or land on schedule, it lost Fr100 million in June alone. It is, of course, immeasurable what the delays cost the passengers in nerves and high blood pressure.

Those who want to swap their snow-bound cities for sunny beaches or ski slopes, may encounter traffic jams at Christmas or, though very rarely, be exposed to one of the oldest ogres that still haunts aviation.

ICING
  on the wings, and frozen flight controls, have caused countless accidents. The fact that icing is still an occasional menace is the clearest demonstration of an essential human failing: the combined reluctance and inability to learn from past mistakes, particularly when the evidence melts away.

On 10 March 1989, winter continued to retain its icy strangle-hold on Ontario, Canada. Two pilots reported for duty at Winnipeg airport at 06.40 to take Air Ontario Flight 1363, a Fokker F28, on a round trip to Manitoba, down to Thunder Bay on Lake Huron and back, with stops at Dryden. The APU (auxiliary power unit) was inoperative, but that was an allowable deficiency. Before take-off, the aircraft had to be de-iced. Some delays en route were caused partly by bad weather, and partly by some late check-ins at Thunder Bay where, after ten extra passengers had been accepted for the flight, some of the fuel had to be unloaded to prevent exceeding the eventual maximum landing weight. Because of that, the aircraft had to be refuelled at Dryden in a heavy snowfall. As the APU was out of order, and no ground power cart was readily available, one of the two engines could not be stopped for there would be no way to restart both without waiting for the cart. The company procedure authorized 'hot refuelling' (with an engine running), but that technique precluded de-icing by the pilots. The aircraft spent thirty-three minutes at the gate, and snow was accumulating on the wings.

This F28, a Dutch turbofan, had been built in 1972. It had been in service with the Turkish National Airlines until 1985 when it was 'mothballed'. It was sold, recertified, and leased to Air Ontario in 1988.

The airline operated primarily as a regional feeder, and had some difficulties integrating its first jets, two newly acquired F28s, into its fleet of turboprops. Both the captain and the first officer were relatively new to jets, and both were on record expressing the opinion that their training on the F28 had been hurried. (Most of the captain's great experience in cold-weather operations had been gained in 'bush-flying'. He had flown jets for only 673 hours, including no more than 82 hours on F28s. The first officer had only 66 hours on the type.) Because of their limited experience, they were subject to higher than standard requirements for take-off and landing minima, such as those concerning visibility.

It would eventually transpire that the captain was extremely safety-conscious. He had given his employers some forty reports (far more than any of his colleagues) about unsafe conditions, and he was regarded as overcautious if anything. He was also known to be very keen on punctuality, and 'felt an almost exaggerated sense of contractual obligation to his passengers'.* Now he had to cope with extra pressures. The crew were on the last leg of a four-day flight segment, and cumulative fatigue might have begun to take its toll. Unserviceable systems were an irritation. Upon their return to Winnipeg, both pilots were due to go on holiday. Flight 1363 was already an hour behind schedule. Any more delay would upset many of the sixty-five passengers who had holiday plans and connections to catch. The weather was deteriorating rapidly. If the flight failed to depart quickly, everybody would be stuck in a small terminal with hardly any facility for accommodation.

It is impossible to say how much all this affected the captain's decision to go, but it is likely that the combination of circumstances created a high degree of distraction and stress. One of the passengers, a policeman, was very familiar with cold-weather operations. He asked a flight attendant if some de-icing would be done. She said there was nothing to worry about, the aircraft had 'automatic' de-icing. That failed to reassure him because, he said, only the leading edges of the wings were so protected, and snow was turning into ice all over the wings. The flight attendant just shrugged, but then mentioned the ice to the captain in the cockpit. His response was acknowledgement but no apparent concern.

*_Aviation Safety_ magazine, 15.11.1992, quoting the Canadian investigation.

Soon after noon, the aircraft left the gate. As it was taxiing to Runway 29, the snowfall greatly intensified. Then there was another six minutes' delay to assist the landing of a Cessna pilot who had no instrument rating. The captain had 6000 feet of runway ahead of him as the F28 began its take-off roll. It is very likely that he did not understand fully how ice could build up, and did not appreciate the effects of ice on his aircraft. (Flight would have been possible only through much greater than normal acceleration, requiring a much longer runway than Dryden's.) On a dry runway, with uncontaminated wings, the F28 would reach V_r (rotation speed) of 125 knots after about a 2500-foot run. The captain actually rotated another thousand feet further on, but the nose dropped back on to the concrete. More power increased the speed to 130 knots, and the nose was lifted for the second time near the end of the runway, at the edge of a forest in a precipitous drop.

The aircraft climbed about 15 feet into the air, and in a nose-high attitude, with its wings rocking, hit the first of the tree-tops at 12.11. The main tank was ruptured. With the type of fuel the airline used, an immediate conflagration was inevitable.* The F28 blazed a 3000-foot swath through the forest and crashed in chest-high snow. The forward fuselage was enveloped in flames that burst into the cabin. Twenty-four of the sixty-nine people on board were killed, twenty-two were seriously injured. The policeman and the flight attendant who had talked about the icing were among the survivors.

As the Canadian Aviation Safety Board, that would have investigated the accident, was in a turmoil because of an overdue reorganization (Board members were still arguing about the findings of a disaster at Gander), a Commission of Inquiry was set up. Its three years' work, one of the longest investigations on record, recognized that, as in virtually all cases, a whole series of coinciding factors contributed to the cause of the accident. The captain's decision to fly, and try to rotate (lift-off) once again, was only the last, irreversibly fatal act. The report, published in 1992, ran to some 1700 pages in four volumes, and criticized the Canadian government, various authorities, the airline and the entire industry because the accident did not happen by chance: 'It was allowed to happen,' said Justice Moshansky of the Alberta Supreme Court who

*When fuel is spilt, fire is always a major risk. Some three decades ago, after a long and fierce battle in which the British Air Safety Group was a leading combatant, the much safer *aviation kerosene* replaced JP4, a mixture of kerosene and gasoline, almost universally, even though the latter attracted users with smaller weight and lower prices. The great advantage of kerosene – higher flash-point, i.e. lesser likelihood and slower development of post-crash fires – can be a disadvantage in cold-weather operations because JP4 lights more readily, and burns at a hotter temperature, even in severe winter conditions. Air Canada, the last major champion of JP4, is still not fully convinced that kerosene can save lives, but loads JP4 only at Edmonton, Victoria BC, Rouyn, Quebec, and Regina, Saskatchewan. JP4, also known as Jet B, is in fairly common usage in Canada, and in 1989 the tanks of the Air Ontario F28 contained a mixture of aviation kerosene and JP4.

chaired the Inquiry. The investigation came to the devastating conclusion that the industry still did not fully understand the causes and aerodynamic effects of icing on the wings; that there had been no 'definitive' regulations that could have prevented the operation of the aircraft in the given circumstances; that not only the captain of the F28, but also his colleagues and de-icing personnel, lacked a clear understanding of the limited effectiveness of de-icing fluids; and that improperly controlled practices had created a trap into which that schedule-pressured captain so tragically fell.

Moshansky expected that Canada, a country with much cold-weather flying, would be a leader in the research and development of safe practices, but found that 'compared with European standards and experience in this area, Canadian de-icing/anti-icing standards, methods, and facilities can best be described as primitive'. Many of the 193 recommendations of the Inquiry were published as interim reports, and implemented by Canada. All that was freely available to the international aviation community so that the hitherto unlearned lessons could serve air safety. And yet, if one disaster at Dryden had been 'allowed to happen', it was allowed to happen yet again just before the publication of the final Canadian report.

On 22 March 1992, New York's La Guardia airport was struck by a snow-storm. A USAir jet, an F28, was waiting for take-off. It was de-iced twice, but ice kept re-accumulating on the wings as the aircraft stood in the snow. Though the formation of ice is not always visible from the cockpit, pilots were still expected to make their own decision on whether to return to the gate for yet another treatment. They chose not to. Thirty-five minutes after the second de-icing, the pilots decided to take off – and used an unapproved technique, rotating at below the 'safety speed for freezing conditions'. The F28 climbed at a sharp angle, stalled, rolled abruptly, and crashed into the shallow waters of Flushing Bay. Hampering rescue efforts, the rising tide covered the wrecked fuselage, but miraculously only twenty-seven of the fifty-one occupants were killed.

If all that sounds ominously familiar to the reader, it gave an even more startling illusion of *déjà vu* to investigators. A month after the accident the FAA decided to issue much stricter guidance and regulations to help pilots make crucial decisions in freezing weather. In 1993, the NTSB found that the de-icing fluid that had been used would be effective only for the first eleven of the thirty-five minutes' wait, and reprimanded the FAA and the carriers for failing to develop a system that could cope with icing. Chris Witkowski, air safety director of the US Flight Attendants' Association, concluded that the La Guardia crash could and should have been prevented. It was revealed that United Airlines and Federal Express were already using a different kind of so-called Type 2 fluid, favoured in Europe, that was not a panacea but could provide up to forty-five minutes' protection in steady snowfall.

Captain Gert Andersson, Sweden's representative on a European de-icing task force, criticized US airlines for penny-pinching (Type 2 fluid could cost twice as much as Type 1), and the new FAA ruling (that nobody may take off with snow or ice *adhering* to the wings, control surfaces or propellers) because the word 'adhering' implied misleadingly that snow might blow off harmlessly during take-off. The Swedish policy was that the aircraft must be *free* of ice and snow.

Andersson must have been speaking from bitter experience in March 1992. Only three months earlier, an SAS MD81 jet, that had been standing all night in humid, sub-zero temperatures at Arlanda airport in Stockholm, was ready for take-off. The conditions were ideal for the formation of invisible clear ice, and a mechanic was worried. He ordered a second de-icing, but failed to double-check the wing with his hand or a screwdriver. (The original operating manual requires a tactile inspection, but either the text or the translation left room for ambiguity.)

That was the forerunner of a sequence of events that could have led to a major tragedy. The Danish captain, who had no idea that a hidden computer programme was working against him (as seen on page 27), prayed, and tried to find a field to land on, alerted his passengers to brace for impact and, avoiding two houses, managed to execute a textbook emergency landing. The aircraft had a wing ripped off, and broke into three, but the seven tons of fuel in the tanks did not catch fire. Nobody was killed, and only two people were seriously injured. Once again, 129 people owed their survival to superb airmanship – a craft that should not be called upon even as a last resort when the industry is facing an old ogre of great notoriety. Better de-icing agents, more research into the effects of freezing weather, and more thorough inspections may not eliminate the hazard itself, and may not amount to more than what investigators call 'rubber gloves for leaking fountain pens', but could still protect many passengers' and air crews' lives.

TURBULENCE

known as the 'angry air', has long been worrying to passengers. It had been blamed for numerous accidents, and filled so many headlines that Bobbie Allen, director of the NTSB's predecessor in the 1960s, once declared: 'If I were to write a best-selling novel, I'd put "turbulence" in the title . . . We don't know if we have a turbulence problem.' Once the industry had recognized that it *did* have such a problem, better weather forecasts and flying techniques eliminated it. Improved radars in the cockpit could pinpoint storms, and gave the pilot the choice of flying above, below or around them.

In the early days of the jets, it was expected that those superb machines would fly 'above the weather', but a strange phenomenon began to play dirty tricks on fighter pilots, the first to venture to those higher altitudes. 'I got lost above the clouds in 1951, ended up miles away from where I thought I was, and I suspected I must have made some stupid navigation error,' Captain Harry Harrison, manager of the simulator division of the British Caledonian Flight Training Centre, told me at Crawley, Sussex. 'It was only several years later that I fully understood that I had been a victim of something we hadn't even known to exist – jetstream.'

Jetstreams, high-velocity wind-tunnels up to a hundred miles wide and two miles deep – in which the air may move at 400 m.p.h. – criss-cross the skies, balancing world temperatures. Aviation soon learned to live with and take advantage of the jetstream (when it is a strong tail-wind, it can save a great deal of fuel), and yet another ogre was buried.

There was, however, no time to relax, for some accidents and hair-raising incidents revealed the existence of CAT (Clear Air Turbulence), another invisible ogre that was not associated with adverse weather conditions as it roamed the airways in clear blue skies. It would strike without warning, shake aircraft severely, and make a flight as rough as if it were bumping over cobble-stones. It could even send a jet plunging towards the ground, and as pilots struggled to pull out of the dive, there was a serious risk that the opposing forces would break off the wings, bend the structure and debilitate the control surfaces. Once again, preparedness for CAT and new flying skills answered the hazard, and modern jets proved their strength to survive violent maltreatment, as was amply illustrated by the China Airways dive and somersault over California (see Chapter 10).

In March 1993, another Jumbo had just left Anchorage, Alaska, when its port inner engine tore off. The aircraft rolled 50 degrees but recovered and landed without any further incident. At first the fuse-pins were suspected, but then it emerged that the cause of the upset must have been turbulence, also experienced by other aircraft flying in the area at the time. However vicious the air might have been, the aircraft was strong enough to withstand the assault. (The fuse-pin would have been the first to crack if there was metal fatigue, as suspected initially, but it was probably the last part of the structure to fail, allowing the engine to break free – and the pilot to control the aircraft.)

GLOBAL WEATHER FORECASTS

have improved to the point where the outlook for aviation could safely be called fair to good. From numerous sources, airports, observation posts, an incessant stream of information is pouring in, via fifteen regional forecasting centres, to the two WAMCs (World Area Meteorological Centres) in Washington DC and Bracknell in the UK. The WAMCs provide and continuously update worldwide wind, temperature, ceiling and visibility data for route forecasts, though news of 'significant weather' changes – thunderstorms, cyclones, mountain waves, sand storms or volcanic eruptions of ash, all phenomena that require an alteration of route or flight level – must often come from the pilots in the air. The data is disseminated to all airports and users of the airways.

Before each flight, one of the captain's essential duties is to study the weather charts, and ascertain what conditions could be expected during take-off, en route, and on arrival. (Surface conditions, the strength of wind along the route, may affect the pilot's fuel calculations. Adverse weather, such as fog or storms forecast for the destination airport, may require extra fuel reserves for extended holding in a stack or diversion to an unaffected airport where it would be safer to land. The reserves are governed by legal minima, but ultimately, the quantity loaded for that purpose is the captain's sole decision.)

The ongoing modernization of the meteorological services, and the faster dissemination of information through communication satellites in real time (to be operational by the middle of the decade) are essential for the ever more densely packed airways and, particularly, for the irresistible advance of twin-engine aircraft for extended range (ETOPs) flights over the oceans. Because of the financial attractions of such operations, the use of those twins has, unfortunately, spread faster than the forecast and dissemination technology in some Asian and African regions where the scarcity of data can leave the meteorological safety net in shreds.

While the regulatory authorities might have felt like dancing on the graves of turbulence, jetstreams and CAT, some mysterious events began to worry accident investigators. They knew that, quite inexplicably, some aircraft had crashed, as if they had been slammed to the ground. Other accidents had been attributed to thunderstorms that strangely enough had not affected in any way other aircraft near the same airports only a minute earlier or later. Could it be some new meteorological phenomenon? And if yes, what could it be? Some sort of adverse wind condition near the ground? They suspected some ferocious, invisible and unpredictable downdraught, which they called 'windshear'.

WINDSHEAR

became the new buzz-word, fit for the titles of more aviation sagas. But as a phenomenon, it was anything but new. Bud Laynor, an NTSB investigator, unearthed a case from as far back as 1943, when pilots, allowed to fly through thunderstorms, were only urged to avoid such 'inconveniences' if possible, for their passengers' comfort. Laynor's find was a DC3 accident, with testimony from a US Air Force pilot, one of the survivors who was in the habit of flying by the seat of his pants, like all his contemporaries, and reported that just before the crash, there had been 'a sudden change of pressure, and a light feeling on the seat, which indicated a sudden loss of altitude to me'. There were, of course, no flight recorders at the time, and the crash detectives, confronted with the intangible, used logic as their main source of evidence. They produced, nevertheless, a theory about some nebulous, stealthy downdraught, and made a series of defensive recommendations that were to be repeated by the NTSB again and again throughout the 1950s, 1960s and 1970s, while year after year that mysterious windshear kept killing planeloads of people.

It was in 1973 that genuine evidence of what had gone before could be found. Drifting fog and moderate rain reduced the visibility at Logan, the International Airport of Boston, Massachusetts, but an Iberia DC10 was cleared to land. Witnesses noticed that it 'came in desperately low' and was too low when it tried to recover before striking the approach light pier, then the harbour embankment, bursting into flames, and skidding alongside the runway. Almost incredibly, there were no fatalities, and it was only in the course of the evacuation that three passengers were seriously injured.

Cockpit voice recorders were not compulsory at the time, so verbal exchanges among the pilots were reconstructed from the crew's memory. It transpired that despite warnings of being too low, and despite the captain's efforts to apply more power to arrest the rate of descent, the aircraft had continued to sink too rapidly – as if it were being pushed towards the ground. It was one of the relatively early models of Digital Flight Data Recorders on board that came to the assistance of the investigation. The data in the battered casing revealed the heading-airspeed-altitude sequence of the descent. From that it was known how an aircraft would normally respond to the pilot's input. If it did not, the too-rapid descent and inexplicable behaviour of the machine had to be due to an outside influence – the force of a sudden low-altitude windshear that appears from nowhere and disappears without trace. Suspicion then fell upon the pilot: did he simply fail to handle the unexpected? All the relevant conditions were fed into a simulator, and experienced fliers tried to cope with them. They could not. They 'crashed' repeatedly.

It was then discovered that several previous accidents, that had seemed to be mysterious or had been attributed to thunderstorms, might have been caused by similar downdraughts. The NTSB recommended that all pilots should be trained specifically for flying out of low-level windshear, and that equipment for detecting, reporting and measuring the elusive phenomenon should be developed without any delay.

Delay, however, was inevitable. Some people refused to believe in 'fairy-tales'. Weren't there, after all, some special circumstances in the Logan crash? And weren't the pilots just too slow to react to windshear in all the incidents and accidents that followed? Ninety-six people were killed at Pago Pago in a PanAm 707 crash in 1974, 113 more aboard

Eastern Air Lines Flight 66 at New York's JFK in 1975. It was then that, equipped with all the data from flight and voice recorders, meteorology expert Professor Fujita of Chicago University studied and laid bare the anatomy and nature of low-level windshear, and coined the punchy expression 'microburst',* a dramatic way to summarize what might ambush the unprepared and the ignorant. As numerous cases were re-examined on the strength of new evidence, 'Microburst' might have been stamped on old reports (yes, that 1943 case, too) proving that the investigators' imaginative reasoning had been right throughout, and that in those circumstances the crew would have had neither the knowledge to identify the problem nor sufficient time to deal with it.

And yet, in the light of bitter experience with icing, it would only be the naïve champion of blind faith in human nature who would expect instantaneous response to newly found wisdom. Too much was left for too long to the individual carriers to choose the level of pilots' training for windshear, and only a few proved to be more caring than the average. Non-American pilots and airlines refused to believe that the risk existed outside the areas of extreme climate, in places like Denver, Colorado, the true home of the phenomenon, where 330 microbursts a year could be expected. 'The FAA produced a Low-Level Windshear Alert system that gave us some patchy protection,' said Laynor, 'but we were still a long way from developing airborne warning devices and ground-based microwave doppler radar to let us *see* the invisible.' (Windshear is not always associated with heavy rain and harsh weather conditions. In the American Mid-West, and regions of the high planes, the hazard is often manifested without any accompaniment of rain.)

So the windshear-related incidents and fatal accidents continued. Though there were some lucky escapes due to more thorough training by some companies, including Eastern and its B727 pilot at Atlanta in 1979, windshear training remained non-compulsory. Some airlines claimed they had no time for it, others issued information to their pilots that read more like entertainment than caution.

In the mid-1980s, by which time microbursts had chalked up a known toll of some 600 deaths, the most concerned American airlines and manufacturers got together to create a common strategy. But it still

---

*Though to the expert it may sound like over-simplification, the microburst is a violent downdraught that hits the ground, and fans out like an inverted mushroom, sending horizontal wind in all directions. If it happens during take-off, the pilot flies into strong head-wind that makes him believe – because of his indicated airspeed – that he is climbing out too fast. As he tries to pull up and slow down, he is struck by the downdraught, and loses his indicated airspeed. Instinctively, he puts the nose down to regain speed, but then he is caught in a strong tail-wind that makes him believe, through the indicated airspeed once again, that he is flying too slowly. Stall-warning and his 'stick-shaker' also tell him that he might be about to stall. In order to prevent that, and to recapture his elusive airspeed, he directs the nose even further downwards – and flies into the ground. The microburst-induced sequence during an approach can be just as menacing and potentially disastrous. The latest technique teaches pilots to disregard misleading warnings and their own instincts.

needed a disaster at Dallas Fort Worth International (Delta L1011 Tristar in 1985) to cut through bureaucratic hold-ups and lead to improved and compulsory training levels, as well as a priority programme for the research and installation of windshear detecting and warning devices. 'Priority', however, was not synonymous with immediacy. The slow progress continued to evoke a great deal of criticism from safety experts, some of whom saw it as just one of the gaps in preparedness for emergencies. (For example, Tony LeVier, one of the greatest names among American test pilots, set up SAFE, an organization dedicated to Safe Action in Flight Emergency, to provide additional tuition, because he does not believe that 'the authorities [such as the FAA] even come close to what a pilot needs in the way of flight emergency training'.)

As recently as in December 1992, a DC10 of the Dutch Martinair wanted to land in stormy weather at Faro in Portugal. The visibility was good, but in heavy rain and gusting wind, the captain abandoned his first approach and decided to go round. On his second attempt, the low-level wind conditions changed suddenly. The right wing-tip hit the ground. The aircraft veered off the runway, broke into three sections, and burst into flames. Of the 13 crew and 327 passengers, 286 people, including the two pilots, walked away from the crash – a testimony to the strength of modern aircraft, and to the new, increased survivability of accidents. But the cause of what happened was one of the old ogres – microburst. The crew made no emergency calls, they received no windshear warning, and could not even guess that they had a problem.

Just a fortnight later, the British AAIB issued its findings about a near-disaster of British Airways. The report read in some respects like a script for Faro. In December 1991, a BAe ATP (a short-range, regional turboprop) had just risen from the runway of Sumburgh airport, Shetland, when it began to roll sharply to starboard. The wing-tip scraped the ground, and the aircraft veered perilously towards a high ridge near by. The pilot could not have known what had rendered his aircraft almost uncontrollable. Had his reactions been any slower or less perfect, a serious crash would have been inevitable. He managed, however, to make a safe landing, and all the thirty people on board escaped without a scratch. The investigation revealed what had caused the incident: the wind, gusting to 70 knots, was so strong that while the pilot was still taxiing, and unbeknown to him, it snapped the control rods of the right aileron that governs the roll of the aircraft. He did not know about the force of the wind either, because the single anemometer of the airport did not give an accurate reading close to the runway surface. The BA operations manual (now amended) gave cross- and tail-wind limits for take-off and landing, but did not mention conditions for taxiing even though the manufacturers had predicted that strong surface wind could damage the controls.

The vital importance of windshear training is at last recognized virtually everywhere (simulator training, that can reproduce the frightening conditions, is expensive, and some poorer airlines hope to stay lucky with their illusory economizing), but people like Harrison warn that 'some microbursts can be of such severity that they're virtually unflyable,' and Laynor admits that 'nothing but avoidance is the ultimate answer to the problem'.

Yet it is only now that airborne and ground-based equipment, capable of predicting and detecting microbursts, has begun to reinforce the armour of flying. One of the newly developed systems is being installed, albeit only gradually, at 102 US airports. The CAA announced that windshear detectors would eventually be available at large airports. The major airlines are planning to replace reactive weather radars by costly predictive ones aboard their aircraft. The best news is that in several recent cases, the pilots did not need to rely on good fortune for their safety. In 1993, Denver airport detected a 95-knot windshear that could have led to the repetition of any of the great disasters. The airport alerted an approaching flight of Continental; the captain had no time to avoid the microburst that slammed his B737 down, but being fore-warned, he took advantage of the latest escape technique (footnote on page 203) that goes against the merely instinctive reaction, and managed to recover from the dive when the aircraft was only 400 feet from the ground.

24

Ageism in the Air

The age of an aircraft tends to elicit wildly contrasting, rational and completely irrational reactions. On a course to combat the fear of flying, a young man asked, 'How do I know that the plane has not exceeded its fly-by date?' The answer – 'You've got to trust us' – did not seem to reassure him. Boarding a just-out-of-the-wrappers Airbus, another passenger once exclaimed in horror: 'But this is brand new! How do I know that all the snags have been ironed out?' And a much-sculpted Hollywood star told me: 'In my next life, I wanna be an airplane. I mean, with all that spare-part surgery they're actually rejuvenated, and they just seem to go on and on . . .'

That film star's idea of eternal youth seemed at first sight to be rather dodgy when in 1992 tourists for a local flight on a Kenyan safari were ushered to an ancient *Dakota*, a Douglas DC3, once the darling of air passengers and the industry. They were not at all sure that they were ready for an historic adventure aboard a museum piece. But they soon grew fond of that 'dear old Dak' that gave them the experience of 'real flying' while reading its biography handed out by Airkenya, its operator.

Bearing serial number 4890, the Dak was born and delivered to the US Army Air Force on 13 March, 1942! Like most of the 10,655 members of its family, it served throughout the war as a Skytrain troops-carrier. When the Daks were 'demobbed' (they already had the reputation as an efficient and comfortable airliner for short and medium range), number 4890 went to Spain, served Iberia in 'civvies' for twenty years, then returned to the military, that time with a Spanish Air Force School, for another thirteen-year stretch. It was sold in 1978, gained a British Certificate of Airworthiness, and joined the Kanana Sugar Corporation in Khartoum. Alas, a year later, retirement beckoned and the Dak became a donor of spare parts to various relatives. In 1986, after several years on the ground, the mutilated corpse was struck off the civil register. But following a take-over, the new owners of the wreck recognized the old twinkle in its windscreen, and in 1990 embarked on a course of rejuvenation. It was a painstaking labour of love, and the old

206

Dak is now one of some 300 still in service, mostly in the Third World. 'They have proved almost indestructible.'*

GERIATRIC AIRCRAFT

'The Boeing position,' says Vice-President Ben Cosgrove, in charge of the Engineering Division, 'is that given proper inspection and maintenance, airplanes can be safely flown indefinitely.' He then proceeded to qualify that brave, sweeping statement, made in 1990, barely two years past a most ominous event that had raised some profound questions. Were all owners of ageing aircraft willing, and technologically capable, to provide that indispensable loving and meticulous care? Could they afford it? Would the regulatory authorities spot any slip-up without the slightest delay?

That most ominous event is remembered as Flight 243. The aircraft, a B737 (hull number 152), had its first, the only compulsory, visual inspection of the day by an experienced crew in the pre-dawn darkness of 28 April 1988. The normal Aloha Airlines schedule called for numerous short 'island-hopping' from Honolulu, Hawaii. By 11 a.m. it had completed three round-trips to Hilo, Maui and Kauai, then returned to Maui, on to Hilo, where at 13.15 passengers boarded through the jet bridge for the twenty-minute hop to Honolulu. One of them noticed a crack in the fuselage, about halfway between the cabin door and the hood of the jet bridge, but did not want to make a nuisance of herself, and mentioned it to no one.

Flying at 24,000 feet, the pilots heard a loud 'clap' followed by a 'whooshing' sound. The first officer's head was jerked backwards. The air in the cockpit filled with floating debris. The aircraft began to roll – and the captain was startled by the view behind him: the door had gone, and he saw only blue sky where the ceiling of the first-class cabin had been. By then there was severe decompression, and the pilots donned oxygen masks as they initiated an emergency descent. The wind noise was such that they could communicate only by hand signals.

In the cabin, there was mayhem. All passengers were seated and strapped in when there was the loud bang – the explosive decompression sounded like a bomb going off – and part of the ceiling and left-hand wall were gone. A stewardess, standing at Row Five, was immediately sucked out through the jagged edges, and disappeared. (The eventual extensive sea search would never find her.) Another one suffered serious head injuries. The third was thrown to the ground and bruised, but got up and tried to calm her passengers who had to dodge heavy items sailing through the air.

The captain decided to divert to Maui that was only ten minutes' away, and asked for emergency services to be ready if the aircraft ever got

*Airliners by W. Green and G. Swanborough (published in the 'Observers' series by Penguin/ Frederick Warne).

down in one piece. Flying as skilfully as test pilots after one of the engines coughed and died, the crew executed a perfect touch-down. The fuselage 'wiggled and buckled' but refused to break up. (Inexplicably, the evacuation took twenty-five minutes.) The pilots, whose 'nursing' had protected the integrity of the structure, received the IFALPA Polaris Award.

Pictures of the 'B737 with the sunshine top' flooded the world press. For the investigators, the good news was the strength of the aircraft. The bad news was that the accident was completely preventable, and worse, that it should never have happened because it was also *foreseeable*.

The 737s started to roll off the production line in 1965. They became popular work-horses for short- to medium-range routes, and some 1200 were sold worldwide. (Later variants brought the total sales to almost 5000.) After hull number 291 had been built, Boeing strengthened the skin of the fuselage to counter the signs of hardly visible corrosion brought about by numerous short flights with frequent pressurization and depressurization and by prolonged exposure to a saltwater atmosphere. Following some research, and service difficulty reports from users, Boeing issued several Service Bulletins for inspection and skin strengthening, but compliance with SBs is never mandatory.

In 1981, a second-hand 737 (hull number 151) of the Taiwanese Far Eastern Air, suffered a pressurization failure in flight. It underwent some minor repairs, was given only limited time for inspection because of the false economy of maximum utilization, and took off again the following day. At 22,000 feet, the fuselage burst open and disintegrated in the air, killing 110 people. (It was suspected that the cabin floor, under which the controls ran, had collapsed because of heavy corrosion that might have been caused by saltwater from the frequent carriage of raw fish. A Boeing internal memo revealed that a skin-strengthening kit had been supplied sixteen months earlier, but that it was still in the airline stores at the time of the crash.) The FAA issued Airworthiness Directives that made corrosion inspections and repairs compulsory. Boeing SBs gained 'Alert' status. And it was at this time – in the mid-eighties, years before the accident – that Aloha found substantial rust and cracks on hull number 152, requiring urgent repairs.

Were those aircraft metal-fatigued geriatrics? And if yes, how come they were nowhere near their proven fatigue-safe life-span? In 1982, the American Blue Ribbon Panel of scientists examined some fatigue-caused accidents, suggested the designation of hazard areas that could lead to uncontained damage to aircraft structure (exactly what might have prevented the Japanese Jumbo crash on Mount Ogura in 1987), and made the seemingly wild prediction that *the top skin of a B737 might just peel off by 1987 or 1988*. In 1986, the Chairman of the NTSB warned against rust (particularly on aircraft flown in salt air and near sulphur-producing industry), and criticized users whose rust monitoring seemed merely incidental during inspections for fatigue. After the Aloha case, accusations and counter-accusations erupted concerning who had warned whom about what, and finally the NTSB's 257-page report strongly criticized the airline's maintenance practices, the quality of FAA inspections, and the lack of forceful intervention by the FAA and the manufacturers. Its twenty-one recommendations pointed in the right direction to prevent, at the irredeemable cost of a young woman's life, any disastrous repetitions.

The much more stringent regulations and supervision that followed were geared to the full assessment of an aircraft's ageing process. Unlike the rings in a tree-trunk, no annual birth certificates are notched up on a fuselage by the number of years flown. So the simplistic statement that an airliner is so many years old is virtually meaningless. Hull number 151 at Taiwan was only seven years old in 1981. Hull number 152 at Hawaii was fourteen. A similar aircraft, tested continuously on a Boeing testbed, was older, and 737s of the same age showed up no serious problems. The great difference was in the use to which they had been put, and in the tell-tale, albeit unnoticed or ignored, effects of the special environment they had endured.

Incessant monitoring and immediate 'stopping of the rot' wherever it occurs, the history of (however minor) damages an aircraft has suffered, and the number of *cycles* flown determine the age and signs of geriatricity.

Every time a jet is pressurized, it is blown up a little like a balloon. Depressurization returns it to its original shape. Aircraft like the 737 are designed to fly at least four times as many cycles as a 747 that plies the long routes. While a DC10 might have been flying from Miami to London with just one take-off and one landing, that 737 with the 'sunroof' was doing its tenth cycle on that single fateful day in 1988 – and still had an afternoon's work ahead of it. (By then it had completed some 90,000 cycles, a record surpassed by just one other 737 at the time.) On the other hand, a long-haul airliner is exposed to the greater pressure differences at the higher altitudes it flies, and will eventually suffer some infinitesimal but permanent stretching that imposes extra stresses on the structure and could become critical.

REJUVENATION

Bearing all that in mind, every airliner is now subjected to even stricter maintenance schedules. With ongoing replacement of parts and skin, nothing but its hull-numbered name will be left of the original.

Rejuvenation is, however, expensive. After Hawaii, it was calculated that the necessary work on the Boeing geriatrics would cost $800 million, and that some 1700 B727s would require the most urgent attention. The expenditure on the smaller McDonnell-Douglas fleet would amount to about $600 million. Modifications on each ageing Airbus took sixty-five man-hours per inspection, and 350 man-hours for the installation of a structural reinforcement kit. Regulatory authorities knew that the immediate enforcement of such expenditures could cripple some airlines, many of which were only too eager to find loopholes that would allow delays in their response. In America, for instance, more than 3000 Boeings were given just one year to comply with the ADs. The FAA reckoned that although many older aircraft of eleven models on the US register were scheduled to be retired before the 1995 final deadline, more than 1000 large aircraft would still be used in passenger transport – with only four-fifths of them having completed all the necessary alterations. That is why in 1993 the US General Accounting Office found it necessary to urge the FAA to obtain a clearer picture of the suspect rate of compliance with the rules for rejuvenation.

The leniency in the time limits for the work exposed a massive gulf between rich and poor. A well-to-do airline may see the effort as a trade-off between the extra cost (a major, so-called D-check may take 80,000 man-hours on an old B707) and the fact that an elderly aircraft has already earned its keep, and any revenue-it brings in is pure profit. A poor carrier may want only the barest essentials done to its geriatrics, just enough so as not to fall foul of the law. So once again, the actual *birth-date* of an airliner matters far less than its operator's *safety disposition*. It is indisputable that an old aircraft can be perfectly safe. There are hundreds of Jumbos, DC10s, Airbuses, B727s, Ilyushins and Tupolevs, to mention but a few types, in their third decade of service, reaching or already exceeding their design life, but the manufacturers, at least in Western countries, use testbeds continuously to keep ahead of actual utilization. (Two DC9s that have flown almost 100,000 cycles – twice as many as their design lives were planned to be.)

Leading airlines constantly upgrade their fleets to the latest models with improved economy, reduced fuel consumption, greater dispatch reliability, additional safety devices, extra comfort, and increased payload. It is an unwritten law of the industry that nobody advertises safety (a single mishap could wipe out the effect of millions spent on promotion), so apart from claims of superior service in the air and on the ground, the purchase of new aircraft is one of the few subjects the airlines like to brag about. Singapore Airlines advertises that it offers 'the youngest, most modern fleet in the world'. SWISSAIR is proud that all its aircraft are under four years of age. An average fleet is about ten years old – ageing quite fast because cash-starved major airlines defer the delivery of new orders and extend the utilization of their fleets. Continental – having sheltered from creditors in 'Chapter 11' bankruptcy protection for twenty-nine months, and using a $450 million investment by Air Canada – can now afford to embark on a massive modernization programme. It ordered ninety-two and took options on another ninety-eight Boeings to replace its older aircraft. It aims to run the youngest US fleet, and achieve an annual operational saving of $300 million.

But what happens to all those old machines? If not sold directly, they join the fleet of more than a thousand laid up in places such as the Mojave desert and Marana, Arizona (where the dry heat protects them from corrosion), awaiting offers from those who can afford to fly only . . .

SECOND-HAND AIRCRAFT

The greater the glut, the cheaper the aircraft. Relatively modern Airbuses and upgraded 737s used to keep their value reasonably well, but these days many bargains are available. (A new B737-400, the latest version of the type, costs between $36 million and $42 million. A good, ten-year-old B737-200 can be picked up for about $8 million.) And the second-hand user is not the end of the line. After a crash at Bombay in 1993, along with allegations of pilot negligence, it was revealed that eight of the twenty-two B737s in Indian Airlines service were between fifteen and twenty years old. The proclaimed company policy was to retire every aircraft over twenty years of age.* Irrespective of geriatricity, the discards could be snapped up by those who want to operate on a shoestring or start up yet another small airline with hardly any capital, relying on the vanity of newly born countries or the gullibility of banks and other investors. That is where the real problems with geriatric aircraft begin – and ageism exercised by passengers would be wholly justified.

For those bottom-of-the-market buyers there is an unwritten dodgy aircraft register known to the trade. Many old aeroplanes on that list are traded repeatedly with an increasingly incomplete or crudely doctored service history. By the time they reach their sixth or seventh owner, they may be sold allegedly for scrap to circumvent the need of certification. Yet miraculously, the scraps often re-appear in the air. It is rumoured that certain African and South American authorities are only too happy to turn a blind eye on the continued use of some clapped-out, badly neglected Tridents, Caravelles or Ilyushin-18s that are well into their fourth decade with more than 100,000 hours on the clock.

At that time, just when a geriatric machine would need substantial modernization and repairs, the most careful nursing in flight, and the greatest expertise in maintenance, the end-of-the-line owners lack well-trained pilots, engineers, mechanics and facilities. To satisfy at least the superficial demands imposed by their governments for domestic flights – not to mention other countries' standards if they venture abroad – they go in search of stamped and signed documents that look convincing. The reputable, internationally known maintenance companies will warn

*Flight International, 5.5.1993.

and advise the operator, and will not agree to do anything less to any aircraft than mechanically and legally necessary. (It could cost them their licences if they tried.) But there is always somebody who chases a fast buck to be made on a scam. Some American outfits have now been closed down – but they operated long enough around Miami to earn the area the name Corrosion Corner. It is suspected that some of them have now set up shop elsewhere. Some Third World maintenance bases are excellent, but others take advantage of the availability of cheap though poorly qualified labour (local rates could be a third of, say, Swedish or French wages), and they may be willing to do only as much or rather as little as the client requires even if it is no more than a fresh coat of paint: after all, it is the operator's and the passengers' problem at the end of the day.

Since not all governments' expertise and caution can be fully trusted to ensure the quality and safety of aircraft on their certification register, it is left to the countries those machines visit to spot dodgy operators, refuse them landing rights, prevent them from taking off if they did manage to land, and keep an eye on maintenance cowboys, some of whom have now been banned worldwide. Bogus, substandard and therefore cheap aircraft parts have crept even into the maintenance workshops of some major airlines. An American nationwide investigation helped to clean up at least the air transport industry, but owners of general aviation and business aircraft might have no idea what risks a cut-price quote for a job may entail. Just as these lines were being written, news was coming in about the investigation of an Ayres 32R accident. It emerged that a Texas maintenance company had made false entries in the records of at least two small aircraft, endangered safety, and installed an unauthorized type of engine that caused the fatal crash. The owner of the workshop was indicted by federal grand jury. If convicted, he could be imprisoned for up to twenty years, with fines of up to $250,000. It would be difficult to impose any punishment that was commensurate to the potential slaughter caused by the negligent repair or operation of a truly geriatric passenger aircraft.

25

Upmarket Sherlock Holmes

An aircraft crashed near a British airport. The pilot had not reported any problems during the flight, so it sounded very ominous when an elderly woman on the ground who was clearly in a state of shock, told a policeman just a few minutes after the accident: 'I saw it. With my sister. It was terrible. It was wavering up and down violently in the air, and then we heard the crash.' An erratic flight path might have indicated control problems. It could be an important lead to the investigators.

'Old ladies are not very good witnesses,' says Eric Newton, one of the now retired gurus of investigation. 'Sometimes they report they *knew* something would crash. How come? "Just felt it in my bones." Yet we can't ignore any potential clues. Young teenagers are excellent witnesses. They just report what they saw. Adults may try to get in on the act. Their memories may be influenced by what they *hear* in the pub or on TV. They might claim to have *seen* something. When we take them to the spot where allegedly they made their observation, we may find there's a mountain blocking their view to the airspace the aircraft had traversed. So we checked the old lady's address: yes, her house faced in the right direction, and there had been no other flights in the area at that time.

'An investigator then visited the house, and took the same chair where one of the witnesses had sat knitting and watching the incoming flight. While he was listening to the sisters' statements, he heard engine noise, looked up, and to his horror saw another aircraft "wavering up and down violently". It was, of course, a flaw in the glass through which all aircraft would appear to be flying out of control.'

Taking and evaluating witness reports is a special skill, but only a small part of the investigation of aviation accidents and incidents – probably the last word in great detective work. It calls for the aircrash detectives' vast combined knowledge of aeronautics, engineering, electronics, air traffic control, meteorology, psychology, pathology, as well as a great deal of brilliant ingenuity, logic and perspicacity to find out and prove what factors have contributed to a disastrous sequence of events, and also to exonerate all other elements (the human one included) of the 'million spare parts flying in close formation' that could not have played a role in the mishap.

The investigation of the first passenger transport aircrash took only about three seconds:* in 1908, five years after his first ever powered flight, Orville Wright had to prove to the US Army that aviation might have a future, and demonstrate that his contraption could carry passengers. With Lt Thomas E. Selfridge behind him, he circled above a parade ground at an altitude of 150 feet, descended to 75 feet, but then his machine began to side-slip. Wright peered out of his birdcage seat, and a single glance told him everything: the wooden propeller blade had splintered and cut the wires controlling the rudder. A nose-dive was inevitable. The cause was known long before the plane hit the ground. Wright suffered a broken leg; the lieutenant was pinned under the engine and killed. The event was reported with understandable consternation because the victim had had no control over his own fate (a factor which sets the tone for the sensational headlines air accidents always attract).

The fast progress of aviation created scores of new conundrums, and until quite recently 'pilot error' and sometimes 'the weather' were blamed if anything baffled the investigators. None of the findings would ever surpass the simplicity of the earnest declaration of a British military Court of Inquiry: 'The cause of this accident is perfectly clear – what goes up must come down.' That startling conclusion during World War I did not even attempt to establish the real cause and thus forestall any potential repetitions, but at that time any pilot who had survived a crash was immediately sent up again 'to restore his nerves'. In 1911, a military pilot had to bear the blame for a crash due to his 'error of judgement' in 'selecting an unsuitable place for landing'. It occurred to no one to impose any limitations on the choice.

The second reason why air crashes receive huge press attention is that they are spectacular tragedies on a large scale, claiming perhaps hundreds of victims in one go, as opposed to the unnewsworthy facts that an appalling multitude is maimed – though only one by one – when falling down ladders and stairs or that in Britain alone more than a thousand people are drowned every summer (almost twice the number killed by the entire world aviation in an average year).

No matter how much the aircrash detectives' work has grown in complexity and preventive determination, the demand for instant answers and solutions is just as vociferous now as it was in the wake of Lt Selfridge's historical death. Reputable journalists fall into the trap of righteous indignation when, the day after an accident, the investigators *still* cannot name the cause. Even *The Times*, noted for its accuracy, let a

Aircrash Detective by Stephen Barlay (Hamish Hamilton, 1969).

report slip through saying, 'When American airliners fall out of the sky, investigators usually take little time to find the probable cause, then apportion blame and advise on steps to avoid a repeat. Now, for once, the experts are stumped' (4.3.1992). In fact, investigators need a *long* time, sometimes years, to discover and publish all the causes of a case, and they *never* even *try* to apportion blame. But it is true that if any of their early findings might help to eradicate a problem, it will be passed on to the industry without delay, and also that, in this particular case, they were 'stumped'. One must add, however, that they were deeply concerned, too: despite lengthy investigation, and the elimination of all conceivable causes, the crash of that United Airlines B737 at Colorado Springs in 1991, on which *The Times* was commenting, is still one of the few mysteries on record.

Aircrash detectives – particularly those who work for the foremost investigative agencies, the American NTSB and the British AAIB – talk about 'wasted lives' whenever, however rarely, a riddle remains unsolved, because those deaths fail to provide the posthumous benefit of saving other passengers' lives. The investigators are often seen as the goalkeepers of safety, but in fact the regulatory authorities, who must act upon the findings and recommendations, are our ultimate line of preventive defence. Such follow-up work may sometimes be called tombstone engineering, improvement brought about by tragedy, but the closure of the gate after the horse has bolted will at least protect the rest of the stable.

Unfortunately, the study of hundreds of case histories and consultations with leading experts force us to claim that . . .

. . . THERE ARE NO NEW TYPES OF ACCIDENT

Every single disaster has its forerunner in the shape of another crash or incident (i.e. the catastrophe that did not happen by luck, the grace of god or the shutting of one of the numerous gates that must all be open before an accident can happen). And in this sense, it is fair to say that although aviation is astonishingly safe, it could be made even safer. If the causes of a crash are not revealed in the first instance (such as the early Comets or B727s) the writing is on the wall, and a carbon copy occurrence is only a matter of time. Similarly, when the findings are not acted upon (such as after the loss of a DC10 loading door), disasters, such as the Turkish one at Ermenonville, are inevitable.

The urge not to let old ogres strike again, the fervent desire for saving lives and an insatiable curiosity are the pillars that safeguard the aircrash detectives' sanity when time and again they confront tragedy, gore and the befuddling aftermath of accidents. They might as well call upon Kipling's 'serving-men' (quoted in Chapter 17) when they try to answer the essential questions: *What* happened *Where* and *When, How* could and did it happen, and above all, *Why*? What is demanded of them used to be called the finding of the cause or causes, the probable cause, the contributory factors, the sequence of doom, etc. – and the words are still subject to extensive debate to pin down the principles. But basically, it is the discovery *how all the single-failure-proof defences of a flight could fall like dominoes* after just one human or mechanical slip-up, that might have been facilitated by the coincidence of detrimental circumstances that could have served up an outright invitation to errors and malfunction.

Facing that intricate task, aircrash detectives, supported by specialists from airlines and manufacturers, attack on several fronts simultaneously. They unearth the history of the flight, the condition and service record of the aircraft, the operator's practices and work regulations, the crew's training, experience, health, work habits and potential fatigue; they check the weather reports, the role played by air traffic control, and the communications inside the cockpit and with the flight, until they can reconstruct all the events that could have been a cause or the consequence of flaws in the system. The reconstruction does not stop at the point of impact. It continues into all aspects of design, survivability, the crashworthiness of the cabin, the post-crash behaviour of the crew and the passengers, and a gradual understanding of all the circumstances that might have contributed to the death or escape of all aboard.

The full details of a single case can (and sometimes do) add up to a book-length story, but let us pick just a few simplified examples of the investigators' logic.

The 'wreckage wallahs' are among the first at the scene of an accident. Thousands of pieces of mangled metal may be strewn all over an ocean, glaciers, swamps or jungles, but if at all possible every piece must be recovered (with the spot where it was found marked on a map) for sorting, laboratory examination, and if necessary the reconstruction of, say, a wing or even the whole aircraft, like a million-piece jigsaw, on chickenwire. At 'the scene of the crime' there is hardly ever a 'smoking gun with convenient fingerprints', but the lay-out of the wreckage as well as individual items may carry tell-tale signs. If, for instance, parts of an aircraft are found miles apart along the flight path, the structure must have begun to disintegrate in the air. The first piece to fall off and land furthest away from the crash site might point a finger at a prime suspect. *Why* it broke off is, of course, another matter. It might have been caused by many reasons including a structural weakness or a violent manoeuvre brought about by the weather or the pilot's action, such as trying to avoid another aircraft. The forward spread of the wreckage could indicate the speed of the impact; aerial photographs of scorched, gradually razed treetops, leading to the crash site in a forest, would be better than a sworn statement about the angle of descent.

Many 'tricks of the trade' are so obvious (to those who have thought about them) that even Dear Watson would see them as elementary. Suppose a broken part of the cockpit is heavily stained by smoke. The pattern may show if it was stationary while picking up the deposits. But was it exposed to flames or smoke before or after breaking free? The piece is married to a formerly adjoining part, and the picture tells a story: the smoke marks stop along the line of the fracture, the break-up therefore must have preceded the fire. Similarly, if one piece is badly scored, but the indentation does not continue beyond the fracture, the damage must have occurred after the break-up. The jagged edges of surface paint may reveal in which direction two adjoining bits were torn apart. If a rod connected to a control surface is broken, and the fracture bears the hallmarks of metal fatigue under the microscope, the cause of the crash might have been found – as long as all other evidence offers confirmation. If a crumpled chunk of wreckage from the tail holds a tattered length of textile that used to belong to the cabin furnishings, something must have happened in the cabin, some force must have torn away and jettisoned that shred of carpet or seat upholstery, before that piece of metal was crushed, capturing it in its jaws. So the damage to that tail section must have been subsequent to another even closer to the start of the mishap.

In the early 1960s an old Britannia aircraft accident produced a classic of medical investigation. The hull was sufficiently undamaged to render a crash-landing survivable, and yet a large proportion of the passengers died in their seats. The pathologists discovered that smoke inhalation had killed them. But why? The fire did not break out until some time after the impact. Why did they fail to escape? Further examinations found that the victims' shins had been broken. The individual injuries, in an almost identical position, were matched to the structures, and the explanation presented itself: there was a horizontal strengthening bar in the back of each seat. As the impact brought the aircraft to a sudden halt, inertia forced the passengers' limbs to flail forwards, the shins broke on those bars, and stunned passengers with broken legs were unable to extricate and save themselves in time. Since then, no similar case has been recorded, because with the exception of some older Russian jets, those strengthening bars have been designed out of virtually all aircraft seats.

'We, like all investigative bodies, have a statutory mandate to determine the cause of accidents, make recommendations, and conduct specific safety studies into problems,' Carl Vogt, the Chairman of the NTSB told me. 'As 65 per cent of the world air traffic is within the United States, and an increase by some 30 per cent is expected in the next couple of decades, ours is a vital function – we must run if we want to stay still at the current level of safety. It is also our duty to ensure that the FAA, the regulatory authority, will act upon our findings and recommendations. These days we try not to be aggressively adversarial. We recognize that the FAA must consider wider aspects and cannot accept all our advice, but we're not in a popularity contest. We watch the fate of every one of our recommendations. If it gains acceptance status from the FAA, that is not good enough for us: we keep track of regulatory action, and we close a case only if we see implementation. Currently we have an 80 per cent success rate. Because of our relatively new non-adversarial approach, we're often asked: is there a danger that the relationship between the investigators and the regulators could become too cosy? Not at all. For if we're dissatisfied with the speed or extent of the FAA's response, we have the power to go public, and turn to Congress if there is no other way.'

NOTHING IS GONE WITH THE WIND ANY MORE

Barely three decades ago, aircrash detectives had to rely on finding Sherlock Holmesian clues. A battered altimeter dug out of the wreckage might have revealed that the pilot had set it, erroneously, to QFE instead of QNH – one relates to the altitude of an airport, the other to that airport's height above mean sea level – and the difference between the two would explain why the aircraft flew into the ground. In some cases, the indentation on a wristwatch set the precise moment of a tragedy. The position of a pointer might have left a tell-tale shadow on a smoke-covered instrument face. Even electrical equipment used to preserve material evidence: the good investigator could tell if a filament-type bulb or valve in the instrument panel was on or off at the moment when the glass was broken, because if the filament was undamaged, it must have been off, i.e. cold, when something violent happened to the bulb – whereas if the filament was on, hot and glowing when the 'envelop' shattered, the wire, suddenly exposed to oxygen, would have stretched and burnt.

Since those days, recording equipment has brought about the greatest revolution in crash investigation. The past is kept alive, every action and the response of the aircraft can be scrutinized long after the event, and even dead pilots talk to us, helping to ensure that no life will be wasted. With filament bulbs gone, when the pilot's traditional 'yoke' is replaced by a joy-stick children use for TV games, when composite materials are introduced in the construction and 'delamination' may occur, when instruments may be no more than perishable images on a liquid crystal or cathode ray tube TV screen, when instead of battered altimeters we may find a shattered computer that has lost its memory, when control rods give way to wiring to transmit ephemeral electronic commands, flight data recorders (FDRs) and cockpit voice recorders (CVRs) are not just new tools of fancy, they are simply indispensable.

Computer-driven electronic systems may be much more reliable than mechanical functions and human performance, but they leave no trace of the past, and if there is a bug in the software, it may be duplicated and safe from immediate detection. Without the recording devices, investigators may be left baffled. Why did the aircraft fail to pull up before hitting a mountain in clear visibility? Was it on wrongly programmed autopilot? Did the pilot send a relevant and timely command signal to pull up? If he did, was it the appropriate one? If yes, was it ever received by the elevators? If not, where was the fault? In the wiring? Did it block the transmission? If not, why were the elevators incapable of responding as quickly and accurately as they were designed to? Some clues or even some answers may be found in . . .

. . . A BLACK BOX THAT IS ORANGE-COLOURED

All containers of electronic information are commonly known as 'black boxes' – a reflection of the mysterious nature of their contents. They are, in fact, bright orange (to make it easier to find), capable of withstanding the tremendous forces of impact and the heat of an inferno – but to call them 'orange boxes' could be derogatory to their importance. Recorders are a major aide to the investigators, but not a miraculous short-cut to the hidden truth. The contribution of the data they produce may vary from the minimal to the invaluable, to be correlated with other evidence.

The early models used metal foil or wire, and later magnetic tape. They recorded just five crucial parameters: airspeed, altitude, direction (magnetic heading), vertical acceleration, and the time scale on the basis of which the others were viewed. (Time meant either local time or the elapsed time from take-off and the beginning of the recording.) Modern machines have the capacity to record a virtually unlimited number of parameters including, for example, fine details of the behaviour of the engines. Strangely enough – explained, perhaps, by the FAA's reluctance to impose great expenditures on the deficit-ridden industry – America has long been behind European requirements. The US minimum has now been increased to eleven, but there are still many airliners flying with 'black boxes' wired for only six of the 270 parameters recorded for safety and maintenance on the Airbus 330 and 340.

The latest, third-generation equipment, such as Fairchild/Loral's, use so-called solid state or semi-conductor memories that can record up to 128 parameters every second, contain no moving parts, and require no maintenance. (The latter is a big advantage because many poorer countries neglect their recorders which then often fail just when they are most needed.)

Crash-tested for extreme conditions, all 'black boxes' are exposed to an impact force of 100g, a fire burning at 1100° Celsius for thirty minutes, corrosion and crush at 20,000 feet ocean pressure, and to attempted piercing by a hardened steel spear that is dropped on them with a 500 pound weight. For one of the tests, Fairchild's constructed a 50-foot-long compressed air gun, used the fragile memory module as a projectile, and then checked if the recording remained intact after the blast. (Some cynics claim that in a crash, an aircraft seat would only be safe inside the recorder.)

'It is, however, a common fallacy to believe that FDRs and CVRs give an easy read, like a book, and offer instantaneous answers,' says consultant Ray Davis, formerly of the AAIB. 'When several airlines, even BOAC, used recordings for disciplinary purposes – it seldom happens these days – pilots were sacked for landing mishaps on the basis of raw data. When the recordings were properly interpreted, they had to be reinstated with apologies. Recordings must always be deciphered, verified, corrected, analysed, cross-checked with the rest of the evidence and that can take months rather than a few hours. But then, we can get real value out of it. The DFDR may reveal *what* happened, and the CVR may tell us *why* it happened.

'After the B737 accident at Manchester, some people were trying to jump to the conclusion that the pilots were responsible for the tragedy. But the recordings soon exonerated them. Combined voice and flight data revealed that the pilots acted with great professionalism and presence of mind. On the CVR we could hear a bang during the take-off run, and although its origin must have been a mystery to the captain, he called for an abandoned take-off and a halt within a fraction of a second. He then warned the co-pilot not to brake too hard because if they had some burst tyres – which could explain the bang – there was a danger of veering off the runway. Then we could hear the fire warning in the cockpit. That would have told the captain that an engine was burning, but he would have had no indication what a disastrous situation he was facing. Normally, such fires are contained within the engine, and do not become virtual flame-throwers directed at the fuselage like in that case. It came only later, when the aircraft was already moving on to a taxiway [it was then still a standard practice with a damaged but not crippled aircraft to avoid blocking the runway] that the tower informed him about the terrible position they were in. By then some valuable time had been wasted, but I am convinced that with their limited information about the true nature of the problem, the pilots helped to make that tragedy survivable for at least some of their passengers.'

The recordings may, of course, reveal damaging facts about the crew. On 16 August 1987, a DC9-82, Flight 255 of Northwest Airlines, was cleared for take-off from Detroit at 20.44. There were numerous witnesses to what happened. The aircraft climbed steeply, as usual, then rolled to the left and right, levelled out momentarily, banked to the left, and the wing tip touched a light-pole in a car park. After hitting another light-pole and a roof, it crashed, still rolling, into cars on a road beyond the airport boundary, and then into a railway embankment, disintegrating all the way. It had spent only twenty-seven seconds in the air – 154 people on board perished; one badly injured little girl survived.

Within a few hours, scores of NTSB sleuths, including two dozen pathologists and forensic experts, arrived at Detroit. There were conflicting witness reports about fire in the air, rumours galore about sabotage, windshear and engine failure (some of which might have been planted in the media by interested parties intent on exonerating themselves), but the investigation continued, eliminating one potential cause after another. While the black boxes, fortunately modern and multi-channelled ones recording fifty-six parameters, were sent to Washington for 'read-out', the wreckage wallahs made a peculiar discovery: the flap handle was in the UP/RET position. It might have moved, of course, during the crash, and they treated it as yet another of the red herrings that crop up, because no right-minded pilot would ever try to take off with no flaps or slats that are essential for lift and stability. Nevertheless, Jack Drake and his team began to look for the material evidence in the mangled remains of the flaps and slats mechanism.

In the Washington flight and voice recorder laboratory, NTSB specialists replayed the voices and sounds retrieved from the cockpit. As the recorders worked on a loop – erasing and starting afresh after a while – only a limited amount of past action would be evidenced, but there was enough for Dennis Grossi to discover some peculiarities in the crew's work pattern. Compared to the operations handbook, there were several irregularities during the flight's arrival and fatal departure. The crew had made some mistakes with radio frequency changes, left the weather radar 'on' despite the landing checklist instruction, failed to locate the correct taxiway, and experienced difficulties with the engagement of the autothrottle, but only because of their omission to read out the relevant item on the 'taxi' checklist. It showed that the crew were inclined to abandon that essential safeguard, provided by rigorous adherence to compulsory procedures against the complacency pitfalls of 'boring' routine.

As Grossi's team listened to the dead pilots' monotonous dialogue – one reads out items on the checklist, the other affirms that the required check or action had been followed to the letter – peppered with banter, laughter, irrelevant and irreverent remarks (that are supposed to remain strictly confidential) they heard no mention of the flaps and slats! The person reading out the checklist must have somehow skipped that crucial point, and the other, despite his long experience, must have failed to notice it. Even so, nothing should have been lost. Without flaps the aircraft would be improperly configured for take-off, and an alarm would sound if they tried to go ahead. The CVR recording contained numerous sickening sounds – the stickshaker and the stall warning, the expletives of fright and sudden realization of impending drama, the noise of seven impacts in seven seconds, but no trace of the appropriate 'no flaps' alarm. The news and a warning were flashed to Detroit: the crew might have tried to take off without flaps – but the absence of verbal reference to flaps could not be seen as proof because, possibly, they might have moved the handle without saying so, and if the alarm sounded, it might not have been recorded for some obscure reason. All very ominous, but not enough to substantiate a theory. Drake therefore initiated a concerted attack on every bit of the mechanism, every pulley, roller and track that would operate the flaps and slats, to see if those parts had been damaged in an extended or retracted position. And how about the lack of alarm? Why did it not warn the captain about the mistake?

The Washington specialists embarked on the mammoth task of analysing the available last twenty-five hours' recording in the life of the DC9. Flap and slat positions could be deduced from different sensors four times every second. It was recorded that they were retracted during taxiing on arrival at Detroit – and did not change their positions from then on. Thus the FDR confirmed the CVR. And by then, the wreckage had begun to yield incontrovertible material evidence: when the key cables were severed, they were *not* in an extended position. One question remained: would all that fit in with normal flight characteristics? The investigators dealing with the operational aspects of the case could calculate what would have happened if at least the slats had been extended: Flight 255 would have cleared that first light-pole by some 500 feet. And the alarm? By unlucky coincidence, the system happened to be inoperative on that occasion and, after the human error, its silence must have sealed the fate of that DC9.

Eventually, all the electronic evidence from the black boxes was matched to and brought together with the air traffic control recordings in the form of computer animation – a video presentation using real data, real voices and sounds, in real time, just as it must have happened. That advanced technique is not an investigative tool, but it is extremely useful when a case needs to be presented to laymen. Pilots and regulatory authorities are not well versed in reading tomes of indigestible columns of figures, but can judge other pilots' actions and reactions.

To watch that Detroit video is a painful experience. One hears all that goes on in the cockpit, sees the take-off and each stage of the crash, and it becomes obvious that after the mistake and the coincidence with the alarm unserviceability, there is no way back. (It is a dreadful failure of the American legal safeguards, and the utmost cruelty to surviving relatives, that some party to the investigation – perhaps somebody with an axe to grind – can occasionally leak the 'titillating' details of the CVR transcript to the media. After the Detroit leak, when the horror of the crew's last recorded gasps were played repeatedly to entertain television news audiences, the pilots were right to threaten to 'pull the plug' on all CVRs. They refrained only because the loss of voice recordings would be devastating to future investigations, but it is beyond any doubt that the guarantees of confidentiality must be absolute.)

The flight recorder laboratory of the Canadian investigative authority is now experimenting with an even more advanced application of high-definition moving graphics which take into account all aspects of the flight, including the force of prevailing winds and the weather conditions. In a kind of interactive video, the aircraft flying on the screen can be viewed from any angle, various instrument faces can be called up at will to appear as captions (to show what information was presented to the pilots at any given moment regarding airspeed, altitude, etc.), and experts can then 'take over the controls': they can feed in various commands, and observe how the healthy or semi-crippled aircraft would have responded if the same action was taken by the captain of the actual flight. (Would it have still been controllable after losing two of its four engines?) They can call for close-ups of the real terrain, and with the help of animation, even 'look out through the windscreen' to view what would have been visible to the pilot before the accident.

Computer animation films, so very helpful to those who labour for improved air safety, are now a new aide to lawyers who have already taken advantage of them in some American post-accident litigation when the discovery of the cause was less important than the apportioning of blame, and the whitewashing of those who might have to bear the heavy financial responsibility. But such videos can be manipulated when litigators wish to be somewhat economical with the truth, and try to feed a line to the jury that is more susceptible to the powerful visual reconstruction of an event than to the soporific technical and legal diatribes. (It is no coincidence that in Washington they say, 'A lawyer is the guy who'll make you an offer you can't understand.') At a Royal Aeronautical Society conference, Ken Smart, Chief Inspector of the AAIB, used the Thailand crash of a Lauda Air B767 as an example. A quickly assembled simulation supported the suspicion that although an engine reverse thrust malfunction had created a problem, the pilots had sufficient time to regain control of the aircraft. However, when a missing element, the effect of the exhaust plume on the airflow, was fed into the video, the result was an almost instantaneous dive from which most probably the pilots could not have recovered.

INVESTIGATION BY NUMBERS

Statistics are much maligned – and not without good reason. The same data can be used to support or demolish an argument. This author once made the mistake of beginning a talk in Colombo by congratulating Sri Lanka on running 'probably the safest flag-carrier' (then known as Air Ceylon) because 'statistically speaking, it is verging on the impossibility that a single accident would wipe out an entire national airline . . .' which, in fact, would happen in their case because at the time, apart from three aircraft on lease, they owned just one airliner. Perhaps one does not need to add that the jocular juggling with statistics did not go down too well with the local notabilities of aviation and government . . .

The bare listing of the number of crashes and accident victims can be as misleading as the bland statement that XYZ airline has not had a single fatal accident in so many hours of flying, because such figures ignore the innate hazards in certain types of operations, the number of that airline's annual flights, and numerous other relevant facts, such as that the fatal or non-fatal outcome of an accident may owe more to luck than the carrier's precautions.

Reviewing various causal statistics, James Reason, professor of psychology at Manchester University, raised the question 'Whom should we believe?'* The Flight Safety Foundation that named, in 1986, 'mechanical failure preceded by faulty maintenance' as the main cause of accidents? The NTSB that blamed, in 1987, the weather near airports for 64 per cent of the major crashes? A later NTSB analysis that gave top ranking to pilot error? The even later Boeing and Lufthansa studies that found that 'crew error' was the main culprit in up to three-quarters of the cases? 'In my view, we should believe none of them,' says James Reason. 'Such factors are necessary but insufficient causes. The sufficiency is supplied by a malign chance (Sod's Law) that combines these elements in a moment of system vulnerability.' Reason made out a convincing case for the need to review all the complexities, the interplay of all factors, in order to find the latent causes of a crash.

Those latent causes are not highlighted by the general and otherwise most impressive safety statistics. The number of accidents in which aircraft were a total write-off decreased very dramatically between 1959 and 1968, but has remained fairly steady (apart from four unlucky years) ever since. But what does that tell us? That aircraft were better built or better flown? The figures for fatal accidents per hours flown show only a little fluctuation (one in a million hours in 1984, and the same in 1992), as does the low number of fatalities per 100 million passenger-kilometers (the last ten years' average being 0.05, i.e. one passenger killed per 2000 million passenger-kilometers in the air.)

Statistics can nevertheless help to discover the danger areas of aviation, and pinpoint where safety improvements are most urgently needed. Concerning geriatric aircraft, for instance, they reveal the period (in terms of the length and intensity of service) when the risk of something going wrong steeply increases, necessitating much greater care and more thorough maintenance. Or take the following table that reveals how meaningless the figure for 'hours in the air' really is.† It shows clearly that 66.6 per cent of the risk is concentrated during take-off,

*Paper for the 22nd Annual Seminar of ISASI, Canberra, Australia, 1991.
†'Commercial Transport Safety', a study by Earl F. Weener, Ph.D, Boeing's Chief Engineer in charge of Airplane Reliability and Maintainability, and Safety Engineering, in *Airliner*, a Boeing magazine, April–June, 1993.

initial climb, final approach and landing – barely 6 per cent of the flying time. The least dangerous period is, of course, during the cruise. (Level flight is calculated for an average of 60 per cent of the time, though one must add that during short trips, there is hardly any cruising.) Those percentages vindicate ETOPs and the reliability of new engines, and re-emphasize that the natural aeronautical hazards (low speed, nearness of the ground) still demand the utmost attention of safety improvers.

EXPOSURE PERCENTAGE OF THE VARIOUS FLIGHT SEGMENTS

Based on hull-loss accidents (excluding sabotage and military action) of the worldwide commercial jet fleet – 1981–1992

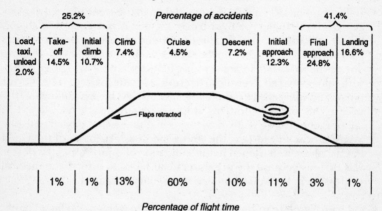

In view of the expected considerable increase in air traffic, the aviation industry knows only too well that it must keep reducing the already reassuring accident rates because the public does not care much about statistics: it is the frequency of crashes and the sensational headlines that may worry (or even put off) the would-be passenger.

26

It's Not Impossible

- In September 1992 a doctor stumbled on to the scene of a rail disaster
at a level crossing in the British countryside. A rail tanker was ablaze,
firemen, ambulances and police surrounded seventy dead or dying
passengers. A helicopter hovered overhead. The doctor climbed into
one of the coaches. He saw a young man screaming, lying face down,
with blood-soaked trousers covering a shattered leg. The doctor
quickly administered a painkilling injection. As he was pulling out the
needle, his patient suddenly stopped screaming, turned, asked in
amazement, 'Do we really have to go that far?' – and passed out. The
'disaster' was an exercise, the young man was a member of the Guild
of Casualties, well trained in the simulation of injuries, and the doctor
was furious because the organizers had failed to inform the medical
profession in the area about the emergency rehearsal.

Good Samaritans may, but precautions could never, go 'too far'. Thanks
to those precautions, it is not impossible – and it is becoming more and
more feasible – to walk away unscathed from accidents. In addition to
crashworthy features of modern aircraft, the passengers themselves can
improve their chances or survival.

The drawing opposite shows some of the most recent improvements
that have been made mandatory by regulations.

Some of these safety features represent victories achieved through
lengthy battles against cautious or reluctant regulators, and the mean or
shortsighted accountants of the industry. Other measures are still in the
offing – subject to research and acceptance, depending on the frequently Quixotic efforts of those who are dedicated to the ideals of
'safety above all considerations'. Regulators, who claim to subscribe to
the same principle, often (maybe too often) feel compelled to quote Dick
Smith, a former chief of the Australian CAA, who coined the phrase 'We
need *affordable* safety. If air transport becomes unaffordable, people will
take to the roads, and we'll have far more casualties.' Cruel as it may
sound, the cost of saving, say, twenty lives per annum is sometimes

prohibitively high. In such cases, available resources must clearly be directed towards the most urgent measures with the greatest life-saving potential, such as the compulsory use of Ground Proximity Warning or windshear detecting systems. On the other hand, timely public outcries, and probing questions by travellers, could put an end to official dilly-dallying and cost-saving delays in borderline cases – particularly when they concern survivability.

ADVANCES IN CABIN SAFETY

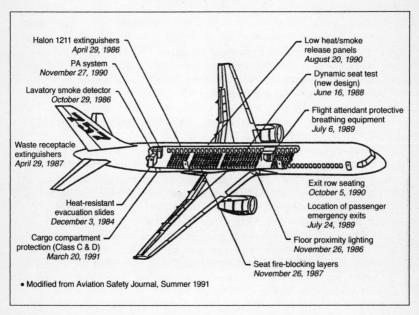

Halon 1211 extinguishers
April 29, 1986

PA system
November 27, 1990

Lavatory smoke detector
October 29, 1986

Waste receptacle
extinguishers
April 29, 1987

Heat-resistant
evacuation slides
December 3, 1984

Cargo compartment
protection (Class C & D)
March 20, 1991

Low heat/smoke
release panels
August 20, 1990

Dynamic seat test
(new design)
June 16, 1988

Flight attendant protective
breathing equipment
July 6, 1989

Exit row seating
October 5, 1990

Location of passenger
emergency exits
July 24, 1989

Floor proximity lighting
November 26, 1986

Seat fire-blocking layers
November 26, 1987

● Modified from Aviation Safety Journal, Summer 1991

STRONGER SEATS AND FLOORS

New, more stringent regulations apply to aircraft (such as the B757 in the drawing) certificated after 1988, but the strengthening of floors and the fitting of more crashworthy seats on earlier aircraft are unlikely to be achieved before 1995. (On the brand-new machine that crashed at Kegworth, the seats were already of the new type, capable of withstanding 16g-s instead of the standard 9g-s – but the floor collapsed.)

Rearward facing seats, promoted by many specialists, could pose various problems. If they need extra-strong anchorage, the weight penalty might reduce airline profitability or increase fares. Are they worth it? They could give protection from forward impact, but many accidents show these days a different pattern – impact can occur from any direction. What would they do then for the passenger? Sadly, there is no concerted research going on to prove or disprove the advantage of such seats. Airlines claim that passengers 'do not like to travel facing backwards'. Unfortunately, the evidence for this argument is less than sketchy. The only time when soldiers on American military flights were questioned, no objections were raised. On the other hand, MALÉV, for instance, still flies two TU134s built with rearward facing seats. It has found that passengers dislike them, but one wonders how they would react if they were told that such a configuration might save their lives.

BRACE YOURSELF

In sudden deceleration, seatbelts are an essential protection from injury. If they were supported by a diagonal over-the-shoulder harness, as in cars, they would be even more effective. Objectors to that innovation hark back to the old argument that passengers would not take kindly to the discomfort. That may be true if they had to sit with a shoulder strap for hours on end. But there would be no need for that. Lapbelts give sufficient protection against in-flight turbulence. The diagonal restraint could be locked in separately for the few minutes of all take-offs and landings.

For emergency landings, we are advised to adopt the brace position. But what is the best form of that? It is most disturbing that the notoriously inadequate drawings on airline emergency cards show at least twenty considerably differing versions. Many of them suggest that the passenger should rest his head on the seatback in front, and place his hands on top of that seat. Others advise resting the lower arms on that seatback, and leaning against them. Yet another version shows passengers crouching down (as much as possible in the confined space of economy class), head against the seatback, hands on top of the head. On the cards of a Turkish Airbus a woman is seen (1) pushing the seat away, (2) embracing her legs under the knees that are used as a rest for a cushion and the head, well away from the seat in front, hoping, presumably, that nothing could throw her forwards. For roomier first- and business-class seats, the most frequent suggestion is that the passenger should lean forward, with the head, cradled by the arms, beyond the knees!

The legs and feet are invisible on many cards. If they are shown at all, their position ranges from resting straight down on the floor to sticking way out under the seat in front. I could not discover a single card that emphasized that the feet should *not* be raised from the floor to form a buffer. (This could easily be told by a picture with the red X in the style of the 'no smoking' sign.)

The problem is that one cannot find a reassuring consensus of expert opinion. 'In the United States, there are only three approved brace positions,' says Matt McCormick, chief of the NTSB Survival Factors

Division. 'The aim is to reduce flailing and the forward travel of the body. In my opinion, the best is, if at all possible, to bend forward, head between the knees, the arms protecting it. If there is no room for that, the head and protective arms should be rested on the seat in front. The tray tables are designed to give and deform, reducing the likelihood of serious injuries. Feet must be firmly on the floor. If you raise them, the force of an impact may be transmitted to and fracture the hips or thighs.'

One of the most experienced British investigators can only suggest what he would do for himself: 'I think it is essential that feet should be firmly planted on the floor, slightly behind the knees. That would help to prevent them from flailing. I'd cradle my head on my knees, space permitting, with one forearm across my forehead and the other on top. I'd try to bring my head as close as possible to the seatback in front, preferably touching it. If a cushion or something like a jumper was at hand, I'd hold it to the back of my head. That would add some protection from objects catapulted from the overhead stowage bins. One other point. I don't want to start a rush for the middle one of three seats, but from what I've seen, it appears to be the safest because the more rigid spar supporting it is less likely to collapse than the outer legs.'

The Kegworth accident (mentioned on page 120) was atypical, but the injuries it caused initiated some urgent new thinking on the best brace position. Numerous crashes were studied and dummies were tested. From April, 1994, a standard position, with new emergency cards, will be introduced by the CAA for all British airlines: *bend forward, chest close to the thighs, with head and knees touching the seat in front; hands must protect the top of the head, forearms the sides of the face; feet, aft of the knees, must be firmly on the floor; seatbelts should be tight round the lowest point of the torso.*

Hopefully, some international standardization will follow, relieving passengers from confusion and the impossible task of making a choice. Meanwhile, it is vital to study the card in the seatback, and take up *some* currently acceptable brace position for an emergency landing. Chris Thomson, a survivor of Kegworth, was quoted in *The Times* (7.10,1990): 'If you fly a lot, you tend not to bother reading the safety card each time.' In a panic, the less recent memories are likely to fade. He just crouched down, and ended up with skull, foot and leg fractures.

OVERHEAD STOWAGE BINS

in the cabin are tested for weight bearing, but have remained liable to disgorging their contents at the slightest provocation because the weak latches pop open as the flexible structure moves – not to mention whenever the dynamic forces of a crash or even of a heavy landing come into play. (The effect could be particularly hazardous if passengers sat facing rearwards, for then the seatbacks would give no protection against flying objects.) After repeated accidents, Boeing, for instance,

developed modifications for safer bins on older 737s and new 757s, but
the time-scale allowed by the FAA for their installation was 'too relaxed'
even for the CAA, which demanded that the job should be done on
British-registered aircraft almost right away. Meanwhile, there are many
types flying with insecure bins, so if cabin crews seem too easy-going
about their contents, passengers themselves ought to object to anything
hard and heavy being stowed overhead.

EXTERNAL TV CAMERAS

could help the pilots in many emergencies because from the modern
cockpit they cannot see what is going on outside (for example, which
engine is on fire or if the undercarriage is locked down properly,
whatever a warning light may erroneously say). The third man of the
flight crew, the engineer, used to amble down the aisle every so often to
take a look outside. Since this job has become redundant, the workload
in a difficult situation may be too heavy to allow one of the two pilots to
go aft and do that. Though Kegworth, Manchester, and numerous other
accidents have fortified the case for external TV cameras, it has taken
much too long to overcome the industry's resistance to the idea. The
current trials on a BA aircraft are helping to eliminate the technical
objections (day and night capability is still to be developed). Pilots'
questions ('Shall we have time to glance at yet another display in an
emergency? Won't a closed circuit TV screen create a distraction?') may
be answered by simulator training. Protestations on cost grounds have
never been more than a flimsy excuse. (Much more substantial investment was required for TV sets in seatbacks to entice customers. On
Japanese domestic flights there is a TV camera in the nose just to
entertain passengers with the thrilling sights of take-off and landing.
Mohamed al Fayed, the millionaire of Harrods fame, had four external
cameras installed for safety on his Gulfstream private jet right after
Kegworth.)

FIRES

have claimed a proportionately very significant number of lives both
in the air and on the ground. Many of the counter-measures, introduced
as 'tombstone engineering' in the wake of accidents, are now proving to
be invaluable in helping passengers to escape even from a threatening
inferno.

Fire hardening of the fuselage skin against penetration by ground fire
has long been recommended by accident investigators, but it is a complex
problem researched currently by the FAA. Eventually, it may become a
part of international airworthiness requirements unless other protective
measures (see Cabin Water Spray on page 233) prove to be a more
feasible solution. Much more could be done, albeit at a considerable

cost, for fire *prevention* through crash-resistant fuel tanks and fuel lines.

Smoke detectors, now installed in the lavatories and cargo compartments, have prevented many a disaster in the last decade. But airlines, manufacturers and regulators have needed much convincing, year after year, case after case, that the flammability of aircraft furnishings, and their toxic fume-producing potential, must be tackled whatever the cost. Firemen had known for some three decades that in every town on any given day, people would be killed in their own homes by smoke rising from foam-cushioned furniture. Yet it was only in the second half of the 1980s that the use of fire-blocking materials became compulsory both in aircraft and household furniture. (Retrofitting in private homes is a hopeless proposition. In aircraft, implementation has been slow because it was allowed to coincide with major refurbishing.) The new materials now delay ignition and the propagation of flames, and in terms of survivability, that means extra time for evacuation. The cost to the aviation industry ran to billions, but it has now begun to pay dividends. (Despite the frightening thought, we are talking about a rather small number of deaths in aircraft fires – some 500 in Britain in twenty years. Not all of the victims would have survived if safe seat covers, costing up to £200 each, were fitted. It has been estimated that fire-blocking sidewall and ceiling panels, for instance, have cost £25 million per life saved by them.)

Many experts are sceptical, nevertheless, about the value of the fire-resistant materials that still produce, when beginning to smoulder or burn, the toxic fumes that make the real difference between survival and death: people who took just one or two gulps of it passed out, and fell easy prey to the conflagration. Some recent tragedies, including Manchester in 1985, and a runway collision between a B737 and a Metroliner at Los Angeles in 1991, demanded urgent consideration of some new measures, including the introduction of . . .

. . . SMOKE-HOODS FOR PASSENGERS

After Manchester, the initial view, shared by British Airways and the CAA was quite straightforward: if hoods meeting their demanding specification were produced, they would be provided for every passenger, as recommended by those who investigated the Manchester disaster. Since then, various models have come on to the market. They cost around £400 each, but promise up to thirty minutes' protection which should be enough even in an in-flight fire. The price would, of course, tumble if the airlines made bulk purchases, but the above goalposts have since been moved.

The only remaining technical objection to the latest types is that they contain compressed air cylinders, a little bigger than a soda syphon Sparklet, that are classified as dangerous goods, the sort banned from passengers' cabin luggage. Yet you find similar ones in great numbers on every aircraft because life-vests need them for inflation. After extensive, though possibly incomplete, international research, the leading American, British, Canadian, French and other authorities have come to oppose the introduction of smoke-hoods. They claim that hoods could in fact be dangerous by giving us a false sense of security, and that passengers, particularly elderly ones, might *waste* precious moments on trying to locate them, fiddling with donning them, and getting confused or panicky when wearing them. However this was not borne out by the British trials in a smoke-filled environment (organized by Dr James Vant), when it was demonstrated that an arguably slight delay *bought* precious extra time for survival.

The issue is far from being settled. Airlines had provided hoods for cabin crews, though 'only for firefighting in the air', long before they became compulsory in 1989. Numerous employees of the above regulatory authorities admit in private that they carry their own smoke-hoods every time they fly, but argue that they have practised their application and so would not waste any time. Other experts and accident survivors are still fighting for smoke-hoods for everyone. Many of them know from first-hand experience that it is the smoke, not the fire, that fatally incapacitates most victims, and blinds them fast with a deposit of thick black soot. They claim with great conviction that 'in a survivable accident, where there were only one or two people trying to don their private devices, they would not be allowed to wear them: it would be our children who used them because we'd snatch the hoods from the owners' heads one way or another'.

Eddie Trimble, a Principal AAIB Inspector, has produced a comprehensive and convincing review of all available evidence in a doctoral thesis. A CAA expert countered his pro-hood conclusions instantaneously, before the full text was circulated, claiming that Trimble had chosen to interpret the data in a way that differed from the authorities' evaluation. Canadian Air Navigation Commissioner Douglas Mien believes that 'smoke-hoods should be declassified as dangerous goods', and their use should be allowed unless there was some strong, hitherto unseen, evidence that they could hinder evacuation.

Malcolm Keogh, the prominent aviation lawyer, introduces yet another angle to the debate: 'I'm convinced that most probably, all the fifty-five Manchester victims could have survived if even the most basic filter-type hood was available to them. Despite the fire-retardant furnishings, they were overcome by smoke before they could even attempt to escape. When the tests were conducted at Newcastle, I was one of the volunteers who occupied the smoke-filled aircraft. None of us had any prior experience, but we had no difficulty with the hoods. Yet the airlines will provide smoke-hoods only if the law-makers compel them to do so. I hope there'll never be another Manchester, Los Angeles or Detroit type disaster, but if there was one, executives of the CAA or other authorities might have to bear not only corporate responsibility but also personal liability for failing to act upon the evidence.

'The regulators' refusal to approve any smoke-hoods might give the airlines a good defence, but if the CAA, for instance, as much as *permits* the use of just one type by individual owners, the airlines could be sued for failing to provide them of their own free will because of the cost. As for myself, yes, I do carry my own simple filter type smoke-hood – carry, that is when I remember to pack it!' Which shows his not unreasonable faith in air safety – for if a lawyer who has dealt with numerous tragedies can be so forgetful, our chances must be good. The question is: why not make them even better?

While smoke-hoods remain unavailable to all, the speed of escape, planned well ahead, is paramount. If there is smoke, it is invariably toxic, so breathe in as little of it as possible. Do not attempt to use the overhead oxygen masks for protection: they have no filters, and the contents may feed the flames. Some cloth, preferably a wet one, covering the mouth and the nose, may be very helpful. And a tip from those who survived conflagrations: do not fly with heavily lacquered hair – in a fire situation, it may be too readily inflammable.

CABIN WATER SPRAY
  systems offer a most promising concept that could prove to be a viable though far from immediate safety development if the remaining technical problems can be solved. The idea is to place nozzles in the ceiling which release a fine mist in the cabin. They could prevent or delay the outbreak of fire, and the occurrence of a devastating flashover (the ignition of hot gases). Above all, they could help to suppress the debilitating, toxic fumes long enough for the passengers to escape. The cost of installing the system on the world jet fleet is estimated – 'underestimated', claim the airlines and manufacturers – at $2 billion. The cost of saving one life could be $30 million. Retrofitting would have technical obstacles, too. If the system was designed as an integral part of new aircraft off the production lines, the cost and technical problems could be reduced, but then we would begin to reap the benefits only in the next century. (That is why many experts advocate smoke-hoods that could serve as a life-saving stop-gap at least until then.)

The seemingly prohibitive weight of necessary water reservoirs and plumbing, 706 kilograms on a B747-400, could now be reduced by zoning the system, and activating it by thermal sensors only in the fire-affected areas. The most astonishing result of tests was that 8 gallons of water in a zoned system provided fifty-five seconds more survival time than the simultaneous discharge of 72 gallons of water all over the cabin. Critical questions must still be answered, however, concerning the efficacy of the resultant cleansing of air in the cabin, and about situations when there is debilitating smoke but no fire to trigger the mist. The airlines are also worried about a possibly inadvertent system discharge. (When water floods department stores, massive damage can be caused to goods on display, and it can lead to compensation claims from soaked customers.) Even if the electronic systems of the aircraft were well protected from such a discharge of mist (not water), the consequences could be ominous. According to a study by Delta Air Lines, it would cost $881,000 to restore a B757 to serviceability, and that excludes 'lost revenue, logistics costs, damage to company image and litigation'.

EVACUATION

No new aircraft is certified without evacuation tests being conducted – albeit in a smoke-free environment. The rule demands a demonstration that all passengers can get out in ninety seconds or less, using only half the exits, for after a crash landing there may be fire outside, or some exits inoperable. Although the maximum distance between any passenger and the nearest exit is governed by design requirements (on charters, there may be up to twenty extra seats crammed in), numerous accidents and incidents have called attention to the accessibility and operation of exits.

After Manchester, the Applied Psychology unit of the Cranfield Institute of Technology was commissioned to pursue an evacuation research project. The trials, with 2000 inexperienced but young and healthy volunteers, brought some startling results. (For added realism, cash incentives introduced competitiveness in the escapers' efforts, and people clambered over seats to avoid delays in the aisles.) It became clear that just as in the real cases, potentially catastrophic bottle-necks would develop at certain points.

Passengers at the overwing exits had hardly any space to stand up and remove the hatch. Under the pressure of others piling up on them, the opening became even more difficult. When better access was provided, the flow through those exits increased, but if too much room was made available by the removal of an entire row of seats, the area soon became overcrowded, and despite expectations, the evacuation through the narrow opening slowed down. Following the Cranfield findings, the CAA ruled that airlines should either remove a seat next to the overwing exit or increase the space between the adjacent rows of seats. That was done in Britain within a year, well before the Manchester report was completed, but in America, it took yet another accident with evacuation problems (at Los Angeles) to convince the authorities. In many other countries, the example is still waiting to be copied.

To eliminate another bottle-neck, Cranfield recommended the widening of the passageway between bulkheads (at the galleys) from 20 to 30 inches. (That was found to be the optimum to funnel escaping passengers, because if even more space was available, dangerous bunching developed in the vestibule areas at the exits.) The CAA made a proposal for a new European requirement in that respect, but action on it is still being delayed, and American experts, for instance, remain unconvinced of its potential advantage.

The operation of the exits by laymen remains a problem. In principle, trained members of the cabin crew are expected to perform that duty, but if they are incapacitated, passengers are supposed to do it for themselves, following the all too vaguely depicted instructions on the safety cards. (Words cannot be used because the industry must cater for all, irrespective of language differences and illiteracy.) However meaningless the guidance with those little arrows and handles on the doors in the pictures may appear to be, passengers are well advised to study the drawings that may help them survive in an emergency. Although not all exits are operated in an identical way, even on the same aircraft, it is useful to take a good look at the doors when boarding or during the flight, and learn something about their *modus operandi*. As mentioned previously, the idea, supported by passengers' organizations, to display demonstration doors in pre-boarding lounges, to let people gain some hands-on experience is resisted by the industry that deems it impracticable.

The opening of overwing exits is the most pressing problem because cabin crew are rarely seated next to them, and the job is often left to the nearest passenger who may be stunned by the weight of the hatch (some 50 pounds, with no hinges to support it) and the lack of room to manoeuvre it. Many emergency cards are downright misleading when a lithesome woman is depicted handling the bulky piece of metal with the greatest ease. The hatch must be lifted inwards until freed, turned sideways, and then jettisoned through the opening. Yet some cards suggest (*wrongly!*) that the hatch should be pulled inside – creating, at best, yet another obstacle – while others show the heavy item being raised over a seatback and deposited gracefully on the seats in front. (Where? Atop some other passengers?)

New regulations now demand that only able-bodied passengers should be seated next to such overwing exits, the crew should brief them for the task, and there should be a special reminder card on the seatback facing them. Unfortunately, there are objections to this most sensible innovation. As mentioned earlier, American associations of the blind campaigned for priority allocation of just those seats for easy egress, ignoring the difficulties that would create. Others feel too embarrassed to say 'no' when asked if they could handle the job. It is impossible to conduct competency checks on the elderly or the infirm, and there were many complaints when the CAA stopped the practice of placing people with a leg in plaster (often seen after skiing holidays) near the exits where there is extra room.

Even though there may be no perfect recipe for emergency behaviour, adding a dash of common sense to the mixture of forethought and careful attention to instructions could greatly improve everybody's chance for survival if the unlikely ever happens.* And although the word 'aircrash' may seem to leave no room for hope, it is far from impossible to walk away unscathed from disasters.

*See also Chapter 14.

27

Arriving Hopefully

Remember the *Berra Doctrine*, preached by an American philosopher (better known as Yogi Berra the baseball player), that 'It ain't over till it's over.' Perhaps it will serve as a stronger reminder than the cabin crew's bored then desperate admonition, shouts and pleading that the flight is not over until the aircraft has come to a complete halt, because a sudden swerve or jolt could cause serious injuries to those who are determined to be first on their feet. (It never occurs to these people that they will then just stand and wait, luggage in hand, wrapped in woollies and coat in the increasingly hot cabin, and stand and wait for immigration controls – there is always another flight still queuing in the hall – and stand and wait some more at the luggage carousel, where there is no guarantee whose suitcase will roll in first.)

Going through immigration can be a long and arduous process, particularly in America. Those who enjoy receiving murderously dirty looks need do no more than start searching for their passports – Didn't I give it to you? Then it must be in that bag . . . No that one – just as they reach the official's desk. The readers' poll, conducted by the *Business Traveller* magazine in 1992, voted Singapore Changi, Zurich Kloten, London Heathrow, Amsterdam Schiphol and London Gatwick the best airports for incoming passport control, but quite frequently it is the luck of the draw. The origin of the flight may heighten vigilance against unwanted, illegal immigrants or a special alert for a flood of forgeries can cause hold-ups. (This author has queued endlessly even at Singapore, coming in from Bangladesh via Thailand, and at Heathrow, where the fifteen-second-per-pass flow lengthens considerably when passports are subjected to ultra-violet tests, especially when arriving from Amsterdam or Luxembourg, the most common markets for fakes). Yet there will be no time lost: the luggage retrieval is bound to be even slower. In the above readers' poll, four of the same airports came best in that respect, with Frankfurt Rhein Main replacing Heathrow.

Arriving hopefully comes to the crunch at the luggage carousels: will your suitcase be there? If it is not, you must file a claim immediately.

Similarly, it is essential to inspect both the case and its contents for damage as soon as possible, because once the passenger has passed through customs, the greater the delay, the worse your chances of compensation. Suitcases are often damaged, and it could be a terrible chore to obtain repair estimates or a 'write-off' certificate, particularly abroad, but timely claims and persistence do tend to pay off.

Airlines cannot and do not argue much about lost luggage, but compensation may vary. The standard is '250 French gold Francs' (about £14) per kilo, but excess luggage that has not been charged for is not covered, and some airlines may offer much less on account of estimated depreciation of the lost or damaged items. Ideally, you should have a list of contents with valuation – and receipts if possible – but the advice from those who handle the worst complaints is more practical: do not give in easily. On American domestic flights, the airlines set a liability limit of $1250 per passenger on a large aircraft (over sixty seats), but they may offer no compensation to start with. Some carriers sell 'excess valuation coverage' at a charge of up to 2 per cent of the value, but general insurance cover may be better. Airlines can disclaim all liability for fragile and perishable items that ought to be in the cabin luggage. Photographic equipment as well as separately checked in items, such as skis, golf clubs, musical instruments, have given rise to many disputes and disappointments, so it is best to insure them, and clarify the position with the carrier. (In America, for instance, the owner may be asked to sign a liability waiver before such items are accepted for carriage. Without that signature, the carrier would have to pay, but the law is muddled to say the least.)

If the luggage is misrouted and delayed, airlines will usually pay for the cost of buying some essentials – the amount depending on their policy, generosity and the length of inconvenience. Frequent travellers of bitter experience practise the art of defensive flying, and protect themselves with packing some basics for such emergencies (change of underwear, toothbrush, razor, etc.) in their hand-luggage.

Those who cannot get satisfaction through the normal channels, may complain to organisations such as the Air Transport Users Committee in Britain or the Aviation Consumers Action Project and the Consumer Affairs Division in America,* and their intervention on the passenger's behalf can speed up the response quite miraculously. The periodic publication of American wrongdoings and the practice of naming names

---

*The British AUC does not see itself as a complaints bureau, but letters of dissatisfaction with compensation claims form the third largest group of cases it handles. Its address is AUC, 2nd floor, Kingsway House, 103, Kingsway, London WC2B 6QX. Handling complaints is a standard function of both ACAP (PO Box 19029, Washington DC 20036) and CAD (Room 10405, US Department of Transportation, 400 7th Street, SW, Washington DC 20590). Do not make the mistake of writing eight- or ten-page complaints. It happens frequently. A brief summary of the relevant facts helps everybody concerned.

are great incentives to all airlines to avoid giving grounds for dissatisfaction. (Baggage complaints rank second highest on the hit parade. Figures for individual carriers depend, of course, on the size of the operation, but it could not have pleased the management of Mexicana, British Airways, Air France, Alitalia, Tarom and Yugoslav Airlines that they were the most frequently mentioned foreign airlines in 1991. In the same year, some of the largest American carriers – including Delta, United and TWA – were among the worst, having exceeded the average 5.38 'mishandled baggage reports' per 1000 passengers.)

Having arrived with justifiably high hopes, the moment of coming to the end of yet another successful flight may still hold a small surge of adrenalin for many passengers: perhaps because 'smuggling' on a minuscule scale is a national sport in most countries. An astonishingly great number of people have a *guilty* look when . . .

GOING THROUGH CUSTOMS

Watching them from behind a two-way mirror as they ambled along the 'Green' nothing-to-declare channel offered a demonstration of human nature: most people know right from wrong, and they are too honest to lie effectively with their body language. A customs officer sized them up at a glance: 'The middle-aged woman with the red scarf . . . doesn't she look suspicious? But I bet she's a born worrier. Maybe she is a first-time traveller. Maybe she didn't wash her underwear before returning from holiday, and dreads the embarrassment of anybody seeing it if her case is opened . . . Behind her, the long-haired chap in the dirty jeans will be stopped, I'm sure.' (As he said it, we saw an officer approaching him.) 'They say we're picking on the type, but it's not true. While we may find a cannabis joint or two on him, we could be missing a real smuggler.' Then why was he stopped? 'His attire doesn't seem to go too well with the luxurious Vuitton case he is carrying . . . ' A young woman came into view: 'Ah, another scared customer. Staring ahead to avoid any eye-contact, sweaty nose, guilt written all over her – might have bought some sexy girdle of black lace, packed it at the bottom of her bag, not too keen to have it exposed . . . ' Pensioner in a deer-stalker, jaunting through Green, with a smile for everyone: 'I rate him at half a bottle of malt over the allowance . . . ' They let him pass. A triumphant tale to tell in his local.

So who are the people who will be stopped and possibly searched? Is it a sixth sense that guides customs?

'No, it's experience,' says Joe Lyons, a Senior British Customs Officer. 'Though the relaxation of regulations have greatly increased the allowances of duty-frees, at least for EC citizens, it is still an offence to overstep the mark. But catching petty offenders is not our main task. The new rules help us, in fact, to concentrate our resources on serious smugglers of pornography, weapons and, above all, drugs.

'Experience has taught us to separate the truly suspicious from the merely anxious, white-knuckled trolley-pushers. Many people come from countries where there's an ingrained fear of uniforms. Clothes can also be misleading. Wealthy youths often travel in rags. So it's a matter of assessing behaviour patterns. Why is he whistling? To demonstrate his innocence? Is he avoiding eye-contact or staring at officers as if challenging them to "stop me if you dare"? Do they talk too loudly to their companions to show they haven't a care in the world? Do they exchange furtive glances? Do they just ooze some well-rehearsed self-assurance?

'Sometimes we stop people to test our own assessments. A light chat, some general questions about the flight and their passports can produce some unexpected results. A woman just fainted when we stopped her: she had bought a set of expensive golf clubs abroad, and hoped to recoup some of the cost by dodging the duty. Some get dismayed, even rude. It surprises them when, as a result, the search becomes longer and more thorough to find out the reasons for their attitude.' (Usually the officers offer help to repack cases, but it is not their duty, and rudeness will not alter that.)

'A Jamaican woman, resident in London, couldn't have been cooler or nicer as she was chatting to us. My colleague was about to let her go without opening her suitcase, when the woman, perhaps trying to gain sympathy, mentioned the hardship of bringing up two kids on social security with no job prospect. That was odd: visa stamps in her passport showed three long-distance trips in two months. A search revealed that cocaine was the name of her game. She got seven years in jail.

'The peculiar things we find in suitcases, such as half a box of washing powder, leftover ketchup or five kilos of cauliflower wrapped in knickers, may look very suspicious and call for a proper search, but it may turn out that people were just too mean to leave them behind at the end of their holiday. A chap carried thirty-two packets of condoms. Another had cases of tea bags bought in and now returned to Britain.

'It doesn't pay to try to be funny when you're stopped and talked to. If someone says, "I admit, I have a kilo of heroin in that bag," we must be thorough because the joke maybe a cover-up rather than a time-wasting false declaration. They don't find it very funny when the tools come out to force open every nook and cranny, and when the knife goes in to probe for a false bottom of the suitcase.

'If nothing is found, and the passenger's property is damaged, we must explain the claim procedure, and compensation may be due. But we have virtually unlimited powers to examine everything, open even sealed items such as tins. Customs and Excise officers, including Robbie Burns and Chaucer, could make arrests long before the police were founded, and in Britain, like in America and some other countries, Customs and Excise can still investigate, detain and prosecute.'

In Britain, the new *Traveller's Charter* sets out our rights (the calculation of a fine, for instance, must be explained, and an appeal can be made), but it is best to know what is legally permissible to carry into the country of your destination – or else nasty little surprises may be in store. For example, chewing gums are banned in Singapore and any quantity beyond a visitor's 'personal needs' may be confiscated.

A word of warning: think twice before you try out some truly original way to trick customs – the chances are that thousands have invented the same long before you. Women who walk the Green, openly flaunting some jewellery with a 'Look! Nothing to hide' expression, ought to know that customs officers, who see such pieces every day, recognize the design and their newness at fifty paces. (A second glance may just confirm that the UK hallmark is missing.) A blind eye may be turned on the odd fake watch or designer-shirt copy, but not if you have dozens of them, obviously for sale or as gifts. A great sigh of relief when you reach the arrival hall can also be dangerous: customs have the right to stop you anywhere.

There are no new excuses. Everybody caught with extra bottles of gin, cartons of cigarettes or an expensive camera seems to have 'received it as a last-minute gift' or 'won it in a farewell raffle'. An old ploy is to go through the Red channel, and declare honestly and voluntarily the Camcorder you bought with the assurance of some Far East traders that the falsely low receipt they gave you as a standard service would satisfy customs. It will not, and it will be checked against detailed catalogues of market prices. In addition to the duty plus VAT, a fine to double the price will be raised. Another device is to declare something petty, say, a bottle of over-the-limit rum, pay the duty, then walk on, waving the receipt from customs, while trying to smuggle in something much more valuable. Do not rely on the idea. You can be stopped even after that honest transaction: many an amateur drug smuggler has been caught in that way.

The best time to smuggle your tuppence worth of goodies is when the arrival of your holiday flight coincides with one from Nigeria and another from the Balkans. Aircraft coming in from countries that are producers of or favoured transit and distribution points for drugs are singled out for special attention. Remote control TV cameras watch the luggage hall, customs officers mingle with the crowd around the carousels, seemingly bored officers listen to the conversation at the immigration desks to pick out suspects (they radio colleagues on the Green channel, 'Watch out for dark-suited C2 type,' one of the six coded categories for easy description), and may also watch the departure lounge as well as the screen at the pre-flight security X-ray machines. Passengers from South America, the Far East, Lagos, Nigeria, Jamaica, Spain and Gibraltar are always closely scrutinized. Lately the Balkans route from Turkey has become a prime suspect. Since the Yugoslavian wars began, drugs are smuggled via Hungary and Romania – yet customs officers find it hard to make their colleagues over there accept that they do have a growing problem.

Drugs are a worldwide menace, and vast quantities are on the move. Even though in Britain alone, £500 million worth of drugs were captured just in 1992, much more evaded detection. But if a friendly stranger asks you – or offers a hefty gratuity – to carry 'just a small gift-wrapped package' for his 'dear old auntie who'll be waiting for me at the airport because she doesn't know that I had to change my travel plans at the last minute,' your chances of getting through with the 'present' are not very good. 'Mules,' the carriers, may easily get eight years in jail (or the rope in Malaysia and other countries) for their kindness. A high-ranking Thai diplomat, who tried to use his immunity to get 50 kilos of heroin into Britain, received a twenty-year sentence.

The hiding places for drugs range from the ingenious to the crazy. Just to mention a few: there were attempts to smuggle cocaine dissolved in alcohol in whisky bottles, and in clothes impregnated with a cocaine solution. The lining of a safe contained five kilos of heroin. Cocaine was found sandwiched inside tin coffee trays, in glued-together walnuts, in raw fish wrapped in cellophane, in jars and bottles where the smell of coffee or spices was meant to mislead the dogs, in fruit full of creepy-crawlies, in personalized lighters sold 'for hiding banknotes for a taxi fare after muggings', in deodorant cans with a screw-on base and a working spray ('a safe for valuables in the bathroom'), and in commercially sealed fruit tins from Jamaica ('Why are you carrying dozens of them in your hand-luggage?' 'I heard it's difficult to get them in London.'). Many would-be smugglers rely on the false expectation that a silver foil or carbon paper wrapping will prevent the X-rays from penetrating the package.

A customs officer, watching the X-ray machine as passengers were about to board a flight to New York, found it odd that a woman, in transit from Ghana, had five pairs of identical sandals in her cabin bag. The machine showed dark patches on the soles, and she was interviewed. As she could not offer a good enough explanation, the sole of one sandal was cut open and, lo and behold, some white powder poured out – cocaine. The woman seemed devastated, but the full weight of her misadventure was yet to hit her: the laboratory examination revealed that the white powder was lignocane, an innocuous non-controlled substance used by dentists to numb teeth. She broke down: she had invested all her savings in cocaine, bought in Ghana, hoping to make a killing in the United States, and she had been ripped off. (As a sideline, she was also carrying fourteen passports, and had a young Ghanaian girl in tow, an intended illegal immigrant.) She was charged with attempting a criminal act, but at last she was in luck: the jury acquitted her and she was only deported.

Professionals make fewer mistakes, and invent plausible cover stories for their frequent trips. They may try to avoid suspicion by changing planes to disguise the origin of their flights. Doctored suitcases and luggage-switching are among their well-tried though known favourites. They may buy two identical suitcases, only to cut off and insert the bottom of one into the other. When the case is opened, there is no sign of the concealed cavity. Customs officers are wise to the technique. If, say, a pencil is held to the outside and then the inside of the case, the discrepancy in the measurements of depths becomes obvious. Smugglers prefer to use the most common types of luggage, with no personal identification inside. They may carry their own through customs, but if they are stopped they claim it is not theirs and they have taken it by mistake. (Only the identification tab would connect it to their ticket, and if it is removed at once in the luggage hall, the game may be up.) 'Mistakes' may also be engineered by smugglers: they may pick up somebody else's identical baggage, let the innocent walk through Green with the drugs, only to discover the error and apologize to the victim when both bags are past customs.

Transit areas are often seen as the soft underbelly of customs and security. Weapons were sometimes smuggled on to aircraft at airports with dubious security, and handed over in transit lounges to would-be skyjackers, coming in on another flight of less suspicious origin. A similar technique of switching identical bags in transit lounges was used by a major Colombian ring to transport drugs and vast sums of cash for laundering. The conservatively elegant final courier's route was concealed: he would be more likely to avoid suspicion on arrival from Switzerland than from Pakistan or South America. The fall of that ring was the result of years of patient investigation with the help of international customs intelligence. Even professional smugglers overlook the fact that the rights of customs officers extend to three miles off-shore, irrespective of the extra-territorial status of the transit lounge. That is how another big ring was broken when drug carriers were seen swapping girdles in the lavatories of transit lounges. Success could be achieved only through lengthy observation of frequent travellers, for there was no question about the gang's professionalism: the Marks and Spencer's labels in the girdles had been removed because they were loaded in an Arab country where wares from Jewish shops were banned; the girdles themselves, packed with heroin, were large enough to be worn by men as well as women.

Sniffer dogs are a great help in the detection of drugs. They work in the cargo sheds, and in areas where passengers' luggage is deposited before it is loaded on to the carousels. If a flight comes in from a 'high risk' country, passengers may be asked to line up with their luggage at their feet. The dogs, such as Raf, a German pointer working at Heathrow, are trained to sit down quietly next to the suspect. They may miss the contraband itself if it is concealed 'internally' but will spot the carrier who had handled the drugs. On one occasion, the dog at Gatwick found nothing, but a passenger from Lagos reacted with extreme irritation to its persistent sniffing: in sealed, airtight wrapping, he had 10 grams of heroin in his shirt pocket, 10 grams of cannabis in his trousers, and condoms containing 200 grams of heroin in his rectum. A computer check of the airline reservations revealed he was travelling with another two passengers. Those two also turned out to be smugglers who had almost evaded detection.

If the suspicion is strong enough, customs officers have the right to go a long way beyond polite questioning and opening suitcases. First they can take you to an interview room where the chairs are riveted to the floor against potential violence, and do a 'rub-down' ('frisking' in America). We have the right to object, and ask to see a senior officer who then decides if there was 'reasonable grounds' for the search. The next step is a strip search. If, innocent as you are, misfortune lands you in that situation, it is just as well to know your rights. You can refuse to be subjected to the embarrassment, and in Britain you can summon a senior person or even a magistrate (they are on call at all times) who can authorize or prevent the intrusion. (When a woman was stripped, 90 grams of heroin of 90 per cent purity was found in her sanitary towel – stained with chicken blood for realistic appearance to keep off the squeamish.)

A further extension of the procedure is an intimate search of all body cavities. It can only be done by a doctor in the presence of a customs officer of the appropriate gender. An objecting suspect may authorize a stomach X-ray and laboratory tests of urine samples in lieu of the search. Nobody can be forced to accede to any of that – but then, customs have the right to detain the suspect, and let nature take its course, however long it may take. Internal carrying is a terrible risk to the mules. Many of them from poor countries do it for a pittance. They are made to practise swallowing honey-coated grapes whole before they down thumb-size, similarly treated condoms that contain heroin. (Larger bags may be hidden in the rectum.) If the carrier is lucky, the pellets will emerge,* eventually, in one piece. If luck runs out, death is inevitable. In 1992, a woman from Lagos collapsed at Heathrow: she was rushed to hospital where pathologists found that two of the eighty-six 5 gram pellets of cocaine had burst in her stomach. She died without regaining consciousness. Such tragedies are a mere routine at Miami, the destination of daily flights from Cali, Medellin and other drug-producing centres, where

---

*The inner sanctum of the customs area has an elevated glass lavatory pan plumbed into a see-through box that looks like an incubator, and has a powerful jet to wash away the sewage from and disinfect the pellets of drugs. Customs officers just wait patiently; it may take up to fourteen days for the contraband to appear, but the longer it stays inside, the greater the risk of a fatal accident that needs only one bag to burst.

smugglers hope to avoid detection by mingling with the annual 6 million passengers who use the airport. Undoubtedly, many of the swallowers get through though almost 200 of them were caught, and four died there or soon after leaving the airport, last year alone. Most of them were poverty-stricken Colombians who had swallowed up to 200 small bags, though they would have enjoyed scarcely any of the huge profits: heroin is selling at about $100,000 a pound in America.

BEFORE LEAVING A FOREIGN AIRPORT

it is useful to make some enquiries in preparation for the return flight: if there is a departure tax, sprung upon the unsuspecting traveller at the last moment, it is payable in their currency – long after you have spent or reconverted your last local farthing.

And remember? *It ain't over till it's over*. Your hopeful arrival and the joy of your trip abroad will be greatly enhanced if you know a little about local customs, particularly if you are on business. In Japan, where the depth of frequent bowing varies with status, polite expressions, if not verbal grovelling, are a matter of basic good manners, though foreigners are not expected to trot out with the equivalent of 'I am a poison to your honourable spirit and shall remain forever in your debt, but may I trouble you for a glance at your watch?' (*The Times*, 8.10.1992.) Indonesians will resent you pointing with your forefinger, Saudis will throw you into jail for kissing in public and will be offended by the sight of the sole of your foot as you cross your legs, it is impolite to refuse a sauna in Finland, and wink or make a fist in Pakistan. Offering a gratuity in the Cook Islands may cause an embarrassment (for the driver is expected to give something in return), shaking your head may mean 'yes' in some parts of the world, and body contact, let alone a kiss from a new acquaintance, may ruin the ignorant visitor's day in Britain. Trousers with bell-bottoms are outlawed in Malawi, and in Argentina single women in low-budget accommodation may be assumed to be prostitutes!*

---

*The *ABC World Airways Guide* contains useful tips for awareness of quaint local customs and etiquette.

28

Flight of Fancy

The future of air transport does not begin with a quantum leap of the imagination. Yet some day, our descendants may travel by pneumatic dispatch, if speed – and being loaded into a tube – is their heart's desire. Until then, the more conservative airline executives predict that 'future' should mean greater reliability, punctuality and economy. For our own sake, we can only wish them luck.

The phase of new developments has already begun. Old workhorses, such as the Jumbo, the B737 and the Airbuses are going to be stretched and upgraded with additional capabilities. Russian aircraft with western technology are about to compete for markets. An A340–200, the first ever built, has set up a new record: it flew halfway around the world non-stop with two crews – though no passengers.*

TRAFFIC FORECASTS
are at the heart of plans for the future. Boeing estimates that by the year 2010, world air traffic will be 2.5 times greater than in 1993. The prediction by Airbus is less optimistic. The 1992 report of the US Scheduled Airline Industry reckoned that its number of passengers would grow from 467 million to 724 million by 2003. (There would be by then 2 million more departures than the current 6 million a year.) The bases of such calculations differ, but everybody projects massive growth. Increased traffic may not guarantee profitability for the airlines if they continue losing more with every passenger enticed from the others, but a combination of more competition, improved safety and greater economy will force them to find the funds for the necessary multi-billion investment. And in that, for the first time, the industry will not be backed by the beneficial by-products of the arms and space race that used to compel, until recently, the governments of all major countries to sink

*It covered the distance of 10,307 miles from Paris to Auckland in twenty-one hours and thirty-two minutes. The return journey, also non-stop, was eighty-five miles, fourteen minutes, longer. The record was a part of the extensive test programme that included an earlier non-stop flight from Toulouse to Perth with just one crew in sixteen hours and twenty-two minutes.

untold billions into aeronautical developments. With the end of the cold war, most countries are trying to cut down on military spending, and the question is how much they will be ready to invest in projects that will *only* help and promote their air industry against international competition.

CREATING NEW AIRCRAFT

has been revolutionized by Boeing whose B777, a machine for the twenty-first century, was designed solely by computers of the twentieth century. Earlier designs had needed a complete mock-up to ensure that all parts would fit together, but in this case eight gigantic mainframe computers worked out every detail, down to the last rivet, and assembled them all in a digital mock-up on the screen. Any interference with other parts showed up in red. The necessary reductions in the intended 500,000 pounds take-off weight – gaining a pound here, an ounce there, by punching a hole in certain parts – were calculated before any part was actually built. When the first huge door was at last manufactured, the computers were proven right: it could be pushed open with one finger, and could be operated even when $\frac{1}{4}$ inch of ice was formed on it. (Many parts were tested in a giant freezer at $-55°$ Celsius.) There were, however, unexpected hitches: they discovered, for instance, that when a toilet seat fell accidentally, it came down with a bang that might frighten passengers, so a device had to be invented to reduce the noise. It was tested in 670,000 cycles, up and down and up again, until it proved to be reliable and cost effective. The two engines (each will be almost as wide in diameter as the fuselage of a B737) were tested for several life-times on the ground and in the air. The aircraft will have to be able to take off, fly for up to three hours, and land on just one engine for certification. To make the aircraft a viable proposition for 1995, and compete with the Airbus 330 and 340 family, international participation was needed both in funds and through farming out the production of various parts to several other countries.

THE SUPER-JUMBO

seating 800 passengers, is already on the drawing boards. The estimated production cost could soar to £15 billion, but the expected market could be worth £200 billion. To cover the vast investment, some of the leading manufacturers will have to co-operate, bringing in Japanese and other backing for a truly international venture. At the time of writing negotiations between Boeing and the four European Airbus partners are at a fairly advanced stage. Twin-engine aircraft created an economical way for increased frequency of service. Super-Jumbos would have an ecological advantage and greater efficiency for the high-density routes – possibly with no more than a cup of tea offered to passengers who could be tightly packed in for short, mass-migratory trips like on some Japanese domestic flights.

Initially, the Super-Jumbo would be a 600-seater double-decker, with a range of 7000 miles, to enter service by the end of the millennium. McDonnell-Douglas is hoping to have a similar aircraft (fewer seats but longer range) by 1996. Passengers may then find themselves in an entirely new environment. Eventually, the 800-seaters may have three floors like a sea ferry, connected by escalators. A catering centre would offer self-service, there could be a lounge with sofas and a restaurant, passengers may stretch their legs on walkways leading to a viewing gallery, an exercise room as well as offices with computers and telephones could be located in the 'basement', individual video sets with microphones in the head-rest in lieu of earphones would help to pass the time, there could be cupboards or individual lockers instead of overhead luggage bins, windows may be replaced by panoramic TV screens, and a corner may be reserved as a 'surgery', equipped for medical emergencies. Although it is likely that among so many passengers there would always be a doctor or two, it will probably be made compulsory that at least one member of the cabin crew should be a paramedic. (For doctors, especially on American aircraft, it would be essential that insurance should cover them against the potential legal consequences of an in-flight Good Samaritan act.)

Those 'flying villages' would create their own problems. Airports would have serious logistical difficulties with handling the masses arriving and departing at peak times. It is envisaged that immigration and customs officers would have to be on board to do their job in the air. The increased wing-span may be too wide for existing runways, and as space on the ground is limited, some thought is given to folding or telescopic wings.

It is feasible that VLCTs (Very Large Commercial Transport) will fly from hub to hub, located perhaps somewhere 'in the wilderness', from where smaller commuter aircraft would ferry passengers to traditional airports near population centres. Another future possibility for such commuting could come with the advanced, next-generation . . .

FLYING BEDSTEAD

Bearing that nickname because of its appearance, an experimental vertical take-off jet with no wings was built and demonstrated in Britain in 1954. The British Harrier 'jump-jet' was the first such machine for military use. Utmost secrecy surrounds the American aircraft and engine manufacturers' feasibility studies of a STOVL (Short Take-Off/Vertical Landing) tilt-rotor type that would combine the capabilities of a helicopter and a jet. The US Advance Projects Agency has allocated $1.75 billion to support building five such aircraft to the Navy's specifications, and it will select the winning concept for flight testing in 1996. By then, an Australian inventor's brainchild may already be flying. Two American prototypes are expected to be ready in 2001, but military needs are still the driving force behind the work. A STOVL strike fighter may enter service in 2010.

Will 'flying bedsteads' be used for commercial air transport? Some urban transportation planners love the idea for a shuttle service between town centres. An American-Japanese consortium for the development of a tilt-wing STOVL aircraft has collapsed, however, due to lack of backing by the cash-starved aviation industry, and Joe DelBalzo of the FAA raises some serious questions: 'Can we build a STOVL for economical civilian service? Will it be safe enough both for the passengers and for flying over heavily populated areas? Will its noise level be acceptable in city centres? And finally, will it be a better mode of transport than high-speed rail? The TGV high-speed train between Paris and Geneva is quiet, comfortable, convenient, acceptable both politically and environmentally. The technology of such trains is more advanced than that of the STOVL. On the other hand, the tilt-rotor has the advantage of flexibility. Railway lines and stations cannot be moved around. If you come to Washington, you arrive next door to Capitol Hill, and that's that. A tilt-rotor may deliver you to a convenient suburb.

'Regarding speed, it could be a toss-up between the two ideas. A Vertical could fly between Washington and New York in about fifty minutes. A high-speed train may take only ten minutes longer. My guess is that eventually, we'll find a suitable combination of the two concepts.'

In Germany, Sprinter trains have an expanding network. In France, high-speed rail transport is already favoured to cars and planes on many routes, and the plan is to spend £25 billion on a 3000-mile network by 2025. With Spain and Italy also joining in, Britain's train service is left far behind. The new fast railways offer great comfort, stress-free travel, and airline-style food service – though the latter is not necessarily an appetizer. In Japan, the famous Tokyo bullet-train has been a great success, but with land being at a premium, a massive project is underway to build hundreds of heliports as an alternative to congested ground transport.

SUPER- AND HYPERSONICS

aircraft were expected to crowd the skies after Concorde went into service, but this did not happen for reasons of economy and the environment. Even though the British and French tax-payer paid for the development, and the airlines received the beautiful supersonics free, fuel (burning twice as much as other aircraft) and the substantial operating costs restricted such fast transport to a small segment of the first-class market. The dream of flights at 8000 or even 10,000 miles an hour is reappearing, however, on the horizon of the twenty-first century.

Subsonic jets fly at some 600 m.p.h., between Mach 0.78 and 0.85. (Mach 1, named after a nineteenth-century Austrian physicist, roughly equals the speed of sound.) The ageing Concorde cruises at 60,000 feet, twice as fast as sound travels. Its much more economical replacement, the Alliance, is planned by a European-led seven-nation consortium. It is intended to fly at 1400 m.p.h., a little faster than Concorde, but it would have twice the range of its predecessor, and more than half its seats would be reserved for economy-class passengers willing to pay a surcharge. If the environmental problems were solved, it could be in service by 2005. The similarly fast Russian TU244 is being designed for 300 passengers to fly at 65,000 feet. NASA and some American manufacturers are researching projects for airliners that would have a speed of Mach 4 on routes at 85,000 feet, and almost halve the fourteen-hour travelling time between Los Angeles and Sydney, including a one-hour stop in Honolulu. An artist's impression of the projected Boeing supersonic resembles the Concorde, but the company wants to eliminate the heavy and expensive droop nose by creating a synthetic over-the-nose forward vision. (It would use a combination of optical and other sensors to provide forward view on a screen in the cockpit.)

At such higher altitudes, passengers would enjoy unique sights of some brighter stars and planets in deep violet skies even in daytime. On the negative side, time-zone differentials and night-time operating restrictions could play havoc with arrivals.

The aviation industry as a whole is fairly sceptical about the prospect. Calling Concorde 'an executive toy, an advertising gimmick for the airlines, and a status symbol for the rich' (excluding the genuine time-pressed commuters between Europe and the United States). It predicts that the economic and environmental problems will be insurmountable. Current research shows that such a gloomy outlook is not entirely justified. The intolerable sonic boom (loud noise generated by shock waves at supersonic speed) could be minimized by better aerodynamic design – a key prerequisite of the authorization of overland routes. (Even then, aircraft may be allowed to go supersonic only when it leaves populated areas or reaches cruising height over the oceans.)

The ever-higher routes now envisaged will penetrate the lower region of the ozone layer. Major objections to the potential harm will have to be overcome by new types of engines that would produce less NO_x (oxides of nitrogen), a prime air-polluting agent, but it is not fully known what effect jet transport has on the upper troposphere and the lower stratosphere. Japan Airlines started an investigation by installing monitoring equipment on an in-service Jumbo to collect air samples, and measure atmospheric ozone and other gas concentrations. Further measurements will be made using Airbus A340s in service with Lufthansa, Air France and Sabena.

All these problems loom disproportionately large when hypersonic flights beyond Mach 5 are contemplated. At Mach 25, aerospace transport would be fast enough to go into a low Earth orbit. Using some cryogenic (very low temperature) fuel, such as liquid hydrogen, hypersonic vehicles could connect any two cities in just a couple of hours, but leaving and re-entering the atmosphere would slow down the operation. It has been calculated that time savings from departure to arrival would be little beyond what could be achieved at Mach 6. NASA's ambitious SSTO (Single-Stage-To-Orbit) hydrogen-powered hypersonic project has been halted, at least temporarily, because of technological, and particularly, financial obstacles: the cost would have been $2 billion a year for the next six years. Neva-M7, a rather secretive project by the Russian Hypersonic Research Institute, has the aim of developing a 9300 m.p.h. airliner for seventy-seven passengers.

FESTIP, the Future European Space Transportation Programme, is investigating the possibility of building a space-plane to be launched, travelling at about Mach 5, in the twenty-first century. A recommendation is to be made in 1995. Two British designs are to be among the main contenders. Hotol, a British Aerospace project abandoned in the 1980s, was designed to be launched by riding piggy-back on a Russian Antonov 225 cargo plane. Skylon, a much more revolutionary invention, would take off without using space rocket pads, gantries, other facilities and vast manpower, to fly commercial satellites into orbit. It could also deliver cargo from London to Sydney in an hour, by taking advantage of the rotation of the earth under its flight path. It is estimated that a Skylon could be driven into the atmosphere for only one-hundredth of the £381 million launching cost of an American space shuttle.

FLYING CATHEDRALS

the hi-tech equivalents of pterodactyls, are about to leave the sphere of imagination. Known as spanloaders, they will need wingspans that will dwarf a Jumbo. Some of them may have two bodies with twelve engines, to carry up to a thousand tons of cargo. A Russian model, exhibited at the Paris Air Show in 1993, offers unobstructed loading space that is 215 feet long, 27 feet wide, and 20 feet high. The McDonnell-Douglas C17, known as Globemaster 3, is a huge jet with very-low-speed flying capacity and highly advanced technology. It combines the main features of the largest cargo aircraft in current use, accommodating enormous objects that now fit only into the Lockheed Galaxy, and being able to use short landing strips that are now the sole province of the Lockheed Hercules. Its wingspan is 300 feet, and it can carry containers weighing 250 tons – half of its gross weight. Boeing's version is designed with a 500-foot wingspan – some two and a half times the total width of a Jumbo – to transport 400 tons at 500 m.p.h. The operation of such aircraft will require far more load-masters than flight crew.

A mysterious Russian flying machine, first detected by military spy satellites over the Caspian sea, has long been puzzling Western intelligence agencies that dubbed it the *Caspian Sea Monster*. Its makers have now begun to reveal details about it – and international bodies cannot yet decide whether it is to be treated as a ship or an aircraft for certification. Its looks have been described as 'the bastard off-spring of a flying boat and a hovercraft'. It can fly at 300 m.p.h., carry 400 people on two decks, skim the water or the ground on an air cushion at 30 feet, but soar to several thousand feet above bad weather. Like numerous aeronautical breakthroughs, it was created to serve military needs – this one for the fast shipment of troops into a war zone – and could revolutionize the sea ferry industry or even the mode of overnight Atlantic crossing.

Where speed matters less than size, lifting power, and staying capacity, there is room for a come-back of lighter-than-air flying. Observation balloons are in service, airships lift and carry awkward, bulky items, such as tree trunks, from inaccessible areas of Canada and forests of the former Soviet Union, and Zeppelins may fly again. Huge airships, a luxurious, relaxed mode of travel, came to grief with the catastrophe of the hydrogen-filled *Hindenburg* at New Jersey in 1937. The fire hazard was too great to carry on with the project, and by the time of World War II, the concept of ocean liners in the sky was thought to be outdated. Now, however, the original Luftschiffbau Zeppelin sees market niches for them, satisfying demands of tourism, the environment, general observation work, and freight transportation in Third World countries. The prototype of the new, 68-meter design, filled with non-flammable helium, will have an all-up weight of almost 7000 kilograms – including 1850 kilograms payload – and a maximum speed of 75 knots. Accommodating a crew of two, and twelve passengers, it will be able to stay aloft for a maximum of thirty-six hours (depending on the payload). The plans envisage take-off in 1996.

WIND-TUNNELS
to test the next generation aircraft will be more accurate, offering extra safety and economy, than the traditional ones. (The wind-tunnels in current use are error-prone: the models inside can only approximate the behaviour of the full-size aircraft in the air; expensive modifications or a shortfall in expected performance may reduce the type's market value, and like in the case of the new MD11, lead to cancellation of orders.) The more advanced European Transonic Wind-tunnel in Germany, a £265 million aerodynamic design facility, will circulate cooled nitrogen up to 1.3 times faster than the speed of sound under high pressure in temperatures of $-180°$ Celsius around the models that will have to be built with precision to the consistency of a hand-finished mirror. (The American NASA has a similar installation but only for pure research, not for commercial application as yet.) The new wind-tunnel could help designers to reduce the £13 billion annual fuel bill of the world's airlines by some 15 per cent, though it is interesting to note that,

due to the efficiency of modern aircraft, more is already paid in commissions to travel agents than for fuel.

THE SAFER FUEL FOR JETS OF THE FUTURE

may well be liquid hydrogen as an alternative to kerosene. Building on Russian research and a German-Russian joint study, an Airbus 310 will be used as a testbed, and liquid-hydrogen-powered aircraft could be in service by 2010. Apart from enhanced safety and reduced flammability, less pollution would be among the advantages so achieved, but there could be a weight penalty, because four times more than the current tank capacity would be needed for such cryogenic fuels. The engines would combine jet and rocket technology.

LOOK, NO HANDS!

Only a couple of decades ago, if a pilot read about ideas for some innovations and flying aids, now in use, he would have felt like being on a ride through Disneyland gone crazy. A couple of decades from now, fly-by-wire technology, weather radars, ground proximity, windshear and collision warning devices, 'blind' all-weather microwave landing and global positioning concepts, thermal ice protection systems, holographic head-up displays on the windscreen of the cockpit (developed, as usual, for military use), flight recorders that monitor continuously all systems as well as the pilots' performance, and 'virtual acoustics' (headphones that give air traffic controllers the impression that pilots' voices are coming from *real* directions on their screens), may look like not-yet-extinct creatures in an aeronautical Jurassic Park.

Fly-by-light controls, using fibre-optic sensors, and power-by-wire with electrically driven actuators may now appear to be science-fiction writers' dreams, but will, in fact, be tested by 1996. The aim is to reduce the weight of a modern jet by some 450 kilograms, increase its reliability, and achieve massive savings on operating costs. Civilian pilots may soon have to wear helmets in which electrodes monitor their brain patterns to detect if they fall asleep, and wake them up. *But will there be pilots at all in the cockpit?* Remote control UAV (Unmanned Air Vehicle) technology is already available. Israeli, Canadian and American drones can be used for reconnaissance over battlefields and beyond enemy lines. Eagle Eye, a Bell helicopter tilt-rotor UAV is being put through its paces in Arizona. An Italian airship-based UAV is suitable for maritime and border patrols. It can stay in the air for twenty-four hours. Its steerable video cameras, infra-red sensors and a 360°-scan radar, offer customs authorities a day and night surveillance facility over the smugglers' favourite routes across the Adriatic.

In commercial jet transport, computers in the cockpit, and air traffic controllers on the ground, could take charge. The obstacle to that is more psychological than technological. The public would react badly to complete automation. On a recent flight to Canada, when the pilot announced, 'You may wish to know that our smooth landing was controlled entirely by our computers,' a few people applauded, while others looked horrified. In the 1970s, when driverless subway trains were designed, public concern forced the authorities to retain the driver. In the cockpit and in air traffic control, automation may minimize the role of the human element, but people would have to continue playing an active (not just monitoring) part with means to overrule electronic commands of the system.

DESPATCH BY TUBES

is probably the wildest dream of transportation. A Swiss company is experimenting with an underground route from Geneva to Zurich. The vehicle would be driven by magnetic propulsion, with no need to counter drag. An American project is also contemplating 'flight through tunnels' with magnetic levitation, unrestricted speed, and propulsion by super-conductivity or other electronic devices.

AIRPORTS

must be developed to cope with twenty-first-century air traffic. Airlines are often used, particularly in America, as unofficial tax collectors to reduce the national deficit. The heavy taxes collected from them – expected to rise to an annual $40 billion by 1998 to pay for ATC alone – will have to help fund the airport improvements, too. The proposed Terminal 5 for Heathrow, for instance, will cost almost £1 billion to cater for 30 million passengers. The first phase, with new roads, express rail service, hotels and other facilities, could be completed by 2002. It would accommodate twenty aircraft at a time, and process 10 million passengers a year. The entire project would be finished by the year 2016. An alternative, more adventurous, proposal for building an airport, on reclaimed land in the Thames estuary, would cost some £4 billion.

The handling of extra arrivals, larger machines, and millions more passengers will require not only expansion, but also new crowd-shifting techniques. Take Washington's Dulles airport. The estimated cost of its development is $1 billion. Its once so imaginative but dreadfully slow mobile lounges would have to be replaced by a 'people-mover' system connected to new roads, railways and the underground. Passengers will enjoy kerb-side check-in and speedier security screening.

Most major hubs are running out of space for expansion. An American concept calls for creating transfer airports to serve only as efficient distribution centres where we just change planes without ever leaving the terminal area. There would be no rail or road connections, no hotels, no car parks, no car rental desks, nothing except perhaps a restaurant. But what if there was a cancellation? Will people readily submit to spending the night in an overcrowded hall?

Once again, the NIMBY factor comes into play. Additional airports, runways and terminals for more frequent services will raise serious objections, particularly because of the noise, pollution and inconvenience to densely populated areas all around them. A clamour by local residents greeted the merest mention of a plan for developing regional airports all over Britain. For example, Farnborough, the home of the Royal Aircraft Establishment, has an airfield that handles some 5000 civilian and 7500 military air movements a year. As a regional airport, it might take 40,000 scheduled flights per annum. Unless the noise could be greatly reduced, that would affect not only the locals, but also anybody who lives under the flight paths. Quite understandably, people's thinking changes when they swap their residents' and passengers' hats.

PASSENGERS OF THE FUTURE

will benefit from the revolutionary technology – but may have a reduced choice when a few truly global airlines will dominate the market with feeder flights connecting major centres to local airports. Flight reservations and billings will probably be handled by computers, the passenger's own computer will have a direct connection to the airline or the travel agent, the need for paper tickets will be eliminated, check-in will be a faster, simpler formality, and it will be less likely that luggage is lost or misrouted.

Noise reduction could become a major source of extra airport capacity because more night flights would be permissible. (Memphis, for instance, is the head-quarters of Federal Express, the airline that conducts a predominantly night operation. The airport is totally deserted during the day though after 14.30, every stand is full, and there is a big rush for about ninety minutes.) With the introduction of flight flexytime, the crafty passenger might opt for a take-off at two in the morning, for to make it attractive night fares would have to be slashed.

So to where shall we fly? Leisure trips to the moon are on the cards. The Earth will *shrink*: any corner of it will be easily and speedily accessible. For the prediction of our favoured, more immediate future destinations, we shall become computer fodder: Thomas Cook is considering a 'neural' computer system to build up customer profiles, and second-guess our next choice for a holiday. The bar round the corner (in Shanghai or Perth, of course) may become anybody's local haunt. One wonders if all towns will look like Miami – and smell like Benidorm.

Glossary of Abbreviations and Some Aeronautical Terms

AAIB	(UK) Air Accident Investigation Branch
Abort	Abandon the take-off already in progress
ABTA	Association of British Travel Agents
ACAP	Aviation Consumer Action Project
ACAS	Airborne Collision Avoidance System
AD	Airworthiness Directive (for compulsory repairs)
AFA	(US) Association of Flight Attendants
Aileron	Hinged control surface at trailing edge of wing to induce banking of aircraft
Airspeed/ groundspeed	Airspeed measures in knots how fast an aircraft is moving relative to the surrounding air; groundspeed measures how fast the aircraft progresses relative to the ground below.
ALPA	(US) Air Line Pilots Association
APEX	Advance Purchase Excursions (ticket)
APU	Auxiliary Power Unit
Aquaplaning	Aircraft runs on wet surface at speed
ASG	(UK) Air Safety Group
ATA	Air Transport Association
ATC	Air Traffic Control
AUC	(UK) Air Transport Users Committee
BALPA	British Air Line Pilots Association
CAA	(UK) Civil Aviation Authority
CVR	Cockpit Voice Recorder
DOTS	Dynamic Oceanic Track System
DFDR	Digital Flight Data Recorder
DoT	(US) Department of Transportation
Drag	Air resistance to flight

Elevators	Horizontal control surfaces for climb and descent – now *tailplanes*
Engines	Turbojets suck in and compress air, add fuel, and burn the mixture that explodes in a white-hot jet of gas at the rear, creating thrust. Turbofans use a large fan at the front of the engine. Turboprops drive propellers of smaller aircraft. Propfans spin large propeller-like blades at very high speed, and resemble turboprops.
ETOPS	Extended range Twin-engine Operations
FAA	(US) Federal Aviation Administration
Flaps	Moving parts of wing to increase lift and/or drag
Fly-by-wire	Flying commands by the pilots are transmitted to the engines and flight control surfaces by electrical/electronic (non-mechanical) means.
FSF	Flight Safety Foundation
g	The force of gravity
Glass cockpit	Instrument readings and all information for pilots are displayed on TV-like screens
GPS	Global Positioning System
GPWS	Ground Proximity Warning System
IATA	International Air Transport Association
ICAO	International Civil Aviation Organization
IFALPA	International Federation of Air Line Pilots Associations
ILS	Instrument Landing System
ISASI	International Society of Air Safety Investigators
JAA	(European) Joint Aviation Authority
Mach number	The ratio of airspeed to the speed of sound which varies with altitude
MEL	Minimum Equipment List (without which aircraft must not fly)
NASA	(US) National Aeronautics and Space Administration
NTSB	(US) National Transportation Safety Board
QAR	Quick Access Recorder (for preventive maintenance)
Reverse thrust	The thrust of the jet engine is reversed: the rearward thrust helps the aircraft to slow down
Rotate	The pilot induces the nose of the aircraft to rise and begin the take-off.

Rudder	Vertical moving surface, attached to the fin, for directional control of aircraft
SB	Service Bulletin (manufacturers' advisory)
SCI-SAFE	Survivors Campaign to Improve Safety in Airline Flight Equipment
Sound barrier	Signifies the speed at which an aircraft breaks through Mach 1 with a bang, and begins to fly faster than sound
SST	Supersonic Transport aircraft
Stall	Unwanted loss of speed in the air that results when an aircraft is trying to climb too steeply – the airflow is disrupted over the wings that can no longer produce sufficient lift
$V_1 - V_2 - V_r$	Critical speeds (velocity) during take-off. Below V_1 take-off may be abandoned; at V_r aircraft must rotate
VTOL	Vertical Take-Off and Landing
Wet-leasing	Aircraft leased complete with crew
Wings	*Swept* wings are angled towards the fin. *Delta* wings are near-triangular like the Greek letter D

Index

The numerous references to various aviation authorities, such as the British CAA, and the American FAA and NTSB, have not been listed in this index. Abbreviations used in the index appear in the glossary on page 256.